Woman in Christian Tradition

GEORGE H. TAVARD

Woman
in
Christian Tradition

UNIVERSITY OF NOTRE DAME PRESS

NOTRE DAME
LONDON

Library of Congress Cataloging in Publication Data

Tavard, George Henri, 1922-
    Woman in Christian tradition.

    Includes bibliographical references.
    1. Women in Christianity. I. Title.
BV639.W7T38   261.8'34'12   72-12637
ISBN 0-268-00490-0

Printed in the United States of America by
NAPCO Graphic Arts, Inc., New Berlin, Wisconsin

To

Dorothy Lukas

Contents

Foreword

Woman needs no introduction, but a book on woman does.

This is a book of theology. It does not indulge in explanations of feminine psychology, or investigations of woman's changing social status, or assessments of either her superiority or her inferiority.

Twice I conducted semester-long seminars on the theology of womanhood, with female students, at Mount Mercy (now Carlow) College in Pittsburgh, Pennsylvania. These seminars were chiefly biblical; but they also included the study of a great deal of contemporary literature.

In 1965 I published an article on "Woman in the Church: a Theological Problem?" (*The Ecumenist*, November-December, pp. 7-10). The present volume is the outcome of the reflections formulated in that essay. As I have explained in a more recent article ("The Depths of the Tradition," *Continuum*, Autumn 1969, pp. 427-437), we need a theological anthropology. Yet I do not think that such an anthropology can be adequately grounded in the phenomenological approach that has been tried by Karl Rahner or Johannes Metz. For theology should be based on theology, not on phenomenology, any more than on Aristotle's philosophy. To the extent that contemporary religious thought turns to man and his world, it should strive to maintain full continuity with, and respect for, the questions and answers of past theology. Only fidelity to the past will allow us to propose bold solutions for the future, because it guarantees our listening to the everliving Christ.

Most volumes I have read on womanhood (and few have escaped my attention) focus on present questions, problems, movements, interpretations while prescinding from an examination in depth of the traditional theological material. Many (for instance, the writings of Sydney Callahan, Dorothy Dohen, Mary Daly) are valuable for the current scene but, to my mind, weak in regard to the historical background of the question of womanhood. Among other authors, Elsie Thomas Culver provides a good survey of history but at the expense of close attention to specific streams of thought. Among more professionally theological authors, there are important studies of related topics (e.g., Helmut Thielicke's investigation of the "Ethics of Sex," or D. S. Bailey's researches on the "man-woman relation"), but hardly any detailed historical evaluation of a theology of womanhood.

My approach to the Bible will not be dominated by any specific herme-neutical school. My concern will not be to give a thorough account of the literal sense of the text: Nor will I (as one of my readers has erroneously thought) use the "theory of *sensus plenior*." My interpretation of the Old Testament is largely indebted to the studies, unfortunately little known in America, of Louis Ligier: *Péché d'Adam, Péché du Monde,* vol. I (Paris, 1960). For the New Testament material, my interpretation is, in some in-stances, my own, as in the matter of the *logia* on divorce. My general purpose has been to discern what elements may provide hints for a renewed theology. Since I always kept in mind the patristic chapters that were to follow, this may have occasionally inspired a "spiritual" interpretation which others may not follow. So be it. One cannot satisfy the requirements of all.

After two chapters on the Old and the New Testament, the first part of this book includes an investigation of the Fathers of the Church, of both East and West, which reaches its climax in the study of Ambrose and Augustine.

Western Christian thinking about woman was given its shape chiefly by Augustine. The technical differences that distinguish Scholasticism and later theology from Augustine himself do not affect the essential structures of Au-gustinian thought on our topic. For this reason, the second part of the book concentrates on the recent tradition and studies models offered to women by the Christian Churches in the nineteen and twentieth centuries. This will lead me to draw the outlines of a theological anthropology and to examine con-temporary questions, focused on woman and women's liberation.

Methodist Theological School   George H. Tavard

Delaware, Ohio

Abbreviations

The following abbreviations have been used:

D.T.C.   *Dictionnaire de Théologie Catholique* (Paris).
D.- S.   Denzinger-Schönmetzer, *Enchiridion Symbolorum* (Freiburg, 1965).
C.O.D.   *Conciliorum Oecumenicorum Decreta* (Freiburg, 1962).
C.S.E.L.   *Corpus scriptorum ecclesiasticorum latinorum* (Vienna).
P.G.   Migne, *Patrologia graeca.*
P.L.   Migne, *Patrologia latina.*
RSV   *Revised standard version* of the Bible.
S.Chr.   *Sources Chrétiennes* (Paris).

PART ONE

The Old Tradition

The Two Traditions

At the roots of the theological tradition about women, the legends of the Hebrews contain rich material which may be called, as far as we are concerned, original. It is original for us because it is the oldest data at our disposal within the sequence of the Hebrew-Christian revelation. But it is not original in an absolute sense. The stories of Genesis express contradictory, or at least divergent, attitudes which themselves testify to a long period of reflection on the male-female relationship as it was experienced in the near East (including in this the Fertile Crescent and Egypt, that is, the geographic universe of the Hebrews and their ancestors). In the prescientific exegesis, these accounts were taken as forming a whole, unified by inclusion in a collection that came eventually to be regarded by the Jews as inspired. More recent approaches to the first books of the Bible divide them into their components, as far as these may be discerned today. In either case, these books escape purely objective analysis. One cannot be certain what they meant in the mind of their authors (or transmitters, or redactors), because we know too little about the times, places, and circumstances of their elaboration. If it goes further than mere philological analysis, reading the first chapters of Genesis becomes an interpretation. Interpretation should of course take account, as far as possible, of all that is known about the historical background, yet it cannot avoid being made in the light of hermeneutic principles that came into being long after the writing of the texts. An interpretation is always made from within a doctrinal tradition, even if the doctrinal element is reduced to a minimum, as is usually the case with literary analysis.

Our reading of the first chapters of Genesis will therefore bring to light a theological or hermeneutical circle; it will be partly guided by the contents of the next chapters of our inquiry. The Old Covenant and the New are complementary; and as read in the Christian tradition, they are so intertwined that the Christian reading of the Old Testament need not necessarily draw the meaning it had for the rabbis, for the prophets, for the kings and the priests of the two Kingdoms. And if Moses was acquainted with some legends about the origins of mankind, we make no claim to know what he thought of them. But this, of course, need not be our problem.

Our problem is to unfold an interpretation of Genesis which makes sense when related, on the one hand, to the text as we have it and, on the other, to the continuing concerns of the Christian tradition as lived in the past and as experienced in the present. The texts of the Old or, for that matter, of the New Testament must not be approached as proofs or arguments in favor of some theological position; and they should not be used simply to illustrate opinions and statements unrelated to their meaning and context. They must be read as links (the first links as far as our direct knowledge goes, but coming themselves at the end of a long prehistory that can only be implied and guessed at) in a chain of unfinished spiritual discovery. And since this discovery, in the matter that concerns us in this book, is focused on anthropology, the chain in question is also a sequence of anthropological experiences. Behind all that we will read or say there looms the question: what is man? Whether they derive from the Old Testament, the New Testament, the Fathers of the Church, or more recent theologians, the texts formulate partial answers to this question. It is not for us at this time to pronounce these answers tentative or definitive. This may be decided later, if at all. Meanwhile, we ought to be concerned first of all with theological consistency, for even though the texts may be at odds with one another, interpretation needs to be consistent. Since hermeneutics tries to discern an intelligible pattern, it must be itself intelligible, even when the data take the form of a mosaic of unrelated insights. The task of the interpreter is to suggest relationships that the texts themselves do not clearly show. As those relationships largely depend on the total picture that he wishes to convey, the sense of the earliest texts may not fully appear until much later in his investigation. Thus there will be no cause for surprise that our interpretation of the biblical data will remain tentative and will need to be tested by the later links in the anthropological tradition that will be uncovered in the course of this book.

So we are led to the first chapters of Genesis and to the account of the creation of woman as both the starting point of our story and the first outline of our theological understanding of womanhood.[1]

We will begin with Genesis 2:18-25 on the assumption, granted by contemporary scholars, that this represents an older strand than the creation account of chapter 1.[2]

Yahweh God said, 'It is not good that the man should be alone. I will make him a helpmate.' So from the soil Yahweh God fashioned all the wild beasts and all the birds of heaven. These he brought to the man to see what he would call them; each one was to bear the name that man would give it. The man gave names to all the cattle, all the birds of heaven and all the wild beasts. But no helpmate suitable for man was found for him. So Yahweh God made the man fall into a deep sleep. And while he slept, he took one of his ribs and enclosed it in flesh. Yahweh God built the rib he had taken from the man into a woman, and brought her to the man. The man exclaimed: 'This at last is bone from my bones and flesh from my flesh! This is to be called woman, for this was taken from man.' This is why a man leaves his father and mother and joins himself to his wife, and they become one body. Now both of them were naked, the man and his wife, but they felt no shame in front of each other. (2:18-24)

In this text, the creation of woman is contrasted with that of the animals. These are made and brought by God to Adam, with the twofold purpose of being named by him, who thereby affirms his understanding of and his authority over them, and of providing him with companionship. The point is linked to a polemical criticism of Canaanite or Egyptian cults of animals. Animals should not be worshipped, since they suffer from a double inferiority in relation to man: it is from him that they obtained their names and they are unable to fulfill his expectations. Be that as it may, the chief lesson of the text refers to woman's relationship to man. The creation of woman is also essentially related to Adam, since Adam's solitude provides the occasion for her creation. Is she to be understood as an afterthought, as a being whose place could conceivably have been filled by animals, as one who, being created like the animals to remedy Adam's loneliness, stands little higher than they? This would hardly be compatible with the whole tone of this section of Genesis, in which Yahweh is shown as knowing exactly what he is doing and as doing everything for a purpose. The God of this creation story is not a hesitant potter who tries one thing after another with the hope of finally achieving success. He is indeed the Almighty, whose actions contain lessons of paramount importance. Instead of seeing the creation (or, as the text says, the modelling) of woman as the lowest in a series of creation attempts that begins on a triumphant note with the making of Adam and follows a descending scale to that of Eden, of plants, of rivers, of animals, and finally of woman, we should look at it as a creation that grows from Adam to woman, with the intermediate creations serving to establish the stage for the higher creation that is achieved with the modelling of woman.

The creation of Adam is told in these terms:

At the time when Yahweh made earth and heaven there was yet no wild bush on the earth nor had any wild plant yet sprung up, for Yahweh God had not sent rain on the earth, nor was there any man to till the soil. However, a flood was rising from the earth and watering the surface of the soil. Yahweh God fashioned man out of dust from the soil. Then he breathed into his nostrils a breath of life, and thus man became a living being.

(2:5-7)

Who is Adam? If the word means man, it designates him by what can only be a nickname: the one from soil (*adamah*). For Adam is created from the dust of the soil before anything else appears. before even the soil has been made into a garden. He comes from the stuff of the earth, before even rain falls from heaven, at a time when the dust is slimy from the water rising up from inside the earth. The first name of man, Adam, is a name of humility. It is significant that woman is not directly related to it, but to another name of man, *Ish*, by which she is called *Ishah*. In other words, the appearance of woman facing man implies the revelation of a new name destined to replace, or at least to accompany, that of Adam. From his origin in the earth, man had received a name translating the lowliness of his condition. For the name, in Hebrew philosophy, unveils the true meaning of the reality it designates. From his companionship with woman, man obtains his name of glory, that which expresses his condition as a being-in-relationship.

Another point deserves to be noted concerning the name Adam. In the Hebrew language it is a collective rather than a singular word: that is, it fits man as mankind rather than man as individual; It denotes a quality, that of being from dust, which belongs to all those who will eventually be called men. It has no connotation of sex. The sex-name of man is his other name, *Ish*, by which he relates to woman, *Ishah*.

We are thus invited to read the second chapter of Genesis as picturing mankind struggling to get out of a self-contradiction, being collective and yet reduced to one. Adam is plural, but still alone. He cannot yet be several; he is not yet a society. The passage deals with Adam's attempt to form a society. to pass beyond his undifferentiated state as mankind to a stage of differentiation. "It is not good that Adam should be alone." This is not a matter of moral goodness, but of basic, ontic reality. In contrast to the first chapter of Genesis, in which God, looking at the work done during the day, always says, "This is good," God here looks at Adam and says, "It is not good." This of course need not mean that Yahweh has fumbled: it implies that the work is unfinished. God looks at his work when it is half done and pronounces the verdict that the work should be brought to completion. Paradise and plants have already been made. Now the animals. Adam invents their names, but finds no companion among them; he can establish no society with them. They answer his call, but nothing else happens. Adam himself is not transformed and completed by his experience. He does not find "a helpmate suitable to himself" or, as the Septuagint has it, a "a helpmate similar to himself." For society requires distinction within unity, and man enjoys no basic unity with animals.

This failure to form a society with animals is of tremendous importance for the differentiation of Adam into *Ish* and *Ishah,* of mankind into male and female, arises from it. It is God's answer to mankind's original dilemma: how to be a society when you are one. Had Adam chosen—if it had been possible for him so to choose—one animal as his companion, he would have made himself an animal, to live at a purely animal level. He then would have fallen into a sin which would be quite different from the original sin recognized by the Christian tradition: the original sin of beastliness, of siding with the beast over against the spirit. By refusing society with animals, Adam committed himself to the spiritual element in mankind. He was dust from the soil, and he had received the breath of life. He now desires something higher. This choice sets the final stage for the creation of woman. Mankind yearns to be a society to express this spiritual capacity and longing in itself; and yet it cannot enter interpersonal relationships with equals, since it has no equals and has not yet been built into a person.

Woman, *Ishah,* is therefore made. But there is a fundamental difference between the creation of Adam out of the soil and that of woman: Yahweh "fashioned" Adam, but he "built" the rib (taken from Adam in his sleep) into woman. This upbuilding of woman is clearer in the Septuagint than in Hebrew, as usually understood: He "took one of his ribs, and closed up its place with flesh" (RSV, Hebrew), or he "enclosed it in flesh" (Jerusalem Bible, LXX).[3] The first version speaks of the surgery undertaken on Adam, an interesting but secondary point; the second shows the beginning of the upbuilding of the rib into woman. Whatever text is correct, the ultimate meaning remains: as far as mankind as a whole is concerned, there is only one creation, that of Adam. The next step does not come as a second process of creation, but as a step within the total process or as a further development of what began with the fashioning of Adam. We should therefore understand woman not as an addition to the mankind that already was in the person of Adam; rather, Adam himself (in that part of him which was his rib) is built up into woman.

Ishah, then, does not walk in on Adam from the outside as an alien element. She proceeds from inside of Adam, where she was already present as that to which mankind was destined, as the development that would bring it to perfection, as the identity with a difference which makes society-building possible. "This is bone of my bone and flesh of my flesh." Mankind recognizes itself in *Ishah.* It speaks of itself as being present in woman. It knew itself hitherto as Adam; and now there comes the revelation of itself in another and thereby of itself as no longer an "it," but a "he" related to a "she." Adam receives his name of glory, *Ish,* companion of *Ishah,* who is his own companion. In this revelation Adam perceives clearly what his confrontation with the animals had only weakly hinted at, his personality. Adam becomes a person, aware of himself, reaching consciousness as mankind at the unveiling of woman. For woman also is mankind. She is no other than Adam; but she is

Adam as bringing to perfection what had first been imperfect. She is mankind as fully aware of its status, as the goal and perfection of man. Thus, woman is not made as Adam's helpmate just because he is lonely; she is created as the perfecting element, to the revelation of which he aspired when he refused companionship with the animal world.

Seeing each other, *Ish* and *Ishah* know each other to be one. For this reason (besides this, no doubt the author wanted to emphasize the point that this was taking place in Paradise), the text adds that although they were nude, they were not ashamed. They could not be ashamed because they were not viewing each other as strangers, but each saw the other as himself. *Ish* saw *Ishah* as the perfection of the Adam which he had been. *Ishah* saw *Ish* as the Adam that she was bringing, by her advent, to completion. In one way, *Ishah* was made for mankind, as she was to bring it perfection, to be its perfection. In another, mankind was made for *Ishah,* the less perfect, the uncompleted, the undifferentiated being preparatory of the more perfect, the fullness, the being-in-relation. In the oneness of man and woman, it is woman who brings perfection. Marriage proceeds from the memory of this perfection, from a hankering after the differentiated oneness which was no longer the primordial state of indetermination and not yet the present state of self-estrangement of mankind. "This is why a man [*Ish*] leaves his father and mother and joins himself to his wife [*Ishah*], and they become one body"—or rather, one flesh.

The ecstatic discovery expressed with the phrase: "bone of my bone, and flesh of my flesh" presents still another facet. The symbolism of house-building is not absent from this text. A man's house is a symbol of the race to be born from him. Israel as a people was so called because it was the house of the man Israel. The Messiah will be born from the house of David. The house in this sense is built by Yahweh himself in a process which prolongs, in our case, the building of woman from Adam. When the text reports that the rib is built into woman, it includes all the descendants of woman in that process; and when *Ish* acknowledges her as "bone of my bone, flesh of my flesh," he salutes in her all his descendants, all mankind.

The revelatory dimension of the advent of woman is better suggested in the Septuagint than in Hebrew. Whereas the Hebrew Bible speaks simply of a "sleep" into which Adam has been plunged by Yahweh, the Septuagint refers to an "ecstasy." Adam enters a prophetic trance, in which all that follows takes place, the removal of the rib, its upbuilding into woman, and their ecstatic encounter. In this perspective, mankind and its energies are not dormant during the formation of woman. For ecstasy implies the silencing of the faculties only so that they may be transformed. It implies access to a new world, transfiguration no less than recognition.

If we now read the account of man's creation at the end of the first chapter of Genesis, we find a much shorter text with a different orientation, yet one which is also highly sophisticated.

God said, 'Let us make man in our own image, in the likeness of ourselves, and let them be masters of the fish of the sea, the birds of heaven, the cattle, all the wild beasts and all the reptiles that crawl upon the earth'. God created man in the image of himself, in the image of God he created him, male and female he created them. (1:26-27)

We can barely touch here upon the relationship of this account of the creation of man with that of chapter 2, which we have just studied. In the modern analysis of Genesis, chapter 2 belongs to the Yahwist tradition, originating in Judea under David and Solomon, and therefore dating back to the ninth century. Chapter 1 belongs to the Priestly tradition, probably written down in the fifth century, after the Exile, although it contains much more ancient material. It would therefore constitute a more recent account. In this case it is tempting to regard the two verses on the creation of man as summing up the longer story of chapter 2, pruning its anthropomorphic aspects, and instead of paying attention to details of the process of creation, throwing a sharp light on the core of it: God creates man in his own image, and he makes man male and female. The Priestly tradition would have extracted the essence of the religious teaching of the Yahwist tradition.

I do not propose to read the text in this way. Its connections with the other story of the origins of mankind are of less importance than the framework in which it appears, the creation of the universe in six days. This framework sets the stage in terms that are both cosmological and liturgical. The six days followed by the day of rest are naturally the week, based, in the Hebrew calendar, on the lunar month. They are also the six days of work leading to the day of worship of the religious calendar. And it may not be purely accidental that the name given to the creator in this first chapter is not, as in chapter 2, the unique name Yahweh, but the plural name Elohim, which is not reserved to him but applies also to the gods of other nations and occasionally designates the inhabitants of the invisible world above this one, which is glimpsed at night when the multitude of the stars shine. Thus, in verse 26, Elohim speaks in the plural: "Let us make man in our own image...," whereas the next verse refers to Elohim in the singular: "God created man in the image of himself."

The dialectic of the one and the many thus still dominates the creation story; but the theology of this tradition has not restricted it to the world of

Adam, struggling to reach beyond a state of undifferentiation. The dialectic belongs to the divine sphere itself, where Elohim is one and yet his name is plural. There is even a hierarchy of Elohim (plural), at the head of which stands the one Elohim who is also called Yahweh .

From this perspective, the expressions "image" and "likeness" become all-important. The six days of creation end with the fulfillment of a new purpose. Until then the creator had made the heavens and the earth, and he had filled and adorned them. He finally starts something else, the creation of one who will be like himself, in whom the dialectic of the one and the many will also be realized. This is related to the liturgical context of the story, for the sixth day is the final preparation for the seventh, the Sabbath, when the many come together into one for worship at the Temple. This is in keeping with the concerns of the Priestly tradition, which argues for the Jerusalem cult against the cults that are still carried out in old Canaanite shrines on the mountains of the countryside.

Adam is therefore made one and many, singular and plural. One and the same sentence passes from the singular to the plural: "Let us make *man* ... and let *them* be...." The singular is Adam, the collective term for mankind which in itself has no connotation of sex. The plural, with which Adam is identical, is explained in the next verse: "... in the image of God he created *him,* male and female he created *them.*" The balance of the terms in this verse suggests, besides the poetic form in which the story has suddenly been couched, that the image and the likeness of mankind consists in being male and female. Neither male nor female alone is in the likeness of Elohim, but both together. There is no special emphasis on the mutual relationships of man and woman or on their distinct origins. On the contrary, there are no two origins of mankind; the creation of woman is not delayed, as in the Yahwist account. This tradition is interested in the identity of the collective, Adam, with the plural, man and woman. In its anthropology, man and woman are not only two, they are also one. Their oneness in distinction is the image and likeness of God.

Furthermore, the terms for "male" and "female" are not *Ish* and *Ishah* (man and woman), which can be used for human being only; they are now strictly sexual terms, like male and female, applying to animals as well as to men. That is to say, if the image of Elohim in mankind resides in sexuality, then sexuality cannot be primordial. Whereas other creation myths of the Fertile Crescent place sexuality at the origin of all, the Priestly saga sees it at the end of the process of creation. In *Enuma Elish,* the Babylonian creation epic, it all begins with the begetting of the gods in the womb through the mingling of Apsu and Tiamat. Genesis 1 contradicts this openly by placing sex at the end of the process, and only at the level of the created world. Elohim is not involved in sex. Yet he gives meaning to human sexuality beyond that of animal sexuality: in being male and female, mankind is "in the image, according to the likeness" of Elohim. The injunction to use sex follows naturally: "God blessed them, saying to them, 'Be fruitful, multiply, fill the earth and conquer it. Be masters of the fish of the sea, the birds of heaven and all living animals on the earth' (v. 28). By thus multiplying, they will fulfill themselves as "image" of Elohim, by becoming numerous like the Elohim in the heavens. By dominating the earth they will also become the image of the divine power.

   The originators of these two traditions probably lived at the beginning of the monarchy, when the rise of a small-scale empire-consciousness contributed to the development of strong cultural traditions. The Yahwist poet of chapter 2 depicts his *Ishah*-Eve in opposition to the feminine idols of Canaanite religion, whose fertility cult, centered on the Mother-Goddess, wielded great power over the imagination of Hebrew women. Israel has already passed from a nomadic-pastoral to a settled agricultural existence, in which the seasonal fertility of the earth focuses attention on the mysterious correspondence between the forces of the earth and the female cycle. In this context, the author tries to woo the Hebrew woman away from Canaanite examples by extolling the primordial status of womanhood, whose present dependence on fertility cycles and whose submission to the domination of her husband derive from sin, whereas her pristine vocation was one of completion and perfection.
   When the main layer of chapter 1 was composed, the Temple was already built and a regular weekly liturgy followed the lunar calendar. But the lunar calendar is also the female calendar. That is to say, the female cycle had then been taken as a pattern for Temple worship and, accordingly, for the life of worship. Thus the entire People, as represented at the Temple, became feminine in relation to Yahweh. Woman had begun her ascent back to her original, prelapsarian, position as the spiritual ideal and embodiment of mankind. The Canaanite fertility cults—as witness the prophets of the ninth and eighth centuries, Elijah, Amos, Osea, and Isaiah—present a lasting and attractive temptation, particularly appealing to women. One can hardly decide if this orientation of the chapter is preexilic—in which case it would show an early and prolonged attempt at transforming popular themes of Canaanite religion into acceptable material for Hebrew reflection—or if it depends on the lunar calendar of the Babylonians, known during the Exile. At any rate, the final form of this chapter is postexilic and corresponds to the reconstruction of Hebrew civilization in its recovered homeland. The adoption then of the lunar-feminine period as the pattern for both liturgical piety and the creation myth was meant to draw the Hebrews toward authentic feminism, away from

the siren songs of Canaanite female worship. Man and woman may now be shown as sexually polarized within the oneness of Adam without making specific mention of the fall and of the dramatic reversal of values which followed upon it.

We may now briefly consider the two accounts of creation together, as they were strung one after the other when the Pentateuch was compiled, around 400 B.C., shortly after the tradition of chapter 1 had found its final shape. As the chief result of this compilation, the two stories are now read as one, so that the characteristics, aspects, and emphases of each are lost on the average reader. The Yahwist account of the creation of woman is mistaken for an amplification of the Priestly account. The two chapters form two episodes of one story, where their common points rather than their divergences and their distinct orientations keep the limelight. Read in this way, the creation of woman becomes a straightforward account of the creation of mankind in two stages. Its first moment coincides with the making of Adam (chapter 1); its second with that of woman from and for Adam (chapter 2). Verses 27-28 of chapter 1 announce chapter 2, and are not completely understood until chapter 2 has been read. Woman appears as the helpmate through whom Adam will be enabled to multiply and fill the earth. She becomes less a companion and more an instrument. Her creation is read in the twofold light of the previous creation of Adam and of the subsequent fall in which she will play a leading role. From the start she is seen as Eve, the fallen woman who carries the burden of painful pregnancy, although this name does not appear before chapter 3. Thus the very compilation of the Yahwist and the Priestly traditions already betrays a certain lack of perception of their implications and the underlying anthropologies.

With the story of the temptation and the fall in Genesis 3, we are still, as in chapter 2, in the Yahwist tradition. The text of chapter 3, like that of chapter 2, and perhaps more so, is related in many minor ways to several pagan myths, especially to the Epic of Gilgamesh. For this reason a number of exegetes have seen the story of the temptation as conflating two previous legends, the one centered on Paradise, the other on woman. Yet whatever the prehistory of our text, it is to be read now as one myth, set in Paradise, and in which the major actor is *Ishah,* the companion of *Ish.* In chapter 2, Adam, the collective name of man, was differentiated into *Ish* and *Ishah:* this accounts for the origin of the sexes. The collective name gave way to what I have called the names of glory, of man and woman in interpersonal relationship to one another. Chapter 3 will end with the bestowing of a second name on woman, Eva, the mother of the living. The whole trend of the story of the fall, as I understand it, points toward this name, which will be at the same time a name of shame and a name of redemption.

The woman is tempted first not, as male prejudice suggests, because she is the weaker, but because she is the perfection. Only a pusillanimous tempter would strike at the weakest link in the chain of being. But the serpent is not such a petty figure. Although the text shows him to be one of the animals of Eden (who received their names from Adam), an obscure symbolism may hide behind this familiarity: there are serpents among the pagan divinities that surround Israel, and the Hebrews too practiced a certain cult of the serpent as a salvific figure in the times of Exodus. The serpent of Genesis is not evil, and what he tells the woman is not false. But he is clever; he knows more than she does of the meaning of the taboo concerning the tree at the Garden's center, and he speaks to her ambiguously so as to mislead her. In the context, there is no sexual connotation to the image of the serpent. What the serpent exactly is appears clearly enough from what he says and from the curse that Yahweh will pronounce on him.

There may have been in Israel other legends about the primordial sin. Isaiah 14 may be taken as alluding to one such myth:

'How did you come to fall from the heavens,
Daystar, son of Dawn? . . .
. . . You who used to think to yourself:
"I will climb up to the heavens;
and higher than the stars of God
I will set my throne.
I will sit on the Mount of Assembly
in the recesses of the north.
I will climb to the top of thunderclouds,
I will rival the Most High."
What! Now you have fallen to Sheol
to the very bottom of the abyss!" (14:12-15)

In the context, the Daystar (Lucifer) is the king of Babylon; but the prophet may apply to Babylon a myth of the primordial man, who sinned through *hybris*, the pride that pushed him to seek equality with God, to be counted among the Elohim.

Ezechiel 28, polemizing against the king of Tyre, likewise sees him as a type of the primordial sinner. Residing in Eden, richly attired, with a cherub for companion, he was perfect "until the day when evil was first found" in him. "Your heart has grown swollen with pride on account of your beauty. You have corrupted your wisdom owing to your splendor" (v. 17). The outcome has been apocalyptic: "I have thrown you down from the mountain of God, and the guardian Cherub has destroyed you from amid the coals" (v. 16).

In both cases, the sinner is presented as a king, and there is no suggestion of the presence of a feminine element in what brought him to sin. Does that contradict the legend of Genesis 3? It seems significant that in both instances it is kingship which has been corrupted; and kingship, in the world of Mesopotamia and in its cultural client, Phoenicia, is akin to divinity. The king stands as the symbol of his nation, the perfect example of mankind as embodied in a certain political and religious contexture. Only the sin of the perfect acquires the dimensions of tragedy. The same effect is reached in the Yahwist tradition precisely by the involvement of woman in the primordial sin. For Adam does not appear as a figure of glory until he has found his feminine companion. He is lonesome at first and becomes pathetic in his search for companionship among the animals, who cannot fulfill his spiritual needs even though he masters them well enough to give them their names. Only with the advent of woman does he himself reach to the dimensions of glory, when he is transformed in ecstasy. It is through woman, through its very perfection, that mankind sins.

In what does the sin consist? We have recognized the grandeur of the image of woman in Genesis 2 and 3 and identified this greatness with her perfecting function. She brings mankind to its fullness. She contains in herself this plenitude which will be spelled out through time in the upbuilding of the house of man. The temptation is thus set on a cosmic stage. The wish to know good and evil entails neither mere divergence from a legal prescription, nor the breaking of a taboo, sexual or other. Like the woman's origin and function, the temptation concerns mankind as a whole.

> The serpent said to the woman, 'No, you will not die! God knows in fact on the day you eat it your eyes will be opened and you will be like gods, knowing good and evil.' The woman saw that the tree was good to eat and pleasing to the eye, and that it was desirable for the knowledge that it could give. (3:5-6)

The heart of this passage lies in the meaning of "knowing good and evil." Is this intellectual knowledge, comparable to an awareness of the law? Or does it imply also an experience, affective knowledge, knowledge by connaturality? In what way does the knowledge of good and evil bring about a likeness to the Elohim? There is no question at this point of becoming equal to Yahweh. Even the serpent could not suggest this, as it would be opposed to the very experience of the woman, who knows herself to have been built by Yahweh. The world to which she aspires is indeed near to Yahweh; but it is the world of the Elohim, who include the angels, messengers of God, the stars up in the sky, the better world of which one dreams and of which one is more likely to dream if one already lives in Paradise, in the familiarity of that beautiful world. No wonder that the first fruit that is able to open the gates of heaven looks "good to eat and pleasing to the eye."

Woman, therefore, following the serpent's hints, wishes to know what the Elohim are able to know. The problem for her is not to transform herself into what she cannot become. She is well aware of the fact that she is not being built into one of the Elohim. She does not aspire to escaping Paradise and her own destiny on earth. What she wants is to be "like the Elohim, knowing good and evil." She desires, not the status of the Elohim, but their ability to know.

What she wants to know may appear more clear in the light of this statement: "Things hidden belong to Yahweh our God, but things revealed are ours and our children's for all time, so that we may observe all the words of this Law" (Deut. 29:28). In the mythical time of the story of the temptation, nothing yet has been revealed: the Law has not yet induced an intellectual and experiential knowledge of what is legally good and legally wrong. Torah is destined to provide Israel with its very structure; the entire life of the people must center on it; and it is eventually by the standard of Jerusalem and of Torah that all nations will be judged. Thus, that to which the woman aspires is the knowledge of what is still a secret hidden in God: the Law, that is, the structure of her own future as the house of Adam. The woman wishes to know what touches her most intimately: in what way, through what means, by what episodes will the house of mankind be built? Woman wishes to have a foreknowledge of the structure and the history of man. This is the "good and evil" in question: that which is known only to Yahweh and those to whom he reveals it.

If we analyze this further, we shall see that the knowledge of good and evil in this sense implies more than knowing what will happen to mankind. For good and evil, in the Yahwist conception of God's transcendence, proceed from God's action, who blesses for good and curses for evil. Behind the good or happiness and the evil or unhappiness, there looms a divine attitude of benediction or of malediction. He who does good was blessed before doing it, as the evil-doer suffered from God's wrath. Woman wants to hold the key to these acts of God. Were it granted her, the outcome would not be religion but magic. She would attempt to control God's doings. At this level, her wish could not possibly be met. God could not let her know that. We will see in a moment what he revealed to her instead.

Yet the woman's wish is not evil (in our sense of the term). Her wish is good in itself, but it is improper and presumptuous to try to penetrate the secrets hidden in God. Yet, we can recognize the great depth of the Yahwist tradition in that this desire has remained with mankind and still constitutes one of the basic drives of man. The thirst for knowledge about man's future has remained fundamental. Its effects may be seen in the development of all the sciences and in their being marshalled in man's attempt to transform the earth and thereby assure his future. Here again we may perceive the reason why it is *Ishah*, rather than *Ish*, who sins first: as the element of mankind which brought it to completion, she becomes the interpreter of the deepest nisus in man.

What happens as a result of eating the fruit of the tree of knowledge is, however, only a partial fulfillment of this wish. The serpent has not told the whole truth about knowing good and evil; presumably he was not aware of the extent of good and evil that would be known after the experiment he was attempting. There is an unveiling of the future; but what is revealed does not tell much about the future of mankind as it will live century after century. *Ish* eats of the fruit after *Ishah.* In the story, he was present all along, even though he remained silent in the exchange with the serpent. His act unites him to the expressed desire of mankind to acquire the knowledge of good and evil. And, like *Ishah,* he is given only a limited insight: "Then the eyes of both were opened and they realized that they were naked. So they sewed fig leaves together to make themselves loin-clothes" (3:7). In other words, they are initiated to sex. What they had not understood at 2:25 when seeing each other naked without shame, they now grasp. It is through their nakedness that mankind will be shaped. The Yahwist account becomes comparable to the many rites of initiation found all over the world. There will ensue from this the acquisition by *Ishah* of a new name: "The man named his wife Eva because she was the mother of all those who live" (3:20). This they did not know before. Now they realize the glorious function and already (this name is given after the curse) the drudgery of each. They are now not only *Ish* and *Ishah,* man and woman, but male and female. All is now ready for the beginning of chapter 4: "The man had intercourse with his wife Eva...."

The curse should now be examined, as it throws light on the whole issue. Yet we should carefully distinguish between the curse on the serpent, which is a piece of largely nontheological folklore, and the other two curses. The curse on the serpent is highly interesting as a piece of etiological speculation: why, of all the animals, does the snake alone run by wiggling his belly instead of using legs and feet? The answer appeals to a curse pronounced on him as a punishment for tempting the woman. It would seem, too, that the author injected a certain amount of polemical theology into this legend. For by calling the snake "cursed beyond all cattle, all wild beasts" (3:14), he throws discredit on all the ophic cults, those of Canaanites and of Egypt, connected with fertility, those of Mesopotamia, and the prolonged use of the serpent figure in Israel itself as a symbol of life and death.

The enmity between the offsprings of both may well contain a prophecy relating to Israel and the fertility cults of Canaan. These still tempt Israel, striking at its heel whenever there is an occasion; but Israel in the long run will crush the serpent and return to its true God. It seems doubtful that more can be read into this and that a proto-gospel is really included in this passage.

'I will multiply your pains in childbearing, you shall give birth to your children in pain. Your yearning shall be for your husband, yet he will lord it over you.' (3:16)

The curse of woman evokes a reversal of the order of the universe achieved in Eden. Whereas woman in innocence was the acme of creation, woman in experience, following her initiation to sexuality, will be dominated by her sexual desire for her husband, by her husband himself who will rule over her, and by the pains of pregnancy. Literally, it is not only the pains, but also the childbearing, which will be multiplied: "I will multiply your pains and your childbearing...." That is, the punishment will bear on the woman at the very point of which she was curious: this will be her good and evil, the thing she desired to know. The future of the race lies with her, but it will require from her the loss of her original nobility. The higher aspect of mankind becomes enslaved, and the ruder aspect, the man, takes over the leadership.

Admittedly, the order of things is also reversed as regards the man's relationship to the soil which he was to till. It will no longer be the well-ordered Garden; he will no longer live in Paradise. For he will now have to labor for food. He will have to struggle with nature. And at the end he will return to his place of origin, dust.

Read in the light of our previous analysis of the Garden and the happenings in it, the curse contains the clue to the meaning of the entire Yahwist tradition concerning the origins of mankind. The author could look at the problems of the origins of man only from his own situation within mankind. He himself necessarily belonged to the order of the curse, to postlapsarian history. Yet he did not accept the opinion that this order had always existed. The pains of work and childbearing, the drudgery of woman under male domination could not represent the proper order of the universe. The origin must have been different. So, the poet reconstructed a prelapsarian order, a paradise condition, which he depicted as the exact reverse of the reality which he himself knew in his daily life. And when, through the ages, Israel heard these legends and later read them, they were reminded that they experienced the ambiguity of living East of Eden, while yet longing after a return to Paradise. They were nourished by two conflicting traditions: the postlapsarian one, regulating their lives and the order of their society, and the dreamt prelapsarian one which they expected to return some time at the end of their cycle of life, in what will eventually be called the messianic era.

We are thus invited to read the entire Old Testament in this light. There were two traditions about woman. The one corresponded to the order of society, in which woman, though protected by many laws, was inferior to man. The other echoed the legends of the origins as recorded in the Yahwist text: originally, woman was the higher and better part of mankind. The fall from this primitive nobility to the everyday reality was caused by a cosmic catastrophe which provoked a reversal of values. The current anthropology did not fit the order of creation. In my view of the matter, this was by no means a tradition that had been handed down from primitive times. Rather, it was a poetic and theogonic reconstruction with the purpose of explaining how things had come to be what they were. Whatever the exact origin of the story, eventually it became identified with the religious view of primitive times, to the point of itself being taken as the primitive (and therefore the true) account of the relationship between the sexes. The primitive order had indeed been lost. Women had become, in all the societies of the Fertile Crescent, little more than slaves. In Israel itself they kept this inferior status, although Mosaic legislation protected them in many ways from the brutality of the male world. Yet the primitive order can never be utterly lost as long as it is remembered. In the Hebraic concept of the return to the beginning, of *Shoub Sheboth,* the primitive times of Israel—the Exodus and the *Cahal* in the wilderness—were also ideals to be evoked at the recurrence of the yearly liturgies and to be somehow expected again in the future. Likewise, the Eden that had been lost by mankind as a whole could be hoped for. The beginning presented an ideal, and therefore a future. The values whose order had been upset were not forgotten.

The daily life of the people of Israel was naturally led at the level of a society which had itself felt the effects of sin. The traditions of the Old Testament were quite clear as to the origin of civilization, particularly in its technical and urban forms: it came from the descendants of Cain. This society is ambivalent. As the recipient of Yahweh's favor, it experiences the "good and evil" that the woman in the Garden had aspired to know. The ultimate purpose of God remains hidden, but the means to fulfill God's will are known: Torah, the Law. Thanks to this ambiguity, the two traditions as to the status and function of woman could continue side by side. Or rather, the life of the people and its regulation according to the legal system of Leviticus and Deuteronomy reflect the order of the curse, the fallen state of mankind in which woman is legally, socially, emotionally subject to man. The Law is not now given for Eden, but for the real world of time. Indeed, the originators of the myth of the sin of Adam and the woman must have proceeded backwards, reflecting on the legal and natural inferiority of women. This was the data they had to work with. It is therefore to be expected that biblical literature includes many passages where women are berated. The wisdom literature, relatively recent yet going far back, through the proverbs which it incorporated, into the past of Israel, forms a classical source of misogynic statements and antifemine humor. "I find woman more bitter than death," Qoheleth writes during the second century B.C.," she is a snare; her heart a net; her arms are chains; he who is pleasing to God eludes her; but the sinner is her captive" (7:26-28). And the wisdom of Ben Sirach, around 180 B.C., is notorious for its indignation against women, who seem to be assimilated, as a matter of principle, to loose women (e.g. 9:1-13; 25:13-26; 18; 42:12-14). Even Ben Sirach's kinder passages are not flattering for women:

A woman will accept any husband, but some daughters are better than others. A woman's beauty delights the beholder, a man likes nothing better. If her tongue is kind and gentle, her husband has no equal among the sons of men. The man who takes a wife has the making of a fortune, a helper that suits him, and a pillar to lean on. If a property has no fence, it will be plundered. When a man has no wife, he is aimless and querulous. Will anyone trust a man carrying weapons who flies from town to town? So it is with the man who has no nest, and lodges wherever night overtakes him. (36:21-27)

A text of this kind appreciates woman only in relation to man. She is essentially an object man stares at. In herself she has no special wishes, but is ready to take any husband. If she has been well selected, she can be very useful. Above all, she helps a man to settle down and thus to deserve trust. In other words, a wife is better than many prostitutes. In such a view, woman cannot even find an incentive to any values other than those which male society imposes upon her. Ben Sirach's book even includes this ferocious proverb: "A man's spite is preferable to a woman's kindness" (42:14).

No doubt, Ben Sirach's misogynist wisdom corresponds rather accurately to the actual condition of woman in Jewish society.[4] The older books of the Bible, mirroring to a great extent the preexilic society, show woman behaving with great freedom, as is proper in nomadic and rural societies where her toil is necessary to the subsistence of the group. Later books illustrate a growing restriction of her movements. She becomes man's thing. She is bought for marriage from her father, and she may be divorced, at least according to Hillel's opinion, "for any reason whatsoever." As a virgin she is respected but she enjoys no freedom to organize her own life and to refuse marriage. Her official life of prayer is not so extensive as that of man. She has no active function in the synagogue even when she is admitted. The Temple of Herod, unlike the Temple of Solomon and that of Zorobabel, admits her only as far as "women's precincts," where merchants and vendors have their market. After puberty, and in marriage more than before marriage, woman frequently becomes legally impure through no fault of her own: her shedding of blood in her periods and in childbirth render her taboo to her entourage. A good Jew even refuses to be served by a woman and avoids talking to one. At least in Jerusalem and in wealthy society, the growing trend in the Greek period is to confine her to home, which turns into a *gyneceum* or harem. Even when she is outside, her veil is a symbol and reminder of her hidden condition. In her relation to her husband, there is no question of love, only of obedience.

Admittedly, exceptions may be cited. The names of **some prophetesses** have been recorded, although they belong to primitive times. While permitted by the Law, polygamy was never extensively practiced; yet this may have been due to economic reasons more than to respect for woman's personality or wishes. The Essenian communities did not encourage marriage, thus promoting a cult of virginity unknown to orthodox Judaism. In Egypt, the ascetic community described by Philo under the name of Therapeutes included, unlike the Qumran monastery, women as well as men.[5] They lived separately, each in a cell; yet they met for the Sabbath worship in a synagogue where men gathered on one side and women on the other, separated by a wall. They also met for a weekly evening meal. This time they still divided in two groups, "men on the right, women on the left"; after the meal they formed two choirs for liturgical chanting and dancing that lasted through the night. Philo notes that "carried away by the enthusiasm, and drinking, as in Bacchic rites, the generous wine of divine love, they end by forming only one group of singers." It may not be irrelevant to remark that the Therapeutes lived in Egypt, the land where Greek mores were the most permissive for women, influenced as they were by the older Egyptian tradition. Diaspora Jews in general tended to adopt local practices, thus abandoning some of the Palestinian restrictions of women.

Above all, Jesus' behavior, as recorded in the Gospels, does not follow traditional Jewish reserve. To his companions' surprise, he speaks with the Samaritan woman at the well. He heals women as well as men, entertains relations of friendship with Martha and Mary. The group of his followers includes both married and unmarried women. His teaching on marriage implies the equality of man and woman. This will be of great importance for the concept of womanhood in the early Church; it was at variance with the mainstream of the rabbinic tradition.

The Book of Proverbs ends with an alphabetical poem about the perfect woman. Interpreted literally, as a description of the ideal wife, this describes a slave, a person who is entirely dominated by another. This woman in fact does more work than anyone else in her household, looks after everything and everybody, never tires, is the last to retire and the first to rise. She earns a fortune for her husband, while he sits at the gate palavering with the elders of the land. This is an eloquent and puzzling description of woman as pushed by the curse to total devotion to a husband who dominates her and eats away all her substance: "Your yearning shall be for your husband, and he will lord it over you."

Yet, and this will help us to appreciate the ambiguity of the feminine picture in the Old Testament, this text of the Book of Proverbs was also interpreted as describing not a woman of flesh and blood, but the very wisdom of God. The Septuagint identifies this "wise woman" with "the fear of the Lord" (v. 30). Precisely, in the later books of the Old Testament, woman remains also a symbol of what is highest in the proper order of the universe.

This could be illustrated with the stories contained in the various books of the Bible about the great women of Israel. The prophetesses should come first, for in them *Ishah's* desire of knowing good and evil is fulfilled in what is no longer an ironic way: they do share some of the secrets of Yahweh. Among them we ought to mention Myriam, sister of Moses and Aaron, who, in what seems to have been a common rite among the tribes of the Near East, celebrates the victory over the Pharaoh's army by song and dance (Exod. 15: 20-21), and especially Debora, the woman "judge" through whose prophecy Baraq destroyed Sesara's troop (Judg. 4-5). These early examples date from the time of migration and conquest. Later writers will imagine similar figures who would deserve the name given to Debora in the epic poem about her, "Mother to Israel" (Judg. 5:7). Thus Judith and Esther, fictional heroines, yet models for Jewish womanhood. And, in a more subdued light, this other dim figure from the period of the Judges, Jephthah's daughter: she dies a victim of her father's vow to Yahweh to offer in sacrifice the first person who would cross his path on his return from battle. Human sacrifice, forbidden eventually by the Law, was occasionally practiced in primitive times, perhaps under the influence of Canaanite pagan practices. Yet Jephthah's daughter was not the victim of bad luck. "The spirit of Yahweh" had come on Jephthah and inspired him to make this vow. Thus, we touch again this knot of ambiguity which characterizes the woman of the Old Testament: she is both the chosen one and the slave.

There is but one step from reflection on the heroines of Israel's history to the representation of Israel itself, in its role as the people of Yahweh, in the form of a woman related to Yahweh through the bonds of wedlock. This is a classical theme with the prophets, from Osea to John the Baptist. The spark which enabled this theme to catch the imagination of the prophets and, consequently, of the people, seems to have been the historical and religious situation of the Northern Kingdom toward the middle of the eighth century, some two decades before the fall of Samaria in 721. The cult of Yahweh was in imminent danger of being overrun by practices borrowed from the pagan cults which subsisted among what remained of the older inhabitants of the country. The cult of Baal, with its center at the great sanctuary at Ras-Shamra, included sacred prostitution as a fertility rite. This religion continued, in probably a cruder form, in the villages of the Canaanites who still lived within the confines of the Northern Kingdom. And the Israelites in turn sometimes took part in these or similar orgiastic rites. Osea speaks to this situation when Yahweh, through him, blames this sin on the entire population:

So, although your daughters prostitute themselves and your sons' wives commit adultery, I shall not be hard on your daughters for their whoring or on your sons' wives for their adultery, when everyone is wandering off with whores and offering sacrifice with sacred prostitutes. (4:13-14)

In these conditions, the very participation of Hebrews in Canaanite mysteries could easily be seen as an act of prostitution, as a betrayal of Yahweh, whose relationship to his people is likened to that of a man for the woman he woos. Part of Osea's mission was graphically to show this relationship through his preaching and also through the example of his own life. I take here chapters 1 and 3 of the Book of Osea to be a doublet of one incident, namely of his marriage with a Hebrew woman who had prostituted herself by participating in unlawful sexual practices in honor of the "Baalim." This is the starting point for the magnificent development of chapter 2, where a similar sequence of prostitution, atonement, and love describes the position of the entire people of Yahweh.

Yes, their mother has played the whore, she who conceived them has disgraced herself. 'I am going to court my lovers,' she said, 'who give me my bread and water, my wool, my flax, my oil and my drink.' She would not acknowledge, not she, that I was the one who was giving her the corn, the wine, the oil, and who freely gave her that silver and gold of which they have made Baals. (2:7 & 10)

Between the fertility cult of the Baalim, believed to be the dispensers of agricultural abundance, and the worship of Yahweh alone, the people has hesitated. Therefore God denounces it as an adulteress: "She is not my wife, nor am I her husband. Let her rid her face of her whoring and her breasts of her adultery" (2:2), a probable allusion to tattooed marks of initiation.

Up to this point, the analogy is between Israel and the sacred prostitute (or the woman who has somehow participated in these cults). The turning point comes in the analogy when the prophet announces that the sovereignty of Yahweh will be able to change this course of prostitution into a return to Israel's first love: "Then she will say, 'I will go back to my first husband, I was happier then than I am today.' That is why I will lure her and lead her out into the wilderness and speak to her heart.... I will betroth you to myself for ever, betroth you with integrity and justice, with tenderness and love; I will betroth you to myself in faithfulness, and you will come to know Yahweh" (2:9 & 16, 21-22).

The perspective which opens here is a return to Eden. For the renewed tenderness between Yahweh and the woman will be accompanied by "a treaty on her behalf with the wild animals, with the birds of heaven and the creeping things of the earth" (2:20), the three categories of Genesis 1:30 (in the same words, with the exception of the word for "earth"). Thus the woman Israel will be—and, in her moments of fidelity, she is—the woman of the Garden, the perfection of mankind.

This double reference of the theme of the woman Israel recurs throughout the age of the prophets. In Jeremiah (3-4), in Ezechiel (16,23), in the second

Isaiah (62,66), Israel is both the harlot and Yahweh's bride. As harlot, she has betrayed Yahweh through prostitution with false gods; as bride, she is the first fruits of mankind, with whom God takes pleasure because in her the woman of Paradise has retained—or recovered—the state of holiness.

The last of the prophets will still be aware of this. Will not John the Baptist, in what the Gospel of John presents as his last testimony before going to jail, answer his disciples: "The bride is only for the bridegroom; and yet the bridegroom's friend, who stands there and listens, is glad when he hears the bridegroom's voice. This same joy I feel, and now it is complete (John 3:28-29)?

The wisdom literature of the Old Testament, during the last two centuries B.C., offers another kind of illustration of the typology of womanhood. Although much of this literature, is misogynist, books which include some of the most disparaging statements about women also elevate a feminine image to the level of the divine wisdom.[6]

What is the *Hokmah,* or *Sophia?* Admittedly, as in all the wisdom literature of the ancient Near East, Egypt included, it includes the practical and ethical maxims which grow out of the experience of life. Couched in proverbs, in parables, in riddles, these are collected and loosely organized in order to form summaries of the rules of the good life. It is the beginning of a philosophy of ethics in a people not given to intellectual speculation. The books of wisdom (like Proverbs, the wisdom of Qoheleth, the wisdom of Ben Sirach, Job) contain principles and pieces of advice for behavior. They also speak about wisdom as a valuable quality that the human mind ought to acquire. It then becomes the capacity of discernment by which one knows how to behave properly, eschewing the pitfalls and choosing the better and more profitable course of action. As such, it includes the knowledge of Torah. Such a wisdom can be presented figuratively as though it were a substantive entity: it is occasionally made to speak for itself, addressing its listeners and teaching them the ways of wise conduct.

So far, wisdom is not relevant to our inquiry except for the contents of its teaching. However, the Hebrew books of wisdom go further, attributing wisdom also to the Lord. This would not be particularly striking, since the Lord of all things, who gave his people Torah, must know the principles of behavior. It becomes highly important when the writers describe the divine wisdom and, again, make it address the people as though it were a feminine entity belonging to the realm of the divine. In the Book of Proverbs, Wisdom is the first and highest creature of God, identical with Torah in its heavenly state as conceived in God's mind. "Yahweh created me when his purpose first unfolded, before the oldest of his works.... I was by his side, a master craftsman, delighting with him day after day, ever at play in his presence, at play every-

where in the world, delighting to be with the sons of men ..." (8:22, 30-31).
Now this wisdom figure is feminine, and not only grammatically, which is the
case both in Hebrew and in Greek. It is also described like a woman, who invites her children to abide with her and to live in her house. Furthermore, her
opposite number is Folly, also presented with feminine features and explicitly
called *Ishah*, Dame Folly (8:13).

The contrast of Lady Wisdom and Dame Folly shows that we are still at
the level of an allegory or parable. The text is cast in the form of a midrash
and graphically presents the two ways, of life and of death, symbolized by
two women, wise and stupid.

Ben Sirach's personification of wisdom, however, goes further than this.
Wisdom, Sophia (since this book is in the Septuagint and not in the Hebrew
Bible), is here again a creature, though an eternal one (24:9). It is successively identified with the spirit of the Lord hovering over the chaos of the earth
at the beginning (24:3), with the glory of Yahweh which resided in the pillar
of cloud of Exodus (24:4), with the worship in the holy Tabernacle (24:10),
with the Book of the Covenant and the Law of Moses (24:23). This wisdom
presides over Paradise, since Ben Sirach connects her with the four rivers of
Eden (24:25-26). This last notation points to her as to a prototype to be im-
itated and forever followed. She is the feminine model of all those who love
and obey the Lord, the true *Ishah*, of whom Ben Sirach says: "The first [*o
protos*, that is, Adam, the first man] never managed to grasp her entirely, and
the last [*o eschatos*, the ultimate one, the one who comes at the end] has not
found her" (24:28).

With the Book of Wisdom, the personification of Sophia reaches its apex.
Like the book of Ben Sirach, Wisdom is found only in the Septuagint. Yet
Ben Sirach's composition existed in Hebrew before being translated into
Greek and placed in the Alexandrian Bible. The Book of Wisdom, on the contrary, is itself an Alexandrian production; or at least (since we cannot be
quite certain of its place of origin) it was written in Greek around 50 B.C. by
diaspora Jews who were themselves influenced by Greek thought. Alexandria
was a likely place for this to happen, as, a few decades later, in the case of the
Jewish philosopher Philo (20 B.C.–54 A.D.).

Here, Sophia is no longer a creature, but an eternal emanation from God:
"She is a breath of the Power of God, pure emanation of the glory of the
Almighty.... She is a reflection of the eternal Light, untarnished mirror of
God's active power image of his goodness" (7:24-25). She is the repository of
his multiform spirit (7:22-24). She participates in all the powers of God,
being identical with his Word (9:12); yet she is not he. Divine, she is not God,
who remains, as much as in any biblical text, the Unknowable. Wisdom is
that which man can know of God's glory, or, equivalently, that of God which
is communicable to man. In other words, Wisdom is the "good and evil"
which the *Ishah* of Genesis 2 desired to know and never knew. It is the image

of *Ishah* as transformed by the true knowledge of benediction and malediction, the divine antitype of *Ishah*. It shows what *Ishah* would have been had she waited for God's self-unveiling instead of attempting to grasp the secrets of God by herself. Significantly, the account of the beginning of mankind, in chapter 10 of the Book of Wisdom, contains no allusion to the woman: everything seems to stem from "the first-fashioned father of the world, created alone" (10:1). It seems consistent that the Book of Wisdom, placing the primitive feminine figure in heaven with God, would not place her on earth with the first man.

It would be tempting at this point to apply the thesis of this chapter to an interpretation of the Song of Songs,[7] seen as the crowning point of the Old Testament reflections on the theme of womanhood. Admittedly, this meaning could not be attributed as such to the text of the Song when it was written (or compiled), in the fourth century; yet it could fit the Song as found in the Septuagint, placed among the books of wisdom. The lover is Yahweh, wooing Israel. The Shulamite is Israel in its feminine aspect, the bride of Yahweh of the Prophetic tradition. The various episodes of the Song, whether or not they originally belonged together, can be read as poetic expressions of the ebb and flow of the historical relationships between Israel and her God, ever seeking, and often estranged from, each other.

Such an interpretation makes sense only when the Bible is seen as a whole, in which the same themes are used successively, enriched by experience, reflection, and poetry, and reach higher levels of meaning as the tradition of Israel runs toward its fullness.

In the Christian reading of the Bible, this fullness includes the New Testament. Likewise, the theme of woman of the Israelite tradition must be homogenous with that of the writings of early Christianity. The insights that have been opened by the Old must reach their flowering in the New. The full scope of Genesis 2, which, in my view, dominates the entire picture of woman in the literature of the Hebrews and the Jews, will come into better light from a reading of the relevant passages of the New Testament.

Before this, however, the thesis of this chapter may be summed up. The *Ishah* of Genesis brings perfection or completion to mankind as its feminine aspect. Sin itself arises from this feminine aspect of mankind as something good and desirable, but premature, which should be expected as a gift rather than grasped as a possession. Following the fall, the order of history reverses the balance of mankind, making the feminine inferior to the masculine element, and confuses as well as obscures the symbolism of the sexes. But the prelapsarian tradition of the value of feminity is never lost. It comes to life with the prophets, who see Israel as the fiancée of the Lord; in the books of wisdom, where the divine Wisdom is depicted as the primordial woman antecedent to the creation of the world; occasionally in poetry, as in the Song of Songs, where the union of love between man and woman becomes a symbol for the relationship between God and his bride Israel. Israel is also mankind, that is, mankind as loved by God; it is mankind itself which is feminine before God.

2

Return to the Beginning

Considered as the source of Christian thought, the writings of the New
Testament should be treated as a whole since it is as a unit that they have
reached the present-day Church. Yet, seen from the point of view of the historian, they do not at all belong to the same cultural layer. Originating in different places and times, written by several authors, they constitute a conglomeration of disparate works, unified by their common interest in the good
news concerning Jesus Christ, yet diversified by their background and by the
immediate purposes and concerns of their authors and their first readers. My
aim in this volume is theological; and I wish now to study the New Testament
insofar as it shaped later attitudes regarding womanhood (as an idea) and
women (as realities of flesh and blood). Yet the New Testament was not
formed at one try; it contains more primitive and more recent material; it
shows an evolution of concepts to have taken place in the very early Church
at the time of, and immediately after, the Apostles. On account of this, we
may cull diverging views of womanhood from the books of the New Testament. Such a phenomenon is already evident in regard to more fundamental
aspects of the Christian kerygma: as a case in point, the picture of Jesus is not
entirely the same in the Epistles of Paul, in the synoptic Gospels, in the writings of the Johannine corpus. Likewise the picture of woman. Owing to the
influence of the Old Testament and of other Jewish thinking on the first
Christian authors, we may expect the two great streams of Old Testament
thought to be reflected in the New: woman appears in the cursed condition
that she has inherited from the origins of mankind; yet she also is the type of
the heavenly wisdom which presided over the foundations of the world and
which was embodied in the best moments of Israel's existence as the bride of
Yahweh. Just as a prophet like Ezechiel could speak of Israel as being alter-
nately the Lord's unfaithful wife and his beloved companion, so can the New
Testament authors unite in one vision the two images of womanhood, the one
preserving the primitive blessings of *Ishah*, the perfection of mankind, the
other embodying the tarnished image of Eve after the fall. The two perspec-
tives may be found in one and the same author.

This is predominantly the case with Paul, with whom we shall begin. The letters of Saint Paul constitute the oldest historical layer of New Testament literature, having been written before the final redaction of the four Gospels. They also form by far the most comprehensive theological synthesis that has reached us from the primitive Church. The Johannine synthesis may undoubtedly be compared with it by its scope and depth; but the later date of the writings of the Johannine corpus call for a postponement of their examination until we have studied Paul and, subsequently, the synoptic Gospels.[1]

It seems indisputable that, doctrinally speaking, the writings attributed to Paul do not form one consistent entity. The differences that have been discovered between the Epistle to the Ephesians, the Pastoral Epistles, and the rest of the corpus witness to more than the historical growth of one man. They illustrate the fact that we do not read the work of one single author, but of Paul and at least one other person, possibly several. This other person, operating in the context of the Pauline churches and in the light of Paul's authentic teachings, appealed to Paul's authority to justify a development of Church tradition in a way which Paul himself may not have foreseen. In other words, the Pastoral Epistles revise Paul's teaching in view of the settling down of Church organization after the departure of the Apostle. In a similar way, the Epistle to the Hebrews and the Acts of Luke are related to the Pauline corpus. The former adds a theological dimension to Paul's views that Paul himself (if his endorsement of this letter is authentic, as I think it is) acknowledged as valuable. The latter complement the historical knowledge of Paul's mission, relating it to the wider mission of the Apostolic Church.[2]

Be that as it may, Paul's ideas regarding womanhood prove to be ambiguous. They may be, and have been, interpreted in either a misogynist or a profeminine direction. Both the prelapsarian and the postlapsarian traditions of the book of Genesis are reflected in Paul's writings. Paul was a Jew and wrote like one. He could not easily prescind from the theological background to which, with all the primitive Church, he was heir.

The subjection of the wife to her husband in the Christian society of his time, as in Jewish society, to say nothing of the pagan society with which he was familiar, is abundantly illustrated in Paul's letters. The picture of the Christian wife outlined in 1 Corinthians 11:2-6, is that of a person subject to her husband, who is "her head," as Christ is the head of the husband and God the head of Christ. The married woman stands at the bottom of a hierarchy, at the top of which is God. Christ and husband mediate in between, so that the woman seems further removed from Christ and from God than her husband. Looking at this hierarchy downwards, woman becomes the "glory" (*doxa*) of man, as man the glory of God. In the Jewish context of this passage, the glory in question is conceived on the pattern of the *shekinah* of the Old

Testament, the manifestation of Yahweh's presence. In verse 7 Paul explicitly identifies this glory and the image of God which is man. In other words, only man is the image of God, the woman being only the image of man, a prolongation and manifestation of his power.

This is patently a very rabbinic passage. Paul has not yet emancipated himself (and how could he have done so?) from the thought patterns of his Jewish-pharisaic training. In a strongly patriarchal family structure, women are given status in society by the man who acts as the head of the family, whatever moral and effective authority they may actually enjoy within the family circle. Such was the Jewish way of life. Yet Corinth was in a pagan land, and the Corinthian Christians normally followed Greek customs. It is in this context that I understand Paul's injunction, in 1 Corinthians 11:5, "For a woman it is a sign of disrespect for her head if she prays or prophesies unveiled." This alludes to the fact that, at Corinth (whatever may have been the practice elsewhere), women participated in prayer and prophesied in the Ecclesia. They even did it, following in this a Greek custom, without veils on their heads. As at other moments of his career, Paul feels caught between the claims of Christian freedom, for which "all is permitted, although all is not expedient" (1 Cor. 6:12), and the Jewish conventions which cannot be discarded without polarizing the Christian communities to the breaking point. He appeals to a compromise which must have been formerly agreed upon: when women "pray or prophesy" they should at least wear a veil. If they wish to enjoy the spiritual freedom of public prayer and prophecy, let them renounce the material freedom of the Greeks not to wear a veil on their heads. A precedent for such a gentleman's agreement between Jewish-Christians and Gentile-Christians had been set, at the so-called Council of Jerusalem, concerning practices forbidden to Jews. As verse 16 claims, this is the practice in all "Churches of God." This expression I take to mean not all the Churches and not even the Pauline Churches especially, but rather the Palestinian Churches, which Paul, even after he turned to the Gentiles in his preaching of the Gospel, considered the standard to emulate and the model for all Churches. The "Churches of God" of 11:16 are identical with "the Churches of the saints" of 14:33.

Later in the same letter, Paul returns to this question, which, minor as it would seem, must have caused a great deal of discussion at Corinth. This time, Paul does more than express his disapproval of the Corinthian women's behavior. He lays down the law for the future; and, as often happens when it seems urgent to stop a practice which is potentially harmful to the community, Paul's injunction becomes stricter than the agreement he has alluded to. From now on, let the Corinthians apply the Jewish principle as such and imitate the Palestinian Churches: "As in all the Churches of the saints" (by which, again, I understand the Judeo-Christian Churches in Israel, rather than the mixed Churches of the diaspora and of pagan country) "women are to remain quiet at meetings, since they have no permission to speak; they must keep in the background, as Torah itself lays it down. If they have any question to ask, they should ask their husbands at home: it does not seem right for a woman to raise her voice at meetings" (14:34-35).

This old-fashioned Jewish position is hardly in keeping with the principle and the practice of prophecy. Acts 21:9 gives evidence that women were admitted to the ministry of prophecy, even in Jewish-Hellenistic circles; this was the case with the four daughters of the deacon Philip. Paul himself mentioned, in 11:5, the women-prophets of Corinth: but where can they prophesy, if they cannot even speak at the assemblies? On account of this dilemma, I suspect that Paul does not intend this stricter discipline to apply to prophesying by women: women prophets would have permission to speak. His problem is with those who intervene in meetings by asking questions that can very well be asked at home from their husbands.[3] At any rate, the stricter interpretation will be adopted and reinforced by 1 Timothy 2:11-15. As I read them, verses 11 and 12 are intended by the author to be an authentic interpretation of 1 Corinthians 14:34-35: "During instruction, a woman should be quiet and respectful. I am not giving permission for a woman to teach or to tell a man what to do." The following argumentation (vv. 13-14) derives from that of 1 Corinthians 11:8-10; yet the point is made with much more crudeness. In Corinthians, Paul stated: "For man did not come from woman; no, woman came from man; and man was not created for the sake of woman, but woman for sake of man." In 1 Timothy, this becomes: "Adam was formed first, and Eve afterwards, and it was not Adam who was led astray, but the woman who was led astray and fell into sin."

That Paul wished the Jewish subordination of women to men to be enforced in his Churches is one thing; that he was convinced by his theoretical, and strongly rabbinic, argumentation is another. The first point tallies with instructions given elsewhere: "Wives, obey your husbands, as you should in the Lord" (Col. 3:18); "Obey one another in obedience to Christ. Wives should regard their husbands as they regard the Lord, since as Christ is the head of the Church and saves the whole body, so is the husband the head of his wife; and as the Church submits to Christ, so should wives to their husbands, in everything" (Eph. 5:21-24). I will return to this analogy later. For the time being this text of Ephesians may serve to show that, in Pauline circles, the type of behavior enjoined in 1 Corinthians 14, came to be acknowledged as proper. The second point, however, demands another answer. Paul himself remained unconvinced by the objections he raised in 1 Corinthians 11:8-10 against the freedom of the Christian woman. For his next remark ruined the argument he had just used: "However, in the Lord neither is woman without man nor man without woman; for as woman comes from man, so does man come through woman; and they all come from God" (v.11). As I understand "from" ($\dot{\epsilon}\kappa$) and "through" ($\delta\iota\dot{\alpha}$), Paul asserts that woman, in

Genesis, comes from man and, in keeping with the biology of his time, that man is born through (rather than from) woman; yet religiously speaking and in relation to God, this establishes no difference between them, for they both proceed from God.

Paul's theology thus makes room for another principle concerning man and woman in Christ and in the Ecclesia, the principle of equality or, as I think it ought to be expressed, the principle of identity. Early in his writing career, Paul formulated it in his letter to the Galatians:

> Before faith came, we were allowed no freedom by the Law; we were being looked after till faith was revealed. The Law was to be our guardian until the Christ came and we could be justified by faith. Now that that time has come we are no longer under that guardian, and you are, all of you, sons of God through faith in Christ Jesus. All baptised in Christ, you have all clothed yourselves in Christ, and there are no more distinctions between Jew and Greek, slave and free, male and female, but all of you are one in Christ Jesus. (3:23-28)

All Christians, Jew or Greek, slave or free, male or female, enjoy now the same freedom, based on their identity in Christ Jesus. Paul does more at this point than echo the old tradition concerning the paradisiac state of man and woman. It is in Christ, and not in Eden, that he now sees male and female. The pristine state has been restored, not yet for all mankind or to the full extension of nature, but only for those who are clothed in Christ Jesus through baptism in faith. If the world after the fall is dominated by the flesh ($\sigma\acute{\alpha}\rho\xi$), the faithful have been made spirit ($\pi\nu\epsilon\tilde{\nu}\mu\alpha$). It is therefore in Paul's Christology that one should look for the key to the real status of woman in Christ as Paul envisions it from the early days of Galatians. This Christology, fully developed in the latter days of Colossians, was adumbrated in 1 Corinthians 15:45-50:

> The first man, Adam, as Scripture says, became a living soul; but the last Adam became a life-giving spirit. First, the one with the soul not the one with the spirit; afterwards the one with the spirit. The first man from the earth, earthy; the second man from heaven. Those who are of the earth are like the former; those who are of heaven are like the latter. And as we have borne the image of the earthy, so shall we bear the image of the heavenly.

The eschatological passage refers directly to the faithful's future estate, to which they will have access through the resurrection. The fulfillment of Christian life will introduce to a state higher than paradise. We shall not be, like the first Adam, "psychic," but we shall participate in the "pneumatic" state of the second Adam. Both man and woman will be like the second Adam, like Christ. Thus, in the second Adam is to be found the heavenly archetype of both man and woman: they have only one model, Christ, the heavenly mankind. For the word "adam," as we ought to recall, does not primarily designate the male, but mankind. The Christians have access, through Christ, to the heavenly pattern of mankind, at a level that brooks no distinction between "Jew and Greek, slave and free, male and female." As Paul will emphasize in Colossians, Christ is the pattern of all creatures, woman therefore included:

> He is the image of the unseen God and the first-born of all creation, for in him were created all things in heaven and on earth: everything visible and invisible, Thrones, Dominations, Sovereignties, Powers—all things were created through him and for him. Before anything was created he existed, and he holds all things in unity. Now the Church is his body, he is the head. As he is the beginning, he was the first to be born from the dead, so that he should be first in every way; because God wanted all perfection to be found in him.... (1:15-19)

Yet as long as he lives on earth, the Christian is not fully in heaven. Being spirit and still remaining flesh (*sarx*), he finds himself caught in the agonistic dialectic that Paul describes in the letter to the Romans (chapters 7-8). If Christian men and women are raised in Christ beyond the distinction of sexes, they remain at the same time subject to the law of their flesh, which makes them male or female. Accordingly, Paul's injunctions to his communities waver between a vision of the heavenly identity of male and female, to which the faithful have been elevated by the Lord, and the earthly reality of the sexual life. Indeed, we may surmise, from the evidence of 1 Corinthians 7, that much of the difficulties that troubled the Church at Corinth stemmed from the inherent dilemma of belonging to two worlds, Some of the Corinthians attempted to translate their eschatological freedom into their everyday experience. Prophesying without a veil was a minor liberty compared to the boldness of those who tried to experiment with what may be called spiritual promiscuity. Partnership between a man and a virgin woman or perhaps between several of both sexes could be an eschatological sign. The time is short (7:29). The world is passing away (7:31). It is better not to marry (7:28, 32-35). Far from condemning the attempt to lead a heavenly life in the company of the other sex, for those who have the suitable charism, Paul praises it:

> If a man has a partner in celibacy and feels that he is not behaving properly towards her, if, that is, his instincts are too strong for him and something must be done, he may do as he pleases; there is nothing wrong in it; let them marry. But if a man is steadfast in his purpose, being under no compulsion, and has complete control of his own choice; and if he has de-

cided in his own mind to preserve his partner in her virginity, he will do well. Thus, he who marries his partner does well, and he who does not will do better. (7:36-38)

As the attempt at spiritual partnership in Corinth was breaking down under the law of the flesh, Paul agrees to transform these partnerships into regular marriages for those who cannot carry on. The others ought to persevere as they are according to their calling. The ones will live in marriage according to the image of this world; the others will live together according to the image of heaven.

In this light we should read the passage of the letter to the Ephesians relating to Christian marriage (5:21-33). This I take to be a commentary on Colossians 3:18-19); but it is also made in contrast to 1 Corinthians 7. I do not consider it to come from Paul's own pen. As the text suggests, the situation of Corinth was promptly overcome by the disappearance of virginal partnerships. In Ephesians, the marriage itself between two Christians is now modelled on Christ, whereas in Corinthians, it was the nonsexual union and the celibate life which were the images of heaven, untrammelled by the cares of this world and guaranteeing the freedom to wait upon the Lord. There was of course little point in keeping this hierarchy of values once virginal partnerships were no longer practiced. I understand Ephesians 5 to derive from a deliberate attempt to justify theologically the predominance of marriage over celibacy or the nonsexual unions of Corinthians 7, and the simultaneous waning of Christian freedom owing to the social domination of the male over the female in marriage. The heavenly pattern for marriage is sought in the union between Christ and the Church. This followed and reinterpreted the lines of thought of the Old Testament concerning Yahweh and Israel, which Paul had exploited in 2 Corinthians 11:2. Genesis 2:24 ("they will be two in one flesh") is interpreted explicitly of Christ and the Church and implicitly of husband and wife. The "mystery" mentioned in verse 31 is not, as often suggested in translations and commentaries, matrimony, but the secret meaning of Genesis.

We have already noted that the Pastoral Epistles take a restrictive view of the position of Christian women, whose status does not seem any different from the Jewish women of the times. They must be quiet "during the instruction" (1 Tim. 2:11-12), that is, during the didactic kerygmatic part of the worship service. There is no suggestion that women are admitted to the rank of prophets, although there are still deaconesses (1 Tim. 3:11). Their refined dress must not consist, as for pagan women, in "braided hair, or gold and jewelry, or expensive clothes"; on the contrary, "their adornment is to do the sort of good works that are proper for women who profess to be religious" (3:9-10). Both 1 Timothy and Titus include a fairly long admonition to widows. In the communities established by the Apostle Paul, widowhood had become an institution. In 1 Corinthians, the Apostle had advised widows not to remarry; by now they were organized in a sorority fulfilling diverse functions at the service of the Ecclesia.[4] In Titus, their task consists in watching over the younger women, who need to be taught "how they should love their husbands and love their children, how they are to be sensible and chaste, and how to work in their homes, and be gentle, and do as their husbands tell them, so that the message of God is never disgraced" (Titus 2:4-6). The first letter to Timothy is chiefly concerned with making sure that the widows remain faithful to their commitment not to remarry. Such a fidelity is easier with widows who have reached sixty years of age and have fulfilled all their duties by their children or parents. The true widow must be able "to concentrate all her days and nights to petition and prayer" (5:5).

This cannot come, I think, from Paul's own pen. Not because it contradicts 1 Corinthians 7:8 about the remarriage of widows: experience could well have shown that the advice given by Paul to the Corinthians was not normally applicable and could not be made the pattern for an organized order of widows. There is indeed a deeper discrepancy with Paul's former teaching: the underlying understanding of womanhood is, in Pauline literature, entirely new. In what appears like a commentary on 1 Corinthians 11:7-10, the author of the letter to Timothy slants the doctrine in a new direction: "A woman ought not to speak, because Adam was formed first, and then Eve: and it was not Adam who was led astray, but the woman who was led astray and fell into sin" (2:13-14). This contradicts what Paul has clearly said in Romans 5:12: "Sin entered the world through one man," who is identified as Adam, the counter-type of Christ, the second Adam. But in 1 Timothy, sin does not enter the world through Adam—who is even completely cleared of responsibility—since he is said, contrary to Genesis, "not to have been led astray." The burden of sin is now placed on Eve alone. This may be a curious midrash, but it is not Pauline doctrine.

Another fundamental idea in the Pastoral Epistles' view of woman has not yet appeared in the Pauline corpus: "She will be saved by childbearing, provided she lives a modest life in faith, love and holiness" (1 Tim. 2:15). The meaning is plain: she will be saved by the fulfillment of her curse, by which she was condemned to multiple pregnancies and to her husband's domination. Yet, if this is the ture way of life and salvation for the Christian woman, then in no sense can she be said to have been saved by baptism in Christ Jesus; again, this is not Pauline. Furthermore, if this is the correct teaching, then there should be no room, in the Ecclesia, for unmarried women. Clearly, this runs counter to the position of Paul.

The Pastoral Epistles then present us with the picture of a Church at a turning point of its life. The charismatic age of the Apostles and prophets is drawing to a close; the times call for institutional rules and principles. By natural bias, by social pressure, and possibly as a reaction against the allurements of pagan womanhood, the pattern of life of Christian women is being reversed to that of Jewish women. The Pastoral Epistles embody principles that aim at justifying this state of things, as well as rules of conduct taking it for granted that a providential evolution has taken place. The liberty recognized by Paul must now be channelled through regular institutions: that of widowhood stands out; to the younger women, that of matrimony offers the only proper way of life, since it is through motherhood that they will obtain salvation.

To the same concern for updating a view of sex which had proved utopian in the face of human shortcomings and which the extended delay of the parousia deprived of its chief rationale, I would attribute the passages of 1 Peter 3:1-7 on the obedience of women to their husbands. The text is more recent than Ephesians but older than the Pastoral Epistles. If it is of Petrine authorship, which I see no reason to question, it must have been written prior to 69. The Churches are now beginning to settle down in a semicompromise with the standards of surrounding society. Peter, beginning a famous line of Patristic literature, reacts strongly against adopting pagan conceptions of feminine beauty: "Do not dress up for show, doing up your hair, wearing gold bracelets and fine clothes; all this should be inside, in a person's heart, imperishable: the ornament of a sweet and gentle disposition—this is what is precious in the sight of God" (3:3-4). Meanwhile, like Paul, he upholds the Jewish and Gentile principle of the married woman's subservience to her husband: "In the same way, wives should be obedient to their husbands" (3:1). Peter justifies this subjection in three different ways. First, this obedience has an apologetic value, "if there are some husbands who have not yet obeyed the Word ..." (3:2). One may note the difference here between Peter and Paul. In Corinthians 7:12-16, Paul recognized freedom to divorce an unbelieving partner who refuses peaceful cohabitation. But the text of 1 Peter does not seem to agree: on the contrary, cohabitation should bring him to faith. Second, obedience is justified by the example of the holy women of the Old Testament, and specifically of Sarah, "who was obedient to Abraham and called him her Lord." The text adds, for the consolation of Christian women: "You are now her children, as long as you live good lives and do not give way to fear or worry" (3:6). Finally, woman is "the weaker partner" (3:7), a point which is totally absent from Paul's Epistles, including the Pastoral.

Admittedly, the believing wife as seen in 1 Peter is not bereft of her own dignity. Her husband must treat her with consideration and respect. For despite her natural weakness, the wife is "co-heir to the grace of the Life" (3:7). A last remark is addressed to husbands: "Then your prayers will not be hindered" (3:7). This alludes to the belief, which will be long echoed in the later tradition, that sexual intercourse interferes with, and troubles, the soul who wishes to pray. Paul mentioned this in 1 Corinthians 7:5: "Do not refuse each

other except by mutual consent, and then for an agreed time, to have yourselves free for prayer." Peter suggests that such a fear will be groundless if the
man treats his wife properly. It does not seem concerned, however, with a
similar effect on the wife's prayers.

Our investigation of Paul's letters raises a major question: is there further
evidence in the New Testament that the first Christian kerygma included the
promise of a return to the situation of man and woman in Paradise, before the
antagonism of sexes appeared with the fall? Does Christianity imply the abolition in principle of the curse on woman and her subsequent subordination to
the male principle? Was this standard Christian preaching, or a peculiarity of
Paul's interpretation of the kerygma? And if this belonged to the common
paradosis, does it derive from Jesus himself, or is it a subsequent theological
elaboration?

Precisely, if the three synoptic Gospels teach a common message about
sex, it is that the present order of things in the Jewish world does not correspond to the primitive relationship of man and woman.

Let us take Matthew and Mark first.

Matthew 19:1-12 and Mark 10:2-10 present an interesting contrast with
the views of Ephesians 5:21-33. For these pericopes are also presented as
commentaries on the sayings of Genesis: they were made "male and female,"
and "because of that man will leave his father and his mother and will cling to
his wife, and the two shall be one flesh." The commentaries come in answer
to a question about divorce. In Mark, Jesus asks about the law of Moses,
which, as his interlocutors note, permits a man to divorce his wife. Valid reasons for divorce were actually a moot point in Judaism around the time of
Jesus. Following different principles of interpretation of the Law, the school
of Shammai permitted divorce only for very serious reasons, whereas that of
Hillel inclined to greater leniency. The question was therefore a proper one to
ask a rabbi who claimed to teach with authority. Jesus' answer, in the two accounts that we have, is entirely negative: "What God has united, man must
not divide" (Matt. 19:6; Mark 10:9). Mark continues by pointing out the consequences of this doctrine: "The man who divorces his wife and marries another is guilty of adultery against her. And if a woman divorces her husband
and marries another, she is guilty of adultery too" (10:11-12). Hebraic law,
unlike Roman law, did not permit the wife to initiate divorce proceedings;
but Mark, having in view a largely Gentile readership, adds the case of divorce
by the wife, which was a common practice among the Romans.

Matthew and Luke (16:18) are undoubtedly nearer to the original logion
here. Matthew adds a more elaborate commentary with a polemical edge: "It

was because you were so unteachable that Moses allowed you to divorce your wives, but it was not like this from the beginning" (19:8). He then draws the same consequence as Mark, with the notable difference that an exception is made: "except in the case of fornication" (19:9). I am not concerned at this time with the clause concerning "fornication," which has been so debated among exegetes, but rather with the principle which commands the entire passage in Matthew: "It was not like this in the beginning." The eschatological times that Jesus announces imply a recurrence of the primitive order of things between man and woman. For if Jesus speaks to Jews who inquire about his interpretation of the Law, this interpretation is itself given in view of the coming trial and consummation. The messianic day will bring back the prelapsarian situation: the composite quotation from Genesis combines a few words from chapter 1 ("they were made male and female"), which contains no reference to a fall, and a few from chapter 2 ("this is why a man leaves his father and mother ..."), before the occurrence of temptation and the curse. Jesus truly envisions a messianic restoration of the order of innocence.

This is, I think, substantially an authentic logion of Jesus. The radical departure from the prevailing opinions of the dominant pharisaic schools is too sharp to have arisen merely from a desire of the early Christian communities for moral or legal perfection. It could only come from the radical reformulation of the Law which seems to have characterized the preaching of Jesus himself. Yet I am inclined, too, to consider the Matthean clause ("except in the case of fornication") as also belonging to the primitive version of this interpretation as formulated by Jesus. For if the trend of this passage truly evokes a recurrence of the time of innocence with the advent of the messianic day of the Lord, the Jews to whom Jesus spoke had not yet been introduced into the messianic Kingdom. They were not living in Eden, but in postlapsarian East of Eden. For them, therefore, the leniency of Moses remained valid. The sense then would be: when fornication (that is, adultery) has shown that a couple still belongs to the old order characterized by hardness of heart, then a divorce may be pronounced.[5] In this interpretation, the sequel of the Matthean story follows logically, in sharp contrast with this unredeemed legalism: "It is not everyone who can accept what I have said, but only those to whom it is granted. There are eunuchs born that way from their mother's womb, there are eunuchs made so by men and there are eunuchs who have made themselves so for the sake of the kingdom of heaven. Let anyone accept this who can" (19:11-12). Whether or not this is an authentic logion of Jesus, it does contain the correct conclusion and lesson: the eunuchs who "have made themselves so for the sake of the kingdom of heaven" have perceived the coming of the Kingdom and have already, in hope, anticipated the paradisiac state. This is tantamount to what Paul wrote to the Corinthians: "The time is short. Those who have wives should live as though they had none....I say this because the world as we know it is passing away" (1 Cor. 7:29, 31).

If these passages are read in the light of the logia on the resurrection (Matt. 22:23-30; Mark 12:18-25; Luke 20:27-36), it becomes clear that the "eunuchs for the sake of the kingdom" are already "sons of the resurrection"; they are similar to those who have resurrected, who have regained Paradise: "In the resurrection they do not marry nor are given in marriage, but are like the angels in heaven" (Matt. 22:30). Or, in the more Semitic version of Luke, "The children of this world marry and are given in marriage, but those who are judged worthy of a place in the other world and in the resurrection of the dead do not marry, because they can no longer die, for they are the same as the angels and, being children of the resurrection, they are sons of God" (20: 34-36).

More than the other two Gospels, the one by Luke urges anticipation and imitation of the life which will characterize the children of the resurrection. Luke does not include the great passage on marriage and divorce that we have studied in Matthew and Mark, but a brief logion which embodies substantially the same doctrine as the Matthean and Marcian pericopes: "Everyone who divorces his wife and marries another one is guilty of adultery, and the man who marries a woman divorced by her husband commits adultery" (16:18). This parallels Matthew 5:32, which itself duplicates the text of 19:9. In both cases, Matthew includes the fornication clause, which is omitted by Luke, as by Mark (10:2-10). That Luke should leave it out is consistent with his generally strict attitude in matters of sex. In the text containing the promise that one shall receive a hundredfold in the next life, Luke alone mentions him who abandons—not only, as in Matthew 19:27-30 and Mark 10:29-30, his house, brothers, parents, for the sake of the Kingdom—but also his wife. In the logion about carrying one's cross Luke 14:25-27), where Matthew writes: "The one who loves his father or his mother more than me is not worthy of me; the one who loves his son or his daughter more than me is not worthy of me" (10:37), Luke adds brothers and sisters, also wife: "If someone comes to me, and does not hate his father and his mother and his wife and his children and his brothers and his sisters and even also his wife, he cannot be my disciple" (14:25-26).

That Luke recommends the actual separation of husband and wife is unlikely, as this would run against the explicit teaching of Paul and the entire morality of the Jewish background of the early Christian communities. Yet Luke certainly believes that a new way of life, which would include abstention from marriage, is possible and desirable, being in harmony with the coming Kingdom. For, as the pericope of 20:34-36 shows, Luke connects sexuality and death: "Those who are judged worthy of a place in the other world and in the resurrection of the dead do not marry, because they can no longer die...." As the Kingdom will abolish death, so will it do away with sex. At the back of this idea there lurks the Old Testament concept of immortality in one's descendants, of prolonging one's life in one's children, in the "house" built to himself by the father of the race through his wife. In the Kingdom, this will no longer be. The children of the resurrection live forevermore and therefore do not need sex to obtain a substitute for immortal life. The Gospel of Luke contains little hint that the relationship of man and woman in marriage may have another dimension than that.

Luke significantly alters the parables which too openly compare the Kingdom to a wedding feast. The wedding invitation of Matthew 22:1-4 becomes a mere dinner invitation in Luke 14:15-24; and whereas the excuses given in Matthew by those who decline to come include no more than various forms of business, Luke adds the reason: "I have married and therefore I cannot come" (14:20), thus placing marriage among the obstacles to entering the Kingdom. The great parable of the ten virgins who wait for the bridegroom well into the night (Matt. 25:1-13) does not appear in Luke, who, on the contrary, has alone preserved the parable of the prodigal son who swallows up his property with harlots (15:11-32). Likewise, Luke omits Matthew's statement that "publicans and harlots will go before you in the kingdom of heaven" (Matt. 21:31). Thus, Luke refers to evil relationships rather than to proper marital intercourse. He also tones down considerably the Old Testament analogy between woman and faithful Israel, which holds a significant place in the other Gospels. Admittedly, Luke keeps the wedding analogy in 5:34-35 (Matt. 29:14-17; Mark 2:18-22; John 3:29): "Surely you cannot make the bridegroom attendants fast while the bridegroom is still with them? But the time will come, the time when the bridegroom will be taken away from them; that will be the time when they will fast." For this passage stresses the contrast between Jesus (the bridegroom) and John the Baptist or the Pharisees, rather than the marriage relationship: the bride is never identified, even indirectly or implicitly.

Yet Luke's position is not encratic. For encratism would devalue sex as being somehow evil in itself. There is no such suggestion in the Gospel. Sex, however, belongs to this world, not to the Kingdom. The disciples may be married, for they still live in the world. Yet they primarily live in hope, already participating in the Kingdom, in which the sexual polarity will be abolished. To the extent that the Kingdom has been inaugurated the functions of the sexes have been overcome. This would seem to be the gist of the "proto-Gospel" of Luke, where the annunciation, the conception of Jesus without sexual intercourse, the visitation, and the birth of John in his parents' old age show that the order of the universe is changing radically. Such an insistence of Luke on these marks of the messianic times throws light on his view of celibacy as a way of participating in the Kingdom. Luke's perspective is dominated by the prelapsarian tradition on man and woman in paradise: the relationship of Adam and woman before sin has been restored. It is a spiritual, not a sexual, relationship. As a point of fact, Luke alone mentions that a number of women "who had been cured of evil spirits and ailments" accompanied Jesus and his disciples: "Mary surnamed the Magdalene, from whom seven demons had gone out, Joanna the wife of Herod's steward Chuza, Susanna, and several others" (8:1-2). In these women we may see the prototypes of the "women-sisters," who, according to Paul (1 Cor. 9:5) travel with "the other apostles, and the Lord's brothers, and Cephas." They are the feminine part or aspect of the new mankind inaugurated in Jesus.

We now come to the Johannine corpus. My inquiry will prescind from the debated question of the authorship of these pieces. Whether or not John the Evangelist is also the Apostle makes no difference to his teaching. I tend to think he is not the Apostle, but this need not affect our reading of his work. That the Gospel and the first Epistle come from one writer is normally accepted. That the other two letters have the same author is more questionable, though I tend to think that they do. That the Apocalypse comes from another pen I would myself hold. Yet all these writings may be treated jointly as belonging to one school of early Christian theology, and it is with this assumption that I approach them here. Though, still early, this theology is not as primitive as those of Paul and of the synoptic Gospels. The Johannine corpus dates from the closing year of the first century.[6]

The Gospel of John shows no hesitancy in giving considerable importance to the analogy of the wedding and to the place of women among the disciples. A number of events are to be found only in this Gospel: the wedding at Cana (2:1-12), the conversation with the Samaritan woman, who ends up by believing and herself spreading the Gospel (4:4-42), the friendship of Jesus with the two sisters of Lazarus, Martha, and Mary (11:1-44; 12:1-11), the women at the Cross ("his mother, his mother's sister, Mary, the wife of Clophas, and Mary of Magdala") together with the "disciple he loved" (19:25-27), the early visit of Mary of Magdala to the tomb, by which she became the first witness to the resurrection (20:1-18). To this must be added the story of the woman taken in adultery (7:53; 8:11), which, although originally not a part of the Gospel and not written by the same author, does fit the general tone and orientation and thus rightly belongs to the Johannine corpus. In this Gospel, too, the nuptial image is used in relation to John the Baptist; yet it is now John who speaks rather than, as in the synoptics, Jesus referring to John: "The bride is only for the bridegroom; and yet the bridegroom's friend, who stands there and listens, is glad when he hears the bridegroom's voice. This same joy I feel and now it is complete" (3:29). We are in the Prophetic tradition: the bride is clearly Israel and the bridegroom is Christ; the comparison is much more realistic than in the comparable synoptic pericope where the bride is never mentioned (Matt. 9:15; Mark 2:19-20; Luke 5:34-35).

The prologue to the Gospel throws additional light on the analogy. For close connections relate the image of the *Logos* in chapter 1 to that of *Sophia* in the books of wisdom. "In the beginning [ἀρχῇ] was the *Logos*" (1:1). This "beginning" may be identified not only with that of Genesis ("In the beginning, Yahweh created the heaven and the earth ..."), but moreover with that of Proverbs 8:22 ("The Lord created me as the beginning [ἀρχὴν] of his ways ..."). With these texts alone, the *Logos* of John could be seen as latent in the Wisdom of God, and the sophiological reflection, which has appeared several times in the history of Christian thought, especially in Russian theology, would be provided with a starting point. But we should read John 1:1 also in the light of Wisdom 9:1-2: "God of the Fathers, Lord of mercy, who, through your *Logos* made the universe, and through your *Sophia* formed man...." That is, the *Logos* of John, which is not created, but simply "is" with God, must be identified with the Wisdom of God through which all creation takes place: "All was made through it" (John 1:3). In this case, the nuptial elements of the image of Sophia should be now transferred to the image of the *Logos,* who then becomes the feminine companion of God, pregnant with all creation. On the one hand, John sees the mystery of femininity at the level of Israel's relationship to God; on the other he also sees it at the level of the Divinity itself, as manifested in the Logos-Wisdom of God.

This Word (*Logos*), who, in 1:2-3, is said to be "with God," is reported, in 1:13, to have been "born, not of human stock, or by the will of the flesh, or by the will of man, but from God." True, the Greek expression may be used of both the male or the female principle of generation. Yet the opposition to man (that is, male), on the one hand, and, on the other, the reference to the eternal presence of the *Logos* with God suggest his emanation from God as from a womb. This is confirmed by the wording of verse 18: "No one has ever seen God; it is the only Son, who is in the bosom of the Father, who has made him known." The "bosom" may admittedly evoke a seating arrangement at table: the only Son lies next to the Father, that is, figuratively speaking, "in his bosom," as John next to Jesus at the Last Supper. It may also suggest something else. Like the ancients generally, the Jews thought the future human being to be already preformed in his male ancestry. The female womb, recipient of the seed, provides a protective environment for its growth into a viable child. Likewise, the *Logos* is in the Father, but not as a lifeless seed still contained in its male principle. The Father acts as womb which provides the *Logos* with all that he is and he knows. The Father is actually a female womb. Finally, in another bold allegory, John compares the expectation of the Kingdom to a woman's pregnancy: "A woman in childbirth suffers because her time has come; but when she has given birth to the child, she forgets the suffering in her joy that a man [*anthropos:* a human being] has been born into the world" (16:21).

The prevailing atmosphere here is rather distant from that of the synoptic

Gospels. Starting with the image of the *Logos* in the bosom of God, the Gospel of John introduces the disciples to a transcendent mystery of nuptiality. Certainly, by now the first century is far advanced; there is less need than formerly to be hesitant about the belief that the old Israel has been displaced by the new Ecclesia as the bride of the Most High. If indeed, according to the tradition recorded by Irenaeus and Eusebius, John lived at Ephesus,[7] the nuptial image provided a telling contrast with the Ephesian cult of Artemis, the many-breasted mother goddess, whose devotees had rioted against Paul and the first Ephesian Christians during Paul's third missionary journey (Acts 19:23-41). The communities of the province of Asia, for whom John writes, are not, like Corinth at the time of Paul, caught in the throes of a trend to licentiousness. Speculation on the preexistence of the Lord is now far advanced, and a Christian gnosis is already taking shape. Women have acquired standing in the Church, witness the second letter of John, which I take to come from the same pen as the Gospel. It makes little difference to the argument whether this short note was addressed to an actual woman or to a Church figuratively called "the Lady." In either case, it fits the pattern of the Johannine corpus in its free approach to the symbolism of woman.

With the Apocalypse the feminine image in the New Testament reaches its apex, and the nuptiality which dominates the Johannine vision is fully elaborated.[8] Whether or not the seven letters to the Asian Churches originally constituted a separate document makes no difference here as to the content of Johannine theology. If they are read as originally not part of the book, they help us see John as a generic name for a series of authors writing in the same milieu and with identical leading concerns and ideas. Be that as it may, the seven letters sufficiently depict the fully developed Christian life as a return to Paradise: to Ephesus the promise is made that "those who prove victorious I will feed from the tree of life set in God's paradise" (2:7); to Philadelphia, the pledge is that "those who prove victorious, I will make pillars in the sanctuary of my God, and they will stay there forever; I will inscribe on them the name of my God and the name of the City of my God, the new Jerusalem which comes down from my God in heaven, and my own new name as well" (3:12). Precisely, in both Jewish and Christian apocalyptic literature, the symbols of woman and of the New Jerusalem are fused together so that the thought freely flows from the one to the other, as in the vision of a woman in tears reported in the *Fourth Book of Esdras* (a Jewish writing with early Christian interpolations): "And I looked. And behold, the woman no longer appeared to me; but a city was a-building, and a place with powerful foundations was shown to me" (10:27). The woman of the Apocalypse is the woman of Paradise, who is also the City of God, the New Jerusalem, the Ecclesia.[9]

The Apocalypse of John makes full use of this theme. Chapter 12 is focused on the image of the woman, and chapters 21 and 22 on that of the New Jerusalem, while the negative picture of the great prostitute, Babylon, in chapters 17 and 18 stands in striking contrast with the vision of the woman as City of God. No need to detail the parable of the prostitute, which derives straight from the Prophetic tradition: idolatry is a prostitution. Likewise Apocalypse 14:4 ("These are the ones who did not defile themselves with women, for they have kept themselves chaste, and they follow the Lamb wherever he goes. They have been ransomed as the first fruits of humanity for God and the Lamb. No lie was found on their lips; they are faultless") speaks of the true believers as opposed to the idolators. The text says nothing of marriage, but assumes the Prophetic image, fornication-idolatry.

The woman of chapter 12 appears in heaven, "adorned with the sun, standing on the moon, and with the twelve stars on her head for a crown" (v. 1). That is, she is a counterpart to the "heavenly man" appearing on the clouds of heaven in the book of the prophet Daniel (7:13; 10:5-6). She is pregnant and about to give birth to a "male child," to whom, after he has been raised up to God and his throne, is given "all authority," "victory and power and empire" having been won by God (v. 10). This child is the very man seen by Daniel in heaven, to whom also all power is given after he has been led into the presence of "the One of Great Age" (Dan. 7:13): "On him was conferred sovereignty, glory and kingship, and men of all peoples, nations and languages became his servants" (Dan. 7:14). There is one major difference between the two visions: The Apocalypse of John shows the man from heaven being born of the woman (the People of Israel, the Ecclesia) and not as coming by himself, as in Daniel, on the clouds of heaven.[10] The carrier, so to say, is now the woman, who is seen in heaven with the celestial bodies as her attendants, as the man of Daniel is seen on the clouds. In both cases, the faithful people share in his victory: in Daniel, sovereignty belongs to "the saints of the Most High" (7:18-22); in John, "our brothers," persecuted by the dragon, "have triumphed over him by the blood of the Lamb and by the witness of their martyrdom" (12:11). In both cases this victory takes place after a cosmic battle in heaven and on earth between Michael and "the prince of the kingdom of Persia" (Dan. 10:13) or "the great dragon, the primeval serpent, known as the devil or Satan" (Apoc. 12:9).

We may conclude from this that the vision of the woman with her child is a deliberate elaboration on the Danielic vision, which purports to convey the full meaning of the arrival of the man from heaven: this is the son of the woman Israel, sent by God as his divine Wisdom, who flees to the desert when the dragon tries to destroy her after failing to devour her son. John explicitly identifies the dragon with the "primeval serpent" who tempted the woman in Paradise, thus proceeding to a further identification of the heavenly woman with the woman of the restored Paradise. This woman, Israel, the People of God, mankind as God's elect (cf. "the elect Lady" of the second letter of John) is neither Babylon (the Roman Empire) described in chapters 17 and 18 nor the old Jerusalem. She appears again in chapters 21 and 22 in the shape of "the New Jerusalem."

The opening verses of chapter 21 recall the beginning of Genesis, when "the heavens and the earth" were created, and the Spirit hovered over "the water." The seer of the Apocalypse witnesses no less than the new creation: "Then I saw a new heaven and a new earth; the first heaven and the first earth had disappeared, and there was no longer any sea" (Apco. 21:1). The scene is thus set for a complete overhaul of the genetic enterprise, in what is both a recapitulation and a reversal of the first creation. The first creation led progressively to Adam and then to the woman as Adam's perfection. The recreation now unfolding starts with the woman, in the form of "the holy City, the New Jerusalem, coming down from God out of heaven, as beautiful as a bride all dressed for her husband" (v. 2). The traditional Prophetic themes of the bride of Yahweh, the building up of the City through the woman, the Wisdom, are intertwined in this complex picture. The vision continues with an inversed reenactment of Osea's naming of his son. Born to Osea from his harlot-wife in his prophetic acting of Yahweh's wooing of Israel, this child was called "Not-my-people." On the contrary, the new bride, mother of the people, opens up a perspective of divine filiation: "Here God lives among men. He will make his home among them; they shall be his People, and he will be their God. His name is God-with-them" (21:3). To show how far-reaching is the naming of this child "His People," John associates a renaming of God to it.

Another version of this vision follows, inspired this time mainly by Ezechiel's description of the holy City: "One of the seven angels that had the seven bowls full of the seven last plagues came to speak to me, and said: 'Come here, and I will show you the bride that the Lamb has married.' In the spirit he took me to the top of an enormous high mountain, and showed me Jerusalem, the holy City, coming down from out of heaven ..." (21:9-10). There follows a detailed description of the City and its measurements, which leads to the remark that the City has no Temple: "I saw that there was no Temple in the city, since the Lord God Almighty and the Lamb were themselves the Temple, and the city did not need the sun or the moon for light, since it was lit by the radiant glory of God, and the Lamb was a lighted torch for it" (21:22-23). That is, whereas the first creation led from Adam to the woman, the second goes from the bride to the bridegroom, to the new Adam, to the perfect mankind, which is no other than God and the Lamb. The adornments of the first creation, the sun and the moon, have become obsolete, for now the bride, having in herself the one who is "the alpha and the omega, the first and the last, the beginning and the end" (22:13), encompasses the fullness of all things visible and invisible.

Thus the Johannine corpus, and by the same token the New Testament, ends on a vision of woman restored both to the all-holiness of her companionship with God and to the universality of her own dignity as the fullness of mankind. In the liturgical appendix to the Apocalypse, the ultimate dialogue is between the Spirit and the bride, between God and mankind: "The Spirit and the Bride say: come!" (v. 17).[11]

The evidence of the New Testament, as analyzed in the present chapter, may be summed up in the following points:

1. From Paul, from the Gospels, and from the Apocalypse, we may gather the fundamental thought of the authors of the New Testament regarding woman and the division of mankind into two sexes: the advent of the New Creation has, in principle, restored mankind to a paradisiac, prelapsarian state. The Christian woman is therefore no longer under the curse by which she was made servant to her husband and bound to a chain of painful pregnancies triggered by her desire for him. The Christian woman has become free.

2. Accordingly, as long as they expected a speedy return of the Lord, the early Christian communities (or at least those which were most sensitive to this aspect of the Christian newness) felt the call to discover a new type of relationship between men and women in the Ecclesia. The attempt was made, at least at Corinth, to lead a life of celibacy or even of nonsexual common life, these being favored by the Apostle Paul. This endeavor soon broke down under the impact of human weakness and the disenchantment occasioned by the unaccountable delay of the parousia.

3. The Gospel sayings on marriage and the injunctions of Corinthians, Colossians, Ephesians, 1 Peter to married persons trace a curve of thought by which the spiritual freedom of the married Christian woman, under the influence of both Jewish and Gentile customs, gave way to the older, although spiritually abolished, domination by her husband. Pious justifications were sought for the maintenance of this status quo despite the principle of Christian freedom still affirmed in the texts.

4. With the Apocalypse and the last apostolic writings, the image of woman is inseparable from that of the Ecclesia, a union already far advanced with Paul. What this meant for the Ecclesia, as Bride of the Lord, was fairly well indicated, but what it may also mean for woman was left in the dark. One may presume that Paul, sobered by the Corinthian experience, was eventually satisfied with letting well enough alone instead of pursuing the avenues that this could have opened. This conformed to his way of dealing with other delicate problems, like the relations between slaves and masters. As to the Apocalypse, its redaction came too late in the evolution of the early Church for such a line of thought to be adequately developed in it. The delay of the parousia and the necessities of day to day living had already reduced Christian marriage to a secular pattern. The Apocalypse marked a reaction back to the full implications of the Gospel. Yet it could not stop the trend to secularism.

5. At another level of thought, both Paul and John envision nuptiality, and therefore womanhood, as already part of the heavenly mystery now being

revealed. The pattern for earthly womanhood is set, not only in the celestial image of the Church, but in God's own Wisdom and Word.

Taken in its entirety, however, the New Testament, it would seem, left fundamental questions unanswered: how is Christian freedom to be embodied in the sexual relationship? How is the paradisiac state, to which Christians have been reintroduced by baptism and faith, to be experienced while the faithful, waiting in hope for the fulfillment of the promises, live and act their Christian love in the human forms of love? How does one live a prelapsarian life in a postlapsarian world? How is the disciple to participate in the mystery of transcendent nuptiality?

A question may legitimately be asked before this chapter closes. How many of the New Testament ideas about womanhood may be traced back to Jesus himself? If the Gospels were written after a few decades of Christian experience, though with the help of previously written or oral material, they inform us about the Christian communities more directly than about the ideas and deeds of Jesus. Yet it is reasonable to hold that Jesus, standing in the Prophetic line of Israel, would have occasionally used the feminine analogy to designate Israel's relationship to Yahweh. Hence the parables comparing the Kingdom to a wedding feast, the allusions to the bridegroom and the bride, or the bridegroom and his friends (some of them already belonging to the preaching of John the Baptist) have a good chance of having preserved a core which genuinely goes back to the Lord. Jesus could then be seen as the last link in the perpetuation of the "prelapsarian" tradition about women. As they have come down to us, these parables make Jesus the bridegroom, thus placing redeemed mankind in a unique feminine relationship to the Savior. Yet in their original form they presumably maintained the Prophetic identification of the bridegroom with Yahweh. At any rate, the apostolic kerygma, which eventually came to the point of including an important item about Jesus as the new Adam with his feminine counterpart, the new Israel, was itself an interpretation of the function of Jesus as providing in himself the heavenly pattern for womanhood, the pristine perfection of mankind.

In another set of problems, the logion on marriage and divorce, in Matthew 19, Mark 10, Luke 16, may be considered authentic; and, as I have explained, this includes the "fornication clause." With the inclusion of this clause, the logion testifies to the eschatological orientation of Jesus' teaching, which sees womanhood in the light of the paradisiac restoration soon to be expected. The underestimating of the marital relationship which is evidenced in Luke does not derive directly from Jesus; it is Luke's translation of the eschatological urgency which characterized Jesus' preaching of the Kingdom and which Paul and the other evangelists expressed differently. All in all, the message of

Jesus very probably included the chief item of the developed teaching of the New Testament, namely: the curse on the woman has been removed in the Ecclesia. The principle of the typological identity of woman with mankind in the Kingdom is part of the original good news.

3

Seeking the Kingdom

The very ambiguity of the symbolism of womanhood in the Old Testament and in Christian writings of the first century placed the Church of the second century in danger of falling into some form of encratism which would condemn sex and, by the same token, womanhood. This danger was bound to be greater in the circles that remained tied to the Jewish cultural universe, that is, in the Judeo-Christian communities. From the start, these thrived in Palestine; then, after the first destruction of Jerusalem, in 70, they migrated chiefly to Syria and to Egypt, where they survived until some time in the second half of the second century. The second destruction of Jerusalem in 135 and the rebuilding on its ruins of a purely Gentile city, Aelia Capitolina, tolled the knell of Judeo-Christianity as an organized form of Christian life, while it also doomed Palestinian Jewry to its final dispersion. Whereas Judaism survived, Judeo-Christianity died out.[1]

A logion attributed to Jesus in the apocryphal literature may illustrate the encratic temptation. According to Clement of Alexandria, the *Gospel of the Egyptians* contained the following exchange: "When Salome asked, 'How long will death have power?', the Lord answered, 'So long as you women bear children.'..." [2] Salome remarked: "I have then done well in not bearing children," to which the Lord gave this ambiguous response: "Eat every plant, but that which has bitterness eat not." [3] The heterodox possibilities of this line of thought well appear from the other form of this saying in the same *Gospel of the Egyptians*: the Kingdom will come "when you have trampled on the garment of shame, and when the two become one, and the male with the female is neither male nor female." [4] The "garment of shame" is the body, not in the Platonic sense that it imprisions the soul, but on the ground that it is tied to sin and to the curse. In the undoubtedly gnostic *Gospel of Thomas*, an altercation between Peter and Jesus evokes a similar perspective: "Simon Peter said to them: Let Mariham go away from us, for women are not worthy of life. Jesus said: Lo, I will draw her, so that I will make her a man, so that she too may become a living spirit which is like you men; for every woman who makes herself a man will enter into the Kingdom of Heaven." [5]

Even if the first two above quotations from the *Gospel of the Egyptians* may be given an orthodox meaning, they do imply, if not an encratic doctrine of sex as evil, yet a view of eschatology and ethics which urges giving up sexual relationships for the sake of the Kingdom. This at least comes through in the strongly eschatological interpretation of the logion in the *Second Epistle of Clement,* a Judeo-Christian homily, admittedly orthodox, written in all likelihood in the same Roman circles as *The Shepherd* of Hermas.

We expect at any moment the Kingdom of God in love and in justice, though we do not know the day of God's epiphany. For when the Lord was asked when the Kingdom would come, he said: "When the two are one, and the outside like the inside, and the male with the female is neither male nor female...." "The male with the female is neither male nor female": this means, A brother seeing a sister does not think of her sex, and she does not think of his sex. "When you do this," he says, "the kingdom of my Father will come." [6]

As thus interpreted, the logion contains an open invitation to absolute continence: when all the disciples practice it, the Kingdom will come. That such is the intended meaning of the text is confirmed by Pseudo-Clement's exegesis of Genesis 1:27: "God created man male and female." "The male is Christ," the explanation goes, "the female is the Ecclesia." [7] Thus understood, the nuptial image refers properly to Christ and the Ecclesia rather than to man and woman. At this level, however, the second Clementine letter teaches no degradation of woman, although it does disparage the sexual element in man, considered to be useless to the Kingdom of God. This faithfully echoes the New Testament view of conditions of life in the Kingdom, where men will no longer take wives and women no longer take husbands.

One may acknowledge that contempt for woman, which was fairly common in later Jewish literature as it already was in the biblical books of wisdom, continued in some Judeo-Christian circles. Even an enlightened Jewish philosopher like Philo (d. c. 50), who, in *Legum allegoriae* devised an elaborate allegorical explanation of Genesis, interpreting it of the functions of the human mind, also ascribed to woman the status of a servant and described her as an essentially dependent being:

Why was not woman, like other animals [*sic*] and man, also formed from earth, instead of the side of man?

First, because woman is not equal in honor with man. Second, because she is not equal in age, but younger. Wherefore those who take wives who have passed their prime are to be criticized for destroying the laws of nature. Third, he wishes that man should take care of woman as of a very necessary part of him; but woman in return should serve him as a whole.

Fourth, he counsels man figuratively to take care of woman as a daughter, and woman to honor man as a father. And this is proper; for woman changes her habitation from her family to her husband. Wherefore it is fitting and proper that he who receives something should in return show good will to those who have given it, but the one who has made the change should give to him who has taken her the honor which she showed those who begot her. For man has a wife entrusted to him as a deposit from her parents, but woman (takes a husband) by law.[8]

If this may be considered an adequate description of the status of woman in the Jewish communities of the diaspora (and little change could have taken place in it since the time of Philo), we have no ground to suppose that the Judeo-Christians would have assessed womanhood very differently. There is even some evidence that in certain Judeo-Christian circles, heavily dependent on the wisdom literature of the Old Testament and the apocalyptic tendencies of contemporary Judaism, woman was seen no longer as the perennial child that Philo shows her, but as a dangerous and truly evil creature. Thus, in the *Testaments of the Twelve Patriarchs* which Cardinal Daniélou acknowledges as a Judeo-Christian writing from Syria,[9] using Jewish material of shortly after the fall of Jerusalem, the "Testament of Reuben" gives the following advice:

Pay no heed, my children, to the beauty of women nor set your mind on their affairs; but walk in singleness of heart in the fear of the Lord and expend labor on good works, and on study, and on your flocks, until the Lord give you a wife, which he will.... For evil are women, my children; and since they have no power of strength over man, they use wiles by outward attractions, that they may draw him to themselves.... The angel of the Lord told me and taught me that women are overcome by the spirit of fornication more than men, and in their heart they plot against men.... Every woman who uses these wiles has been reserved for eternal punishment.

The text uses the illustration of Genesis 6, yet with a significant difference. In this version, it was by the fault of the women that the angels (called here, the Watchers) fell: "For thus they allured the Watchers who were before the flood ..."; yet the biblical text is free of any similar suggestion.

As far as the community is concerned, then, the "Testament of Reuben" recommends complete separation of men and women before their marriage: "Command the women not to associate with men, that they also may be pure in mind. For constant meetings, even though the ungodly deed be not wrought, are to them an irremediable disease, and to us a destruction of Beliar and an eternal reproach." [10] Admittedly, the purpose of the Testament is to fight fornication by removing temptation; yet the fear of fornication is explicitly justified by the evil attributed to women in general.

If this is an extreme position, the other extreme having been held by the Corinthians at the time of Paul, there was still room between them for the Prophetic analogy of woman witl. Israel and with the Ecclesia. This was lost neither to the Jews nor to the Judeo-Christians. The *Fourth Book of Esdras* includes the vision of a heavenly woman who turns out to be, as in the Apocalypse of John, the holy City.[11] For Pseudo-Clement, as we have seen, the Ecclesia is the woman of Paradise, corresponding to Adam, who is equated with Christ. In *The Shepherd*, Hermas, a prophet, whom the Muratorian canon identifies as the brother of the bishop of Rome, Pius (141-155), makes full use of the analogy.[12] This volume is held by Daniélou to be a Judeo-Christian writing.[13]

Only the first part of *The Shepherd* is relevant to this inquiry: namely the first four "Visions." The book begins with a piece of autobiography, which can be fictional or authentic. At any rate, Hermas reports that he had been sold by his master to a lady called Rodè, an inhabitant of Rome. Strangely enough, nothing is said about what happened immediately after this; but he met the lady again years later, even helped her on one occasion to come up from bathing in the Tiber, noticed her beauty, and compared her favorably to his wife. Later, Rodè, presumably having died, appeared to him in a dream and told him: "I have been taken up to denounce your sins to the Lord." [14] As he shows surprise at this turn of events, she reveals to him that he had sinned against her by having bad desires.

Another vision follows. An old lady in shining garments, holding a book in her hand, tells Hermas that his real sin lies in his neglect of his children, who have become near-delinquents.

One year later the old lady appears again and gives him her book to copy. After deciphering the text for a fortnight. Hermas understands: he must discipline his children and watch over his wife, who is a bad gossip. Henceforth she will be a sister to him, although he must keep her in his house. He is also to reveal to the whole Church that a promise of forgiveness of all sins has been made for the benefit of all the faithful.

In the following revelation, Hermas discovers the identity of the lady: she is the Ecclesia. She owes her old age to the fact that "she was created before all. This is why she is old: the world was formed for her." [15]

Finally, after the contents of the little book have been read to the Church, in another vision Hermas sees an empty throne. The lady arrives, accompanied by six angels. In a vision within the vision, she shows him a tower under construction. The tower, she says, is herself, the Ecclesia; [16] the stones are the various categories of the faithful. As an afterthought, Hermas mentions the three successive aspects of the lady: "I had seen her, brothers, in the first vision last year, very old and seated in an armchair. In the second she looked younger, though her body and her hair were old. She was standing and more joyful than formerly. In the third vision she was completely young and very beautiful; her hair was still old; she was extremely joyful and seated on a bench." [17] The explanation of this is given at length: the Ecclesia looks old when the faithful do not repent their sins, young when they do. One may surmise, though this is not said here, that her hair remains old all along to symbolize her old age, the fact that she was made before the world, as explained during the first vision.

From the standpoint of our inquiry into the theology of womanhood, the visions of Hermas present several interesting features. The identity of the Ecclesia with the lady of the vision who is also the tower seen a-building derives from the old imagery inherited from the Old Testament and instanced in the New. In the context of *The Shepherd*, the lady is the celestial Church, analogous to the wisdom of God created before all the worlds; and the tower represents the Church on earth. They are one Ecclesia in two forms at two levels. Hermas's concept of the Ecclesia relates her especially to penance, which is not surprising in the middle of the second century in view of the growing moral rigor of the times. Hermas argues against rigorism, this being the main purpose of his writing, in favor of a more open access to penance than was the current practice, yet he himself suffers from a penchant to a mild encratism. Sex is not undervalued, yet Hermas is called on to change his relationship with his wife to a nonsexual partnership. So far, Hermas has contributed to the fields of morality, penance, and ecclesiology. I would propose to see his work also as directly relevant to a theological reflection on woman. For if Hermas does not tell us much about his wife, what he reports about the woman he calls Rodè seems to me highly important.

His autogiography is commonly read in the following way, Hermas would have been a slave. Rodè was the name of his Roman owner. Perhaps because she had freed him, he did not see her for a long time. Then he met her again and noticed her beauty. The visions start at this point. On the whole, such an autobiography would be a rather awkward introduction to the book.

One may wonder, however, if Rodè is not a symbolic name: it could be a barely concealed play on the word Rome (this comes out more clearly with the Greek spelling: *Rhodè-Rhomè*).[18] In the vision, Rodè fulfills a task which will later be shown to belong to the Church: she brings the faithful to penance by revealing their sins to them. In this case, Hermas' slavery would correspond to the time before he believed, and he would have been converted to Rodè (the Church) in Rome: "My Master" (a title that is sometimes attributed to God) "sold me to a certain Rodè in Rome." [19] After travelling for a long time he returns to Rome, loves and helps the Church by the side of the Tiber (perhaps fulfilling some official function), sins against her by some vaguely evil desires, and has his visions, which tend to teach proper moralism. The old lady who appears to him would still be Rodè. Thus, a triple imagery draws attention to the woman in Rome by the Tiber, who is beautiful though elderly, to the heavenly lady, who is old but appears younger when the faithful repent their sins, to the tower being built by the faithful, whose completion will mark the advent of the parousia. Furthermore, Hermas is called to an encratic relationship with his wife, that is, to the sort of relationship he has, at the beginning, with Rodè. Thus, Hermas envisions a close connection between the Ecclesia and the woman image. For that reason the Church takes a feminine shape; evil desires toward women are sins against her; and Hermas should treat his wife like the Church herself, loving both in the same manner.

In this reading, the image of Rodè is far from extraneous to the story. For her very femininity and her identity with the celestial lady introduce the comments about Hermas's wife. Thus, instead of constituting an awkward opening, the first lines of the work present a very sophisticated doctrine of the symbolic ties between the Ecclesia and woman. The Church may be seen, not only in the eerie picture of a shining feminine form coming from heaven, but also in the realistic sight of a woman bathing in the Tiber. By the same token, however, Hermas's wife, in order to be assimilated to Rodè and thereby to the Ecclesia, must be deprived of her sexual life. Thus, Hermas has expressed the basic identity of woman and the Church, but at the expense of the integrity of the woman's female endowments. Although, once more, this does not amount to the complete encratic doctrine which condemns marriage, as well as fornication, as essentially evil, it does make manifest that the image of woman in the early Church is not free of encratic elements and tendencies. The return to Paradise, which remains the *leitmotif* of Christian reflection on our theme, is taken to entail the victory of mankind over sex, sex being interpreted as part of the curse which was imposed on man and woman after the fall and has been lifted in principle through baptism in Christ.

Many Christians fell into the pitfall of encratism. There is no need here to speak in detail of the encratic heresies which abounded in the second century.[20] Tatian the Apologist notoriously taught encratism, even forming a sect of his own in 172, according to the records of Eusebius. Marcion, with the basic opposition he claimed to discover between the God of the Old Testament and that of the New, dug a seedbed for encratic ideas. Various forms of gnosticism included a more or less total condemnation of the flesh and assimilated marriage to fornication. Other purity sects, which appeared later, especially in the fourth century, were duly catalogued as heresies under a variety of names: Apotactites, Apotaxamenes, Saccophores, Hydroparastates.[21] Such a widespread disparagement of marriage could not but leave traces even among the orthodox. Thus the remarriage of widows and widowers, always frowned upon since apostolic times, was occasionally compared to adultery.[22] Even with the passage of time, the further delays of the parousia, and the progress of Christian experience and reflection, traces of encratism survived for a long time, right through the patristic period. However, encratic exaggerations also provoked a reaction in favor of marriage, as may be seen in the works of Clement of Alexandria.[23]

While this struggle was taking place, a prophetic movement, Montanism, brought several women into prominence. Since apostolic times, women had been admitted to some official church functions. They were deaconesses, especially entrusted with the pastoral and, in regard at least to the unction of baptism, the sacramental care of women.[24] They were prophetesses, like the four daughters of the deacon Philip (Acts 21:9), of which the Churches of the province of Asia were so proud that they argued from the location of their burial place in Asia to prove their own apostolic origin over against the apostolic claims of Pope Victor.[25] Widows had official standing in the Church. Early, although how early escapes us, an official order of virgins was established for women who consecrated their virginity to the Lord and who spent their life, under the watchfulness of the bishop, in prayer and good works. With Montanism, several women prophets rose to the leadership of an important spiritual revival. Beginning in Phrygia (whence the name of Phrygian prophets sometimes given to the adepts of the movement) with the preaching of Montanus, Alcibides and Theodotus, Montanism presented itself as a spiritual awakening.[26] It marked, or so was it taken by its followers, the Advent of the Paraclete. Far from being a heresy, it neither deviated from the traditional teachings of the Churches, nor did it organize, like so many heterodox groups, a hierarchic structure of its own.

Discouraged by the great Church and formally condemned, as for instance by the bishop of Rome, Zepherinus, in 200, the movement did not exactly go into schism, though its partisans, like Tertullian himself in his Montanist period (after 213), held their own private gatherings, where prophecy was actively experienced. By that time, of course, prophecy as a regular Christian activity was all but forgotten in most of the Churches. Thus the dynamic strength of Montanism was allied to an anachronism which helped to bring it into ill repute with the progressive circles of the times, while others saw this as a token of its traditional character. Thus, Saint Irenaeus of Lyon (c. 130–c. 202), strenuous opponent of the gnostics, was sympathetic to the prophetic movement: there are some, he notes, who reject the Gospel according to John, because they refuse to acknowledge the validity of the promise made in it that the Lord "would send the Paraclete; but they reject both the Gospel and the spirit of prophecy." By the same token, they reject Paul. "For in his Epistle to the Corinthians he spoke in detail of the prophetic charisms, and he knows men and women who are prophets in the Church."[27]

Thus Irenaeus links together prophecy and womanhood. As a point of fact, one of the traits of the Phrygian prophets was their recognition of the rights of woman to prophesy in the Ecclesia, as long as she had received the gift. Woman prophets were prominent in the Montanist movement. Two of them, Priscilla and Maximilla, who were close to Montanus himself, were held in high esteem as mediums of the Paraclete. In his hostile description of Montanism, Hippolytus blames its adepts for "reverencing these young women more than the apostles and than any charism." Some of them, he adds, "go so far as to say that there is in them something more than was in Christ."[28] Epiphanius reports that one finds the following among the false prophecies of Maximilla: "After me there will be no more prophet, but it will be the end," [29] a mistake, indeed, as far as the end goes; still a defensible proposition as regards the popularity of prophecy, especially of prophecy by women. The same Epiphanius refers to a sect of heretics, whom he calls Quintillianists, Prepuzianists, Priscillianists, and Artotyrites, and who seem related to Montanism. "Among them," he states, "there are women-bishops and women-presbyters." [30]

According to Eusebius, the Churches of Gaul—presumably of Vienna and Lyon—wrote to Eleutherus, bishop of Rome, about the Phrygian prophets "when there was a difference of opinion about them"; and "they submitted their own careful and orthodox conclusions on the question." [31] Eusebius, who judges the movement harshly, refrained from quoting the letter. From which we may suspect that the Christians of Lyon (among whom a number were originally from Phrygia or of Phrygian descent) looked favorably on the prophets. Irenaeus' sympathy for prophecy confirms this. And the Churches of Vienna and Lyon had themselves experienced prophetic charisms during the severe persecution of 177, under Emperor Marcus-Aurelius. The account of the ordeal of the martyrs of Lyon and Vienna, as sent by the Churches of these two cities to those of Asia and Phrygia, emphasizes the transformation, by the grace of God, of a young girl slave, Blandina, whose mistress feared that she would not bear her sufferings, into a strong, frank and fearless confessor. Blandina "proved that things which men regard as mean, unlovely and contemptible, are by God deemed of great glory, because of her love for him shown in power and not vaunted in appearances...." During the several days of the games in which the Christian prisoners were martyred, Blandina became the very soul of their resistance. Thus she showed herself to have been, not just an insignificant young girl, but the mother of them all: "Last of all, like a noble mother who had encouraged her children and sent them before her in triumph to the King, blessed Blandina herself passed through all the ordeals of her children and hastened to rejoin them, rejoicing and exulting at her departure as if invited to a wedding supper...." [32]

Another of the remarkable documents known as Acts of the Martyrs also links together the spirit of prophecy, martyrdom, and the dignity of woman in the Ecclesia, which surpasses her status and achievements in the world. The *Acts of Perpetua and Felicitas* originated in Carthage during the persecution of Severus (202 or 203). As we know from the career of Tertullian, Carthage was still strongly influenced by the Montanist movement. Precisely, the Acts (the introduction to which may have been written by Tertullian himself)[33] highlight the role of Perpetua, a twenty-two-year-old married woman, recently baptized, as a prophetess. Her prominence does not reside only, as in Blandina's case, in her constance under torture, but in her being a prophetess. Her own brother, who shares her captivity, suggests that she can ask for a vision and obtain it: "Then my brother said to me, 'Lady sister, you are now highly honored, so that you might ask for a vision which would show you whether suffering or release awaits you.' "[34] She duly obtains the vision, followed in the next few days by three others. In one of these she sees herself as transcending her own sex: "An Egyptian came out against me, evil in appearance, with his helpers to fight against me. And there came to me also goodly young men as my helpers and supporters" (that is, facing the devil and his bad angels she finds herself surrounded by good angels as her assistants). Then, "I was stripped and became a man; and my helpers began to rub me with oil, as is done for a contest."[35] Thus, Perpetua has "become a man," while remaining a woman, for to the end she is addressed by her companions and by Christ himself, in feminine terms. At the end, together with Felicitas, a young slave girl who has just given birth to a child and whose breasts are dripping with milk, Perpetua is tossed to a mad heifer, for the devil "wanted to match them with a beast of the same sex."[36] Both women are finally executed by the sword with all those who have survived their encounter with the beasts.

What meaning can we find in this conjunction of the emergence of a prophetic movement which admits women among its leaders, the prominence of women as recipients of charismatic graces, and the suggested symbolism of the overcoming of sex? It would seem that the devil, by matching Perpetua and Felicitas with "a beast of the same sex," tries to keep them at the low level at which femininity has been placed by the world, whereas the Paraclete raises them to the angelic realm in which sex has been transcended. Thus, a young woman can be a wife and, seeing herself nude in a vision, perceive that she has become male, while others still see her as "a delicate young woman" when she is brought nude into the arena.[37] Blandina can be a young girl and yet mother to her fellow Christians and thus a type of the Ecclesia. In the realm of grace, when the Paraclete leads the faithful, there is neither man nor woman.

There is a thin line between the idea of overcoming sex (thus arriving at male-female equality by the denial of differences) and that of degrading sex as evil (and, in a masculine world, placing all the opprobrium on the woman). Montanism promoted women to prophecy, thereby recovering in part the primitive discipline on women prophets. It also taught a strict asceticism, which seems to have reached its climax on African soil. As understood by Tertullian, it enjoined prolonged and rigorous fasts; it utterly condemned remarriage; it recoiled at the "laxity" of the bishops who, in growing numbers, admitted apostates to penance and reconciliation, as well as that of the *Pontifex Maximus,* "bishop of bishops" (presumably Pope Zepherinus [198-217], who decreed leniency in favor of repenting adulterers and fornicators).[38] Flight to other areas to avoid persecution became a grievous sin; the veiling of a woman's hair, a strict obligation. On flight in persecution, Tertullian the Montanist judged more harshly than Tertullian the Catholic. Yet on other points he does not seem to have significantly hardened his line of thought. Naturally prone to excess, he adopted extreme positions in matters of morality. But in such questions he still claimed to remain what he always wanted to be, namely a faithful interpreter of the Scriptures and of the universal tradition. His arguments against remarriage remain the same, from his *Ad uxorem* (between 200 and 206, well within his Catholic period), to his *De exhortatione castitatis* (around 206, a transition work written after his acknowledgement of the "new prophecy," but before his verbal outbursts against "the psychic," those who denied and condemned it) and his *De monogamia* (after 213, that is, during his avowedly Montanist period). Based on Scripture, both on the Old Testament and on the New, especially on the Epistles of Paul, and on the traditional discipline of the Church, they also appeal to reflections on nature and to the examples of the sages of paganism. Tertullian's argumentative method, as described in *De virginibus velandis* (c. 206), applies to most of these works: "The defense of our opinion is based on Scripture, on nature and on discipline. Scripture promulgates the Law; nature supports it; discipline demands it."[39] The only new arguments used in the later writings are borrowed from "the new prophecy."

We conclude from this that Tertullian is aware of nothing more than of being faithful to Scripture. But, and this is undoubtedly the fundamental weakness of his position, in his exegesis he is a literalist. Embarrassing or puzzling passages are not interpreted allegorically as applying to other contexts than those immediately indicated in the text; nor are they assessed historically as being relative to a given culture, so that their injunctions must be adapted to other periods and cultures. On these points Tertullian was not a traditionalist, since the New Testament itself used allegory to explain the Old, and since previous authors were anxious to stress the historical differences between the Old and the New Covenants. Tertullian makes little distinction between the two moments of the Revelation when he is looking for texts supporting his doctrines.[40] And once he is convinced of the sense and the value of a text, he pushes its logic to the end with what may be called fanatical zeal. What the Book of Genesis says, for instance, about Eve, is the ultimate truth about every woman. Paul's direction about the veiling of women in church stands for all times, all places, and all conditions of womanhood. His views of marriage and continence are not a counsel but a decree from which no exemption is admissible. In this, we face no more than Tertullian's conviction that Scripture is *lex veritatis*, the law of truth, and that accordingly it teaches the principles of human behavior as revealed and willed by God. Tertullian's personal bias enters the picture and colors his conclusions when, confronted with two interpretations of a text, he adopts the perfectionist one that seems to him to fit better a morality of absolute perfection. Such is the case, in *De monogamia*, no. 11, with his interpretation of 1 Corinthians 7:39: "A wife is tied as long as her husband is alive. But if the husband dies, she is free to marry anybody she likes, only it must be in the Lord." To Tertullian, this does not permit remarriage. Paul refers only to the hypothesis of a new convert, who was married before her baptism: if her husband dies, she may enter one Christian marriage. Her previous marriage does not count. Her new marriage is the first after baptism. This is still literal interpretation, though with more eisegesis than exegesis. Tertullian reads into his text the conviction he has acquired from other sources.[41]

A last remark should be made on Tertullian's method. As a literalist, he took much more seriously than most Christians of his times the eschatological expectations of the New Testament. The arguments of Paul that we have little time—that, given the imminence of the parousia, taking time for marriage is rash, that it is wiser now not to be divided but to give oneself totally to the coming transformation—makes good sense for him: "Therefore we marry everyday; and while we marry we are caught by the last day like Sodom and Gomorrah, when there will be fulfilled the curse on those who are pregnant and those who are nursing, that is, the married and the lustful. For to marriage belong the belly, the breasts and the babies."[42]

Tertullian's thought had definitely archaic features. He looked back to the beginning, even when he believed that the new prophecy was leading into all the truth: this still remained the truth as originally delivered.[43] Significantly, return to the beginning became the *leitmotif* of his anthropology. He clearly formulated the principle with which we have summed up the New Testament data concerning womanhood: "If such was the case at the beginning, we find ourselves directed by Christ to the beginning.... As the apostle writes to the Ephesians, God intended, as the way to fulfil the eons, to recall to the head, that is, to the beginning, all things in Christ, those in heaven and those on earth in Him." Commenting on Alpha and Omega of Apocalypse 1:8 and 22:13, Tertullian concludes: "He would thus show in himself the conjunction of the beginning with the end, and of the end with the beginning.... And thus in

Christ all things are brought back to the beginning."[44] The problem comes with the application of this admirable principle. For Tertullian, the curse belongs to the beginning; it therefore remains after baptism and determines the status of the Christian woman and the symbolic horizon of her being.

What, then, is Tertullian's view of woman? In the light of the first chapters of Genesis, including chapter 6 and the legend of the sons of God who married the daughters of men, woman is Eve:

> You give birth, o woman, in pains and anxieties; and your desire goes to your husband, and he will lord it over you. And do you not know that you are Eve? God's judgment over this sex continues in this eon; its guilt must also continue. You are the gate of the devil, the traitor of the tree, the first deserter of divine Law; you are she who enticed the one whom the devil dare not approach; you broke so easily the image of God, man [*hominem*]; on account of the death you deserved, even the Son of God had to die.[45]

The practical consequences of this reading of the Old Testament are far-reaching. For Tertullian reads Genesis 6 in the same perspective: in reward for her intercourse with the angels (Gen. 6), woman was taught by them methods of pigmentation and adornment that pagan women later developed into the elaborate art of make-up. This comes from the devil, the "disturber of nature."[46] Yet Tertullian is no ordinary misogynist. His wife he calls "my beloved companion in the Lord's service."[47] Christian women, to whom he dedicates his blast against make-up, he addresses in terms which express both a profound affection and the predominance of his ethical concerns for all human beings, men as well as women:

> Handmaids of the living God, my companions and sisters, by whatever right I am sent to you—ultimately by my right of companionship and brotherhood—I dare to speak with you not indeed in affection but acting with affection as your advocate in the matter of your salvation. This salvation—not only for women but also for men—has been decreed to consist mainly in chastity.[48]

In Tertullian's ideal, the Christian woman rejects all the arts taught by the devil. She feels no need for beauty, for beauty passes away with the figure of this world. And whatever natural beauty has been given her by her maker, she does not artificially cultivate; rather she hides and neglects it, for fear it should turn out to be a source of sin for men. The Christian woman recoils at the notion that someone might desire her.[49] Yet if she is married she need not fear that her neglect of her natural beauty should repel her husband: "Be at peace, blessed ones. No wife is ugly to her husband. She pleased him well when she was chosen, whether she was commended to him by her behavior or by her beauty."[50]

For Tertullian proposes a high ideal of the unity of man and wife. The prophecy of Genesis, "They will be two in one flesh," he takes, like all biblical statements, very strictly and applies it to married Christians to the letter. In marriage, he recognizes, the same act is performed as in fornication and in adultery. Yet, what a difference: "There is marriage when God joins two in one flesh, or, finding them joined together, baptizes them in the same flesh. There is adultery when another, an alien, flesh, of which it cannot be said: This is flesh of my flesh, and that is bone of my bones, intrudes between two who are somehow disjoined."[51]

Once a marriage has been blessed by God, either when it took place in the Ecclesia, or by the subsequent baptism of the married partners, it becomes a school of holiness in which the two are never without Christ. Tertullian's style, always terse, often eloquent, gains softness in this beautiful picture of marital unity:

> How can we be equal to the task of singing the happiness of a marriage which the Church unites, the Eucharist confirms, the blessing consecrates, the angels proclaim, the Father ratifies? Not even in the world do sons marry rightly and properly without their fathers' consent. What is the tie of two believers with one hope, one discipline, one service? There are siblings; they are companions; there is no separation of spirit or flesh. They are truly two in one flesh; where there is one flesh, there is also one spirit. Together they pray, they work, they fast, teaching, exhorting, helping one another. Together in the Church of God, at the banquet of God, in anxieties, in persecutions, in joys; no one hides anything, avoids the other or is disagreeable to the other; willingly the sick is visited, the poor is helped; alms without afterthought, sacrifices without hesitancy, daily zeal without obstacle; no greeting is hurried, no congratulation lukewarm, no blessing unspoken; among themselves they sing psalms and hymns, and challenge one another to sing better for God. When he sees and hears them, Christ rejoices and sends them his peace; where the two are, there he also is, and there is no evil.[52]

In such a marriage the wife is spiritually equal to her husband: both are co-slaves of God, and they share in all things. One could hardly describe their unity better than Tertullian's sharp pen does. To them he applies the saying of the Gospel, "When two ... are gathered in my name, there am I, in the midst of them" (Matt. 18:20). Their oneness is so profound that death does not break it, hence the theological argument against remarriage. In his view, such a marriage does not break virginity, and Tertullian can speak in these terms: "I pray you virgin—whether you are mother, sister or daughter, according to the title that fits your age—veil your head."[53] All these are without a husband, the mother in question being a widow. The other kind of Christian women comprises the "women of the other chastity, who have fallen into marriage,"[54] that is, those whose husbands are still living. These too, in Tertullian's view, should wear the veil.

Such a married woman is not interested in procreation. For, like Tertullian, she expects the parousia as an imminent event and the Gospel warns her: "Woe to those who are with child or with babies at the breast, when those days come" (Matt. 24:19). Why such a curse? Tertullian answers: "because the trouble of that coming day of flight shows up in the excess baggage of children." This does not condemn marriage as such, since it cannot apply to widows, who will run first at the trumpet's call: "They freely bear all torment and persecution, with no product of marriage burning in their womb or at their breast."[55] Yet it forbids a second marriage. Those who remarry in spite of the Apostle's warning, will be punished by being made unfit for the last days. The fruit of their womb will be antichrist. Upon them Tertullian turns his savage irony: "with their renewed marriages they harvest fruits well fitting the last days, dripping breasts, stinking wombs, crying babies."[56]

Clearly, Tertullian does not envisage Christian marriage, even the one and only union that he considers to be permitted and holy, in the perspective of procreation. He explicitly denies that this provides a good reason to marry. To wish to survive in one's descendants is a Judaic illusion that has been now dispelled. Some men, he objects to himself, seek to justify marriage by "concern for posterity and for the bitter joy of children." Such a consideration is loathsome to Christians: "This is hateful to us." For we live in the expectation of the imminent parousia, a time fit for no frivolities. "Why be enthused about bearing children, and, having them, send them off because of the imminent catastrophes, wishing to leave this wicked world and to be received with the Lord, as the Apostle also wished?"[57]

The Great Church will reject Tertullian's rigorism, as already happened in his own time. Those whom, in his Montanist period, he scornfully entitled the "psychic," in opposition to the spiritual ones who received the Spirit, will eventually triumph. The prophecies of Montanus, Priscilla, and Maximilla will be, for all practical purposes, relegated among the rantings of pseudoprophets. The veil will not be imposed on woman as an obligation. Remarriage will become fairly normal, at least entirely permissible. Fasting will be reduced. Apostates and fornicators will be offered forgiveness. Yet, even apart from his major contributions to the theology of the Trinity and to sacramental reflection, Tertullian will continue to influence the mind of Western Christendom. To a greater extent than we may wish, he will shape the understanding of womanhood for a long time. His encomium of the unity of marriage will be forgotten, whereas his sarcasms against women who paint their face and braid their hair will be remembered. As to his indifference to procreation as an element in Christian marriage, it will eventually be countered by the still more powerful voice of Augustine.

We turn now to Clement of Alexandria (d. c. 211), who lived and worked at one of the great intellectual crossroads of the ancient world.

We may wonder how much unorthodox influence may have been felt by the Christians concerning the meaning of womanhood and the place of woman in Christian reflection, to say nothing of her practical status in the communities. I need not speak again of the Jewish influence which must have been powerful in all the Churches especially in those of Judeo-Christian origin and predominant membership. In Alexandria the thought of Philo was certainly felt by the Christian thinkers who worked in the same milieu as the great Jewish philosopher and the neo-Platonists who made the city a great intellectual center.[58] Philo's allegorical interpretation of Genesis applied the myth of Adam and the woman to the creation in man of the two faculties of mind and of sense perception.[59] Here woman symbolizes the lesser aspect of the human being, while the male represents the nobler aspect. What is the reason for this? The accidental correlation between the myth of woman's formation from Adam and the secondary place of sense in relation to mind can hardly justify the symbol. It is more revealing to look at the notions which then prevailed about the genetic aspects of womanhood as reported by Philo himself. Philo sees man and woman as "sections of nature, equal in one harmony of genus, which is called man."[60] In this philosophical view, each section appears as "a half of the whole," along lines that evoke the myth reported by Aristophanes in Plato's *Banquet*.[61] But there is more. Philo turns to physiology to prove that "woman is a half of man's body.... For this we also have evidence in the constitution of the body.... For all things are seen as if in double proportion. Inasmuch as the moulding of the male is more perfect than, and double, that of the female, it requires only half the time, namely forty days; whereas the imperfect woman, who is, so to speak, a half-section of man, requires twice as many days, namely eighty." The belief that the formation of a female body takes twice as long as that of a male suggests that the quality of the product and the time required to make it are in inverse proportion. "When the nature of the body and the construction of something is in half-measure, such as woman's, then the moulding and forming of that thing is in double measure."[62]

This point explains why Philo sees woman as a "very necessary part" of her husband, who must watch over her as part of himself, whereas she "should serve him" as being the whole of which she is only a part. Thus, in the harmony of male and female in one genus, the male constitutes the whole, in which the female must be incorporated. Now, this very point happens to be a fundamental axiom of the gnostic approach to our problem. Thus Philo brings us to gnosticism. And gnostic influence on orthodox Christianity remains one of the major unanswered questions relating to the history of this period.

Gnosticism was a vast movement with a multitude of early forms.[63] We are better acquainted with the Valentinian school than with the others, for Valentinianism, because of its success, was better described and refuted by the orthodox authors.[64] The contemporary testimony of Hippolytus distinguished broadly between an "oriental" and an "Italian" or occidental gnosticism, both of which had inherited the doctrines of the great Valentine, who, according to Tertullian, had established a school at Rome at the same time as Marcion, whose doctrines had some affinities with his own.[65] In the occidental school, we are informed about Heraclion through Origen and more exhaustively about Ptolemy through the *Adversus hereses* of Irenaeus of Lyon.[66] All our sources, however, stress the doctrine of the syzygies, or eons which emanate from the first principle (called, in Irenaeus, *Bythos,* i.e., Abyss). The first eight emanations constitute the Ogdoad, the primary form of the divinity. Referring to these eons, Irenaeus says: "Now each of these is masculo-feminine." A syzygy is the unity of an eon with its female counterpart; in this unity the female is not other than the male but part of it. Thus, according to Irenaeus, "Propator [*Bythos,* Abyss], was united by conjunction with *Ennea* [Thought]; then *Monogenes* [Firstborn] or *Nous* [Mind] with *Aletheia* [Truth]; *Logos* with *Zoe* [Life]; *Anthropos* [Man] with *Ecclesia* [Church].[67]

In the *Excerpts from Theodotus,* preserved by Clement of Alexandria, Adam is described as originally containing in himself both the male and the female elements: "All the female seed, extracted from him, became Eve, from whom all females come, as all males come from Adam."[68] By the time we reach Adam, we are at the bottom of the emanations. From Sophia there stems the emanation of the Call (male) and the Called (female), also named Angels and Higher Seed. This feminine component (Called, Higher Seed) constitutes the Church of the earth, destined to union with the male *Logos* (Call) in the course of her return to the primordial oneness of the *Pleroma.* This union to the male element of the syzygy actually reintroduces the female into her male principle, of which she was only temporarily separated. Accordingly, all women must be andronized in the process of salvation: "The female elements, changed into males, enter in conjunction with the Angels and enter the *Pleroma.* For this reason it is said that woman becomes man and that the Church here below becomes Angels."[69] On earth, however, the men are themselves female until they are saved: "As long as we were children of the female only—as of shameful copulation, imperfect, wordless, reasonless, strengthless, formless, abortively brought forth—we were children of Woman; but once formed by the Savior, we have become children of Man and of the Nuptial Chamber."[70] Salvation implies the andronization of females. For this reason the *Gospel of Thomas* attributes to Jesus the already mentioned logion: "Every woman who makes herself a man will enter the Kingdom of Heaven."[71] This should be related to the saying, quoted at the start of this chapter, of which slightly diverse forms are found in the *Second Epistle of Clement*, the *Gospel of the Egyptians*, the *Gospel of Thomas*, and the *Martyrdom of Peter:*[72] the Kingdom will come "when the two will become one, and the male with the female is neither male nor female."[73] The gnostic meaning of this is a far cry from Pseudo-Clement's interpretation. It relates to the syzygic mystery of the original inclusion of the female in the male and their eventual return to unity.

According to Irenaeus, some of the Valentinians admit women to a prominent place in the Eucharistic ceremony. Describing the liturgy of Mark the Valentinian, he shows Mark handing a small chalice to a woman who stands before him. At his bidding, she consecrates the chalice in his presence. After it has been "eucharistized" by her, he pours its contents into a larger chalice which, by some trick, is made to overflow. Irenaeus then shows the woman being thrown into a prophetic trance which ends up in an orgy: Mark, if we are to believe Irenaeus, promised women the gift of prophecy and was not infrequently rewarded in return by the gift of their body in copulation.[74] Perhaps one should not lay too much stress on the suggested orgiastic sequels of this gnostic liturgy. If Irenaeus is correct in his unveiling of Mark's horrible deeds, the ultimate meaning of what he describes may still be the overcoming of femininity and the return to oneness through union with the male principle.

Has this gnostic speculation left traces in the orthodox literature? The main tenets of gnosticism were refuted by many authors who opposed Christian simplicity to gnostic complexities.[75] One type of reaction would keep some gnostic ideas, while entirely changing their context and thereby altering their sense. For instance, in the Pseudo-Clementine novels, the syzygies are reduced to an arrangement of all things by pairs, Within each pair, however, the evil or less perfect appears first, the good or better second. Thus the pairs are conceived as opposites, made of exclusive elements, whereas the gnostic syzygy is a balance of complementaries of which the second is the lesser one and derives from the first, which is identical with the whole. Although both the Recognitions and the Homilies give many examples of these pairs, the pair male-female, or female-male, is not listed.[76] Admittedly, the date of these writings is debatable. Their present form is now dated from the fourth century, although an older document, called the *Kerygma of Peter*, dating back to the second half of the second century, was incorporated into them. In its original form, the *Kerygma of Peter* was certainly related to Judeo-Christianity. While it was once thought to contain the conceptions of some Jewish gnostic group,[77] it is now considered an ebionite document.[78] In this case, the syzygies of the *Kerygma of Peter* would express the Judeo-Christian idea of the "two ways."[79] Even then, however, a polemic antignostic intent need not be excluded: the *Kerygma of Peter* is contemporaneous with the explosion of gnosticism during the career of Valentine.

A more likely reaction against the gnostic concept of femaleness may be instanced by Clement's clear delimitation of the female element in woman. In *The Pedagogue,* a program of Christian education in the light of the *Logos,* Clement asserts the equality of man and woman in everything, including education. While they form two sexes here below, in heaven the reward of victory will not be granted "men and women, but the human being freed from the longing which separates him into two distinct beings. The name 'human being' is common to men and women."[80] In this hominization of women (not, as in gnosticism, their andronization), Clement was supported by Stoic philosophy.[81]

Once Clement has recognized that sex belongs to the human conditions in this world, *The Pedagogue* defines the temporal destiny of woman chiefly in social terms. As "helpmate" of man, she is to give assistance to her husband. She should therefore shun anything that may bring shame on him or on herself. She should give up all the fashions of pagan women, renounce colorful adornments, clothes, jewelry, make-up, hair dying, etc. She should wear a veil and walk with modesty. She should avoid the baths, where any gawker would see her nude. She should not wear silk which, adhering to the skin, makes all her forms visible.[82] Thus, after upholding the human dignity of woman, Clement curtails considerably her social freedom. In common with the Stoics, he affirms her right to the same degree and quality of education as men enjoy. Over against the laxity of pagan mores, he severely restricts her. In Clement's theology, marriage is good, though his demonstration of this remains somewhat pedestrian. the *Stromata* sum up the Christian position in these terms: "They who approve of marriage say, Nature has adapted us for marriage, as is evident from the structures of our bodies, which are male and female. And they constantly proclaim the command, Increase and multiply."[83] Yet one may doubt the weight of the considerations Clement adduces from philosophy, history, and literature to make this point: "We must by all means marry, both for our country's sake, for the succession of children and, as far as we are concerned, for the perfection of the world." A wife is particularly useful to a sick husband, for her endurance and sympathy are more valuable than those of friends. "In truth, according to scripture, she is a needful helpmate." The fourth book of the *Stromata* describes the task of the married woman in

similar terms: "She will charge herself with remedying, by good sense and per-
suasion, each of the annoyances that originate with her husband in domestic
economy."[84] Having granted this to the bourgeois, Clement still prefers the
marriage of philosophers to that of other people. For philosophers do not
practice self-indulgence; they "take advantage of marriage for help in the
whole of life, and get the best self-restraint."[85]

The common sense of worldly approach to marriage is counter-balanced by
a specifically Christian view. In any case, Clement disapproves of forced marriages. The woman must not bow to force or necessity to accept the man who
loves her.[86] But he goes further toward a spirituality of marriage. If the husband is indeed, as in Paul's Epistles, "the crown of woman," marriage itself—
and in this Clement goes beyong Paul—is "the crown of the husband," while
the child is the "flower that the divine Gardener culls from the meadow of
the flesh."[87] In *Stromata* 3, procreation symbolizes recreation through baptism. This obtained in the Old Testament itself, where circumcision fulfilled
the role of baptism: "The Law formerly baptized the sex organ, in order to
symbolize our rebirth through our carnal birth, not as a token of disapproval
of human generation. The injection of seed prepares the birth of man. Not
many acts of intercourse do generate, but reception in the matrix prepares
generation, when semen becomes a foetus according to the course of nature."[88] In the Christian order also marriage is holy. As man's helpmate, woman is particularly destined "to procreation and the care of the house."[89] Clement maintains, however, that continence is good, since the Gospel admits both
marriage and celibacy. As to the logion of the *Gospel of the Egyptians* concerning the andronization of woman, Clement interprets it allegorically, saying that it does not refer to male and female, but to the faculties of the soul.

In contrast with Tertullian, who rejects all compromise with philosophy,
Clement does not shun eclecticism. His conception of womanhood reflects
several views, Stoic, common sense or popular, Jewish (Philo), gnostic or semi-
gnostic, and of course Pauline. In practice, however, Clement's and Tertullian's Christian women receive the same advice regarding fashions and the
arts of womanhood, although Clement tends to leniency when it comes to remarriage and to the use of soft garments. Admittedly, Clement lived in a more
cosmopolitan society than that of North Africa; and his writings have an apologetic and educational orientation, rather than a dogmatic one like those of
Tertullian. His eschatology presents no urgency. His reaction against gnosticism was serene rather than polemic. His image of woman seems more blurred,
less heroic, than that which Tertullian sketched for his wife.

More than any other, Origen (185-255), the genial successor of Clement in
Alexandria, exploited the bridal analogy, which he understood in both collec-

tive and individual terms, applying it to the union of Christ and the Church and to that of Christ and the faithful soul. After explaining that, at the resurrection of the dead, Christ will celebrate his marriage, of which one must not say, "They will be two in one flesh," but rather, "The Bridegroom and the Bride are one spirit," Origen added a caution against mistaking this for gnosticism: "Let us make no mistake about these words, accepting in their wake the mythical fictions about male and female Eons, according to those who have imagined their syzygies: these have no reality, and the Scriptures do not mention them."[90] In other words, the masculine-feminine dichotomy may be applied to Christ only to the extent that Scripture does it. Origen indeed likes to dwell on the biblical passages referring to the hierogamy between Yahweh and Israel and between the *Logos* and the Church or the soul. The true marriage is not carnal but spiritual; and if it is to be realized in heaven between the *Logos* and the soul, it is already achieved on earth, in the Church, between Christ and the faithful to the extent that these lead the angelic life. Bodily marriage is a temporal symbol of it. Bodily virginity, also a symbol and a witness of it, will last into the heavenly life. Spiritual virginity, chastity, is its condition. Origen carries this point so far in his conception of heaven that he not only denies, with the New Testament, the survival of bodily marriage in heaven; he further maintains that the elect will not be aware of the family ties of their earthly life.

In keeping with this, Origen equates virginity (including its spiritual demands) with the Christian ideal, being alone compatible with the life of contemplation of the true gnostic. Alluding to the curse on woman, he adds: "The virgin is free from all that; she has been freed by her purity, for she expects her blessed Bridegroom."[91] In other words, the eschatological dimension of Christian faith, which holds a paramount place in Origen's homilies, justifies the spiritual superiority of the ascetic life over marriage: thanks to it, the curse can be lifted on earth.

For Origen, sex does not belong to the first creation, when "God created man in his image" (Gen., 1:27). This chapter of Genesis refers to the creation of human souls, endowed in their preexistence with angelic bodies. The mention of "male and female" here applies to the creation of the soul of the ideal man, Jesus, joined to the ideal woman, the Ecclesia. Sex belongs only to the present world, to the second creation, which followed the fall: now the soul dwells in a corporeal body which renders it impure. "Every soul is stained because it is clothed in a human body."[92] The soul of a woman is stained by the corruption of the female body. As sexual activity is bodily, it is the source of a spiritual impurity. In this sense every man is born of sin. True, sex need not be sinful, for its use is justified by lawful marriage. Even then, however, it should not be ruled by passion. Reason ought to moderate it, whether sex is the instrument of procreation or, as a "remedy for concupiscence," indulged in only to render the marital debt. Yet sex is never without stain. It always remains impure and a source of impurity. For human bodies originally were not made for this purpose: they were destined to be Temples of the Holy Spirit. Before his fall, Adam had a spiritual body, similar to the resurrected body or to the angelic body, and sexless. Sexuality results from the fall.[93] For this reason sexual intercourse impedes prayer. Origen even thinks that the Spirit does not sanctify it, even within Christian marriage; yet he also teaches that the vocation to marriage corresponds to a divine charism.[94]

Despite this charism, marriage differs radically from the ideal of Christian freedom. Each partner makes himself the slave of the other.[95] In this husband and wife are equal, although the man remains the head. For Origen, this means first that a man should lead his wife and his family in prayer, that he should teach them the right doctrine; but it also implies the right to be obeyed in his decisions in secular matters. Thus, Origen sees the marriage union at two levels. At that of God's action and outlook, men and women are equal and sex has no direct spiritual relevance. "The divine Scriptures do not mean to separate men and women by their sex. Before God there is no distinction of sex; one is called male or female according to the quality of one's soul."[96] Yet sex acquires importance at the level of earthly behavior and achievements. Then Origen, inspired by Philo, constantly and systematically sees the feminine as the very type of moral weakness. In human experience the feminine represents the point where the human comes closest to the corporal. For this reason, Origen can write such amazing sentences: "God does not stoop to look at what is feminine and corporeal."[97] Or, "It is not proper to a woman to speak at the Assembly, however admirable or holy what she says may be, merely because it comes from female lips."[98]

We know too little about Origen's life to speak of his relations with women. He certainly had female acquaintances, but we know nothing of female friendships. He conversed with Julia Mammaea, mother of the Emperor Alexander Severus.[99] and he wrote to Severa, wife of the Emperor Philip the Arab. During Maximinus's persecution he resided for some time in the house of a virgin, Juliana, in Caesarea, Cappadocia. Among the disciples who followed him to Palestine when Bishop Demetrios expelled him, one at least was married, Ambrose who with his wife and children accompanied him and for whose sake Origen later wrote his *Exhortation to Martyrdom*. Unlike Augustine, Origen speaks at length, with reverence and love of his father Leonidas, but never mentions his mother. These indications do not suffice to provide his undeniable misogyny with a psychological explanation. Misogyny was exploited by Origen as a literary, allegorical, and philosophical theme. In some of its aspects, it was also taught by him as a disciplinary principle, as a scriptural doctrine, and as a theological tradition. One of his chief objections to

Montanism was that the Cata-Phrygians did not leave woman where she belongs.

Tertullian divided womankind into two groups, married women and those, virgins or widows, who are happily free from marriage entanglements. Clement considerably reduced the distinctions between these groups by asserting the holiness of both virginity and marriage. Origen, abandoning Clement's leniency and optimism, considered sex a consequence of sin, a stain on the soul, and woman a symbol of weakness and evil. Thus the second half of the second century faced and deepened the dilemma of Paul. Should Christians marry, or should they concentrate all their energies on the expectation of the Kingdom? The eschatological aspirations of Montanism confirmed Tertullian's endorsement of virginity as the better Christian way, even though Tertullian, himself married, described the marriage union in eloquent terms. The philosophical and humanistic interests of Clement of Alexandria oriented him toward a more unquestioning, if also more down to earth, view of matrimony; and the gnostic controversy made a defense of marriage imperious. The mystical bend of Origen turned him away from Clement's pioneering approach and made him see marriage, sex, and the human body as tokens of the evanescence of this life, ultimately incompatible with the final form of the Kingdom.

The gnostic controversy was also responsible for the deepening by Irenaeus of the already old analogy between woman and the Ecclesia, and for its new focus on the image of the Virgin Mary. Whereas Hermas, in a typical Judeo-Christian manner, had joined together the pictures of the Ecclesia, the tower, and woman, Justin of Rome (d. c. 165) in his *Dialogue with Trypho,* had suggested a parallel and a contrast between Eve and Mary as women and virgins, thus opening a new avenue to reflection:

> He is born of the Virgin, in order that the disobedience caused by the serpent might be destroyed in the same manner in which it had originated. For Eve, an undefiled virgin, conceived the word of the serpent and brought forth disobedience and death. But the Virgin Mary, filled with faith and joy, when the angel Gabriel announced to her the good news that the Spirit of the Lord would come upon her and the power of the Most High overshadow her, and therefore the Holy One born of her would be the Son of God, answered: Be it done unto me according to your word.[100]

In this context, virginity contains in itself the possibilities of death (with Eve) and of life (with Mary). The two orientations follow the woman's response to her challenge, the one being given in pride for disobedience and death, the other in humility for obedience and redemption.

With Irenaeus, this contrasting parallel between Eve and Mary obtains a new setting. It is inserted into a radical transformation of the gnostic concept of the syzygies which emanate from the Abysmal Principle. As Adam is the type of Christ, so is Eve the type of Mary. Between type and antitype relation exists by similarity and contrast. Adam sinned and Christ redeemed; Eve disobeyed and Mary obeyed. These two couples, Adam-Eve, Christ-Mary, are not isolated and separated from each other, but actively interrelated. The second couple "recapitulates" and restores the work of the first: "What is tied can be untied only if the movements of the knot are reversed, so that the first unities are untied by the second, the second free the first."[101] I suspect that the term I have translated as unity (*conjunctio*) really means syzygy, Irenaeus replacing the gnostic eons by a totally different scheme. The two syzygies, Adam-Eve, Christ-Mary are in ascending order, in contrast with the descending theory of the gnostic eons. The first is responsible for the fall, the second for the restoration. Each includes a male and a female type. For the gnostics, the male includes the female. For Irenaeus, the female participates in the chief characteristic of the male, sin in the first syzygies and "recapitulation" in the second, so that the two female elements are related by the similarity of virginity and by the contrast of disobedience and obedience: "Thus the knot of Eve's disobedience was untied by Mary's obedience. For what Eve the virgin tied by incredulity Mary the virgin untied by faith."[102] If the female element of mankind is represented by Eve, the Ecclesia corresponds to Mary. The relation of origin is now reversed from the gnostic model: instead of the female coming from the male, Christ is born of Mary. Irenaeus, of course, cannot apply this to Adam and Eve and deny the story of Genesis on the creation of woman from man. At this moment of his analogy, then, he substitutes the virgin Earth (before rain had fallen on it) to Eve, and the counterpart of the virgin Earth is the Word himself as the creator: "As the first-made Adam . . . obtained his substance from the primitive virgin Earth, and was modelled by the hand of God, that is, the Word of God . . . likewise, recapitulating Adam in himself, the Word, born of Mary who was still a virgin was begotten for Adam's recapitulation."[103]

Thus Irenaeus's theology proposes three images of womanhood: Earth as the clay modelled by the Word and the virgin-mother of Adam, Eve as the female element of the first syzygy Adam-Eve, Mary as the female partner in the redeeming syzygy Christ-Mary. Irenaeus does not draw the consequences of this for a typology of Christian womanhood. Yet his rationale implies that the Christian woman partakes of the three, of Earth as virgin and as mother, of Eve as falling and fallen, of Mary as believing and obeying.

With the end of the second century, a period of a great theological fermentation closes. The recession of gnosticism marks the end of the difficult adaptation of Christianity in Hellenic soil. Judeo-Christianity has collapsed as a theological force. With the waning of Montanism, imminent eschatology is no longer a real option. Thus a normalization of Christian life is about to begin—which the persecutions of the third century will slow down by maintaining an apocalyptic atmosphere.

As a result of this normalization, Christian thought runs the danger of excessively relying on worldly patterns, and in this context the concept of womanhood is about to become less symbolic and more commonplace. The apocryphal literature provides uncanny illustrations of conceptions that were eventually abandoned. To give an instance, the *Epistula apostolorum,* written in the first half of the second century, offers an insight into the feminine structure of creation and of the Church. Jesus is the bridegroom. The disciples must be "as the wise virgins who kindled the light and did not slumber, and who went with their lamps to meet the Lord, the bridegroom, and have entered with him into the bridal chamber."[104] In a symbolic map of the soul's faculties, the wise virgins are "faith, love, joy, peace, hope"; the foolish ones are identified, with antignostic intent, as "insight, knowledge, obedience, endurance, mercy."[105] Among believers the latter sleep while the former watch. Among others (or so do I understand the text) gnosis is awake while faith is dormant. Thus, mankind falls into opposite patterns of life, that of faith and that of knowledge. Only the former leads to the bridal chamber. Yet the faithful never forget the bonds of sisterhood that tie them to the gnostics: "They will rejoice that they have gone in with the Lord, and they will be grieved on account of those who slept; for they are their sisters." In this way faith and gnosis raise the question of mankind's filial relationship to the Father. The womanhood of creation postulates the Fatherhood of the creator and its unfathomable mystery. When the disciples object that the foolish virgins ought to be forgiven, the answer appeals to mystery: "This thing is not yours, but his who sent me."[106] Here the connection between God and man is conceived on the analogy of a father-daughter relationship. This can appeal to New Testament precedent. In such an outlook, maleness remains superior, but is reserved to God, whereas femininity is an attribute of mankind. Yet could not the pattern be reversed? These are suggestions in both the Old and the New Testament that God and even Jesus have feminine qualities. The Jesus who wishes to gather the children of Jerusalem as a mother-hen calling her little ones under her wings cannot be seen as a type of maleness. This line of thought also was to be found in the early Church. In the apocryphal *Gospel according to the Hebrews* Jesus speaks of "my Mother the Holy Spirit,"[107] and the Spirit refers to him as "my Son . . . my first-begotten Son."[108] Yet the gnostic speculations and practices offended the sense of the orthodox faithful by placing duality within God in the form of syzygies. The reaction effectively killed for a long time the vision of God that could have grown out of a feminine symbolism.

4

Out of Utopia

As it took shape in the first centuries, the Greek tradition about woman partly reflected and partly reacted against a number of extraneous influences. The Jewish sources of the faith, the pagan environment, sundry heterodox speculations contributed to its growth. The Christian expectation was slowly transformed from a transworldly eschatology based on the Jewish concept of the messianic Kingdom, to a this-worldly way of living based on sacramental experience, faith in the Savior, and ethical principles. This was bound to alter the views of womanhood that we have detected in the New Testament and the earliest writings. When Tertullian condemned female frivolity, he started from a high notion of womanhood which booked no compromise with the world; but his stand was already outmoded, for the pressures of pagan society were unavoidable. A return to a purely eschatological concept of the world, congenial to Montanism, was already utopian. Christian though they were, man had to live as man, and woman as woman. Like it or not, their standards of behavior would be set by the ethos of surrounding society no less than by doctrinal principles. Faith needed to reach a compromise with a world that was not coming to an early end.

At the beginning of the third century, the trend was clearly set against whatever utopian elements lingered in the Christian view of woman. Despite the fundamental overcoming of the fall through baptismal regeneration, the theology and experience of womanhood effectively restored a "postlapsarian" conception of woman and her place in the Christian order. True, especially with Irenaeus, the Ecclesia and Mary provided types of the Christian woman. Yet the view of woman as an embodiment of evil—and, at the root of all, sexual evil—waxed strong, gaining the support of the powerful voice of Tertullian and of much popular apocryphal literature. In principle, the writings of the New Testament offered liberation to woman by restoring her to a "prelapsarian" status in keeping with the experience of baptism. But the theology of the Fathers did not follow this consistently. The two pictures that we have seen in biblical material remained side by side, woman as evil slowly casting her shadow over woman redeemed.

In the third century, Christian experience is focused on a new phenomenon, an amazing explosion of social relationships within Christian circles, from which the consecration of virgins and the choice of virginity as a stable way of life, were to lead in the fourth century to an exodus of both men and women toward deserted sections of the Roman empire, there to live in solitude. Out of this heremetical movement there grew the monastic (cenobitic) foundations of both East (Evagrius, Saint Basil) and West (Saint Benedict). Thus, at the very moment when the encratic implications of early heresies had been frankly discarded, Christian experience gave hitherto unknown value to virginity.[1]

The positions of the Christian authors are not unaffected by the social situation of woman at their time. When they protest over forced marriages, the theologians are actually reacting against the mores of the Hellenistic world, where, in keeping with the older Greek tradition, a "free" woman always belongs to some man, who not only must respond for her before the civil authorities, but may also marry her to whom he selects. A childless widow falls back under the authority of her parental relations (father, brother, uncle, as the case may be) until another husband has been found for her. And there is a public official, the *gyneconomos,* who watches over the proper application of the laws and customs concerning the status of women. In classical Athens a wealthy woman may not leave her house without his authorization. Indeed, the Greek world by and large does not promote the dignity of women.

In the ancient world, Crete and Egypt had developed a civilization where women enjoyed nearly as much freedom as men.[2] In the primitive Greece of Homer, woman, although by no means free, was entrusted with a great deal of responsibility and received the corresponding dignity. After the Doric invasions (1200-1000 B.C.) her status was considerably lower.

In classical Greece the legislation of Solon (594 B.C.) in Athens deprived her of the right of ownership; thus she lost the very basis of public influence.[3] Destined only for procreation, wives belong to their husbands. This reaches the point where the husband lists his wife in his will as a piece of property to be passed on to someone else. The wealthy classes confine her to the *gyneceum,* the equivalent of the oriental harem. She goes out infrequently, on a shopping expedition or to attend a religious ceremony. Her education does not go beyond music, dance, and some society games.

The benefits of education and culture are shared with men by the *hetairae,* or high-class prostitutes, who supply sophisticated conversation, for the entertainment of the mind, as well as sexual pleasure. Thus Sappho could be a great poetess. Presumably at a lower level of the scale, Hipparchia, a woman philosopher of Cynic orientation and the author of lost treatises, is said to have demonstrated her contempt of marriage by marrying a hunchback and consummating the marriage in public. Such would be the origin of the feast of Cynogamies ("dog-wedding").

Numerous common prostitutes cannot share the joys of the mind with anyone; yet their head-tax suffices for the upkeep of the Temple of Aphrodite-Pandemos in Athens. Besides these, slave girls, having no ownership of their actions, are at the beck and call of their owner. As to the orphan girl (*epiclaros,* heiress), she may be claimed as wife by her nearest male relative together with the rest of the inheritance from her father. If no one claims her, the *gyneconomos* promptly marries her off.

All this contributed to the low place of woman in Hellenic society. Whatever was left her as mother or playmate could even be contested by the Athenian penchant for boys as acceptable partners in friendships that were not entirely Platonic.

The principles and customs of Sparta, which dominated the Peloponnese peninsula from 700 to 500 B.C., differed greatly from those of Athens and of the other Greek states, even after Sparta's defeat by the Athenians in 506. Here, little distinction was made between men and women in the duties and responsibilities of citizenship. Boys and girls received the same education, which stressed physical exercise. Nudity was the rule for their jousts and games. Because they were trained to fight, women were respected. Marriage customs remained primitive: marriage ordinarily began with the kidnapping, sequestration, and rape of the girl. But given the girl's ability to defend herself, this was little more than an act played by the two parties. The parents had no say in the matter. (By contrast, the Athenian girl was married in great solemnity, but she had no choice in it and was practically sold by her father.) In the Spartan ideal, which inspired Plato's *Republic,* women belonged to the state which should be able to distribute and redistribute them among men according to needs, just as it organizes the men on a military basis and sends them here and there for action. In fact, however, state ownership gave the Spartan woman more freedom than any other Greek woman enjoyed. She even owned property and could receive legacies.

Women indeed held a special place in Greek religion. Delphi and other shrines featured popular prophetesses. Yet power belonged to the priests rather than to the Sybil, herself no more than a passive, often a drugged, instrument in the hands of the divinity. Several cults and feast days gave women a unique place, such as the cult of Eleusis and the later forms of the cult of Dionysos. Isis, imported from Egypt, became a popular type of divine womanhood in later Hellenism. On the frieze of the Parthenon, women are shown taking part in a solemn procession in honor of Athena. They play a prominent role in the feast of Adonis, at the beginning of summer. And the Thesmophorae are celebrated by women only, while their husbands, if they are of means, pay the expenses of the feast.

In the world of philosophy, criticism of the customary and legal status of woman was fairly common. The school of Pythagoras seems to have made no distinction between sexes. Plato, however, endorsed the usual prejudices, as did the Socrates of the *Dialogues*, Aristotle justified the social inferiority of women by their presumed biological deficiencies. Thanks to their concept of a universal *logos* underlying all nature, the Stoics asserted the fundamental equality of men and women. Together with the Sophists and the Cynics they also disparaged marriage as a source of endless trouble. In this area the Christian authors did little more than imitate the social philosophy of their time. Largely borrowing the rhetoric of the New Sophistic movement,[4] which supported the contempt for marriage spread by the Stoics, they advised women of the drawbacks of the matrimonial condition. Little else could be done as long as the Christian ethos had not pervaded the empire. Meanwhile, the Christian principle of spiritual freedom contrasted sharply with the realities of life in the Hellenistic world. The Christian woman could be persuaded of her intrinsic value; yet the law, recognizing no such thing, placed her always under the power of a man. Some restrictions on her legal rights were removed very late by the Christian Emperor Justinian (527-565).

In these circumstances, the theologians had to take account of two sets of notions: Christian principles (baptismal equality of all; the biblical command to increase and multiply; the desire for spiritual fulfillment; the unreality of the present world as compared with the heavens; the true union, which is between Christ and the soul) and secular realities (the legal status of women; the normality of concubinage, adultery, divorce). Sheer prudence dictated their many reservations about the wisdom of marrying, or, having once had the experience of marriage, of trying it again after the death of the first husband. Add to this the frequency of infant mortality, the dangers of pregnancy in a world where medical care was primitive, the growing number of frontier wars against the barbarians, which sent soldiers away where they incurred the danger of violent death: criticism of the married state by Christian authors or by philosophers seems well justified on empirical grounds alone.

Are there only minor functional differences between men and women? Or do the male and the female principles affect the entire personality?

If the Clementine *Recognitions* are at all indicative of a popular view of the matter, the difference between men and women would be reduced to the distinct shape and functions of sexual organs in the strict sense. Everything else would belong equally to both. A lengthy description of the human body in the eighth book of the *Recognitions* mentions no difference outside of the organs which give or receive the human seed: "The female differs from the male species only in that part of her body where posterity is seeded, received and nourished."[5] If both have breasts, only women's provide milk. Thus woman is made for receiving the seed and nurturing the child. Apart from this her body is the same as man's. This passage praises the wonderful hand of

Providence, who makes all things adequate to their purpose. Woman is defined in relation to procreation; she remains a man in everything else.

If this could correspond to a popular view of the matter, medical opinion was, naturally enough, more nuanced. Basilius of Ancyra (d. c. 366), who had been a medical doctor before becoming a priest and a bishop, drew on his science in his *De virginitate* (written before 358).[6] His detailed account of virginity gives unusual importance to physiological descriptions and to the psychological analysis of sex. Basilius's method is clear: "Let us examine at the start, if you wish, what is the nature of the female sex in relation to the male sex, in order at the same time to perceive clearly the purpose of virginity."[7] In order to fill the world God divided the human creature into male and female, setting "in the nature of each an ineffable desire to be united to the other." Thus woman was to act as a magnet that would draw man to itself. God "placed the female under the power of the male, and charmed the male with the female's attraction." In this natural order, it is not the female that is brought to the male, but rather a "mysterious power" has been placed in woman, so that man is drawn to her "not only for procreation, but through this very desire for union."[8] In this magnetic radiation lies the secret of the female body: delicate and beautiful, it should "soften the male in pleasure" when it "assails him through all his senses", "through the touch, the sight, the demeanor and the sweetness of all its parts."

This very beauty renders woman physically weaker, and this in turn makes her inferior. She needs a protection that she can obtain only from the male whom her endowments have attracted. "For this reason, man will leave his father and his mother; not the female, but the male, urged by his deep desire to be joined to woman. And it is written: he—the male—will cleave to woman: not woman to the man."[9]

In this perspective, the difference between man and woman cannot be restricted to the sexual organs and their purpose. It is the entire body of woman which attracts man, and the entire body of man which pines after woman. "For, as I say, there is a great seduction in the nature of woman, which brings to itself the entire nature of man."[10] Basilius analyzes at length the part of each sense organ in this man-woman polarity. Yet, doctor though he be, fully aware of the importance of the flesh in human nature, and bolder in his descriptions than the modern mentality would expect from a bishop writing a treatise on virginity for the benefit of monks and "sisters," Basilius remains a Greek. His philosophy preserves typical elements of neo-Platonism, the chief philosophy of his times. For this reason, he does not extend to the essence of the soul the polarities which he finds in the male and the female bodies. Souls are equal, both in dignity and in structure. They become unequal only to the extent that they are affected by the differences of the bodies into which they have been thrown and which now clothe them. Could souls converse with each other "naked," that is, without the outer garment which is their body, men and women would never know each other as male and female.[11] In this life, however, souls are clothed, and communicate through a bodily apparatus which happens to be male or female.

In such a context, the ultimate goal of those who decide to live a virginal life is to escape the order of the flesh and to come as near as possible to being pure, naked souls, unhampered by bodies. This requires a thorough reeducation of nature, so that the soul tied to a female body no longer shares in its sex appeal, and that which lives in a male condition no longer feels the attraction of the female. "Seeing that the soul is equal and of the same essence in man and woman . . . the virgin does not cease trying to sever the soul from the love of the body. . . ."[12] "Clearly knowing that the kingdom of heaven belongs to the violent on account of their trials, she must do violence to nature in view of the purpose she has formed. . . ."[13] Basilius accordingly gives advice or mortification of the senses, especially of sight, touch, and taste. He shows how a virgin can take care of her own hygiene without making herself an object of desire to men. He tells her how to dress and how to go to the baths.

Overcoming the nature of the body should eventually achieve the equality of man and woman which belongs to their souls and which is to be fully manifested in the next world, when men and women will no longer marry: "If the soul, in the body where she is, experiences no desire for man or for woman and does not bear the mark of the passions, then there is neither male nor female, neither passion nor concupiscence, but 'in all and for all, it is Christ.' The body has died, since the pleasure instinct of man and of woman has stopped acting, and the soul lives alone in them without corruption through virtue."[14] At the summit, once this blessed indifference[15] has been reached, the disciples of the Lord can approach the other sex without fear, in total equality. "Then such a woman may touch the servant of the Bridegroom, if indeed feminine voluptuousness no longer lives in her flesh."[16] Then, she need not be afraid of those who may harm her body in a persecution. Were such virgins assaulted and raped, their souls will remain virginal, for, "experiencing the death of the flesh, they remain uncorrupted, whatever they may have to submit to."[17]

The text of Basilius of Ancyra clearly shows the movement of thought which underlies the promotion of virginity in the early Church. This is a simple though far-reaching transformation of a New Testament concept. The equality of man and woman through baptism, which Saint Paul expressed in the statement, "There is neither male nor female," has been severed from baptism and made an effect of the ascetic life. In their souls men and women are one and the same, though in their bodies they are not. Destined, however, to be restored in oneness and equality when the soul leaves the body, they may already learn to participate in the heavenly life. This participation, offered to all believers, cannot be achieved without strenuous effort: it requires abstinence from marriage, reeducation of the senses, and an absolute avoidance of the ways of society.

The *De virginitate* of Basilius of Ancyra is unusual in patristic literature for its insistence on human sexuality. Most authors rather see the problem of woman mainly from the social standpoint, which reveals many drawbacks to the spiritual development of woman in marriage. Admittedly, this contrast is not absolute. In his famous encomium of virginity, Methodius of Olympus includes a description of the sexual act which modern exhibitionism could envy. On the whole, however, the Christian theologians do not operate at that level. They feel caught between the dogmatic statement of the fundamental Christian freedom, in view of which "there is neither male nor female," the conditions of the times, which, both in and outside of marriage, subject woman to man, and the patently human experience of dividedness on which Paul had already reflected. Is Christian freedom, promised in baptism (indeed, given, if Paul was to be believed), a present reality? Or, contrary to the expectations of Paul, since the world had not yet been transformed into the messianic Kingdom, is Christian freedom to be indefinitely delayed until the receding parousia finally dawns? By abolishing a number of previous laws including part of Augustus's legislation against celibacy, Constantine in 320 will slightly narrow the gap between Christian theory and secular reality. By this time, however, the main lines of Christian thought will have been set.

In any case, legislation could not erase the problem of men and women divided between sexual attraction and the ideal of the contemplative life. (Owing to the influence of neo-Platonism, virginity and contemplation are tied together in the intellectual conceptions of the Fathers). Likewise, changes in legislation could not do away with the medical views of woman's passive role in relation to man. As a result, whatever theological adjustments could be made, marriage remained a less than perfect way of life, and woman kept her inferior social and legal status inherited from former times. What changed somewhat was the explanation of, and justification for, this inferiority.

The Greek theologians found the only solution that was then possible to the dilemma of the Christian woman. How can woman, who is made inferior to man in the legal and social order, achieve in her own life the equality with him which belongs to her by right as a disciple of Christ? The solution, if difficult to achieve in fact, is beautiful in its stark simplicity: the promise of baptism can be fulfilled through the ascetic life. In the structure of the Church following the Constantinian peace, a woman could be free from entering the bonds of marriage by joining the Order of Virgins or of Widows. This had already been the case, but the more fluent and dangerous situation of pagan times impeded the formal organization of virgins and widows. A woman then remained legally under the authority of her nearest male relative, but the endorsement of her virginity by the Ecclesia protected her, guaranteeing that she would not be married into another man's power. Thus woman's freedom was tied to her choice of a way of life which excluded matrimony. It would be the fruit of baptism indeed, but through asceticism. Thus the accent shifts from a transformation of the old order by the Redeemer (the old order being, primitively, that of the Old Testament and of Jewish society), to an overcoming of the old order by the charism given by the Spirit to the ascetes (the old order now being the pagan order of Greek and Roman society). It is in the microcosmos of each person that this takes place, until a more favorable time when it may extend to the structure of Christian society.

This problematic illustrates a change of perspective in Christian thought, which has altered the structures of its parousiac expectation. From now on, that aspect of eschatology which promises total spiritual freedom is offered as an ideal to be achieved here below through the virginal life. Such a project is clearly presented in all the great tractates on virginity, from the *Banquet* of Methodius of Olympus to the treatises of John Chrysostom, including the *De virginitate* of Gregory of Nyssa and the writings of Basil of Caesaria and Gregory Nazianzen.

The study of virginity and, by implication, of womanhood, is often more symbolic and poetic than in the technical treatise of Basilius of Ancyra. At least one instance of that approach should be given. And we cannot select a better example than the early and very influential work called *The Banquet*, written by Methodius of Olympus between 260 and 290.

Methodius was a most influential author, who left his mark not only on the theory of the ascetic life, but also on the basic categories of Greek theology. Yet all accounts of his life are too short and too confused to provide reliable information. Probably bishop of Olympus in Lycia, and perhaps a martyr during the persecution by Decius (311-312), he lived in the second half of the third century. Of his many works, the most important is *The Banquet*.[18]

The Banquet is a dialogue, in which ten guests plus the hostess, all virgins, pronounce the praises of virginity. Two virgins, Gregorion and Eboulion, introduce and conclude the series and occasionally interrupt the account to exchange their impressions. The speeches are reported by Eboulion, who heard an account of them by one of the guests.

The eleven speeches on virginity (plus a hymn) adopt diverse points of view, so that the whole *Banquet* constitutes a well-balanced survey of the question as well as a complete summary of theology. Much of the material is not particularly original, though its presentation is always interesting. The speeches draw on the New Testament (Paul: Discourse 3; the parable of the wise and foolish virgins: Discourse 6; the Song of Songs: Discourse 7; the

Apocalypse: Discourse 8) and the Old Testament (the description of the Feast of Tents in Leviticus: Discourse 9; the parable of the trees in Judges: Discourse 10). Far from condemning marriage, *The Banquet* devotes one whole speech (Discourse 2) to its defense. All in all, the work is a beautiful rhetorical encomium of virginity, presented from the point of view of women who have chosen it.

Because they are placed in the mouths of women, the discourses contain none of the disparaging remarks about women in which many other authors indulge. On the contrary, woman appears throughout as the high point of creation, exemplified in the Ecclesia, "the woman who appeared in heaven clothed with the sun," our Mother "whom the prophets, in their vision of the future, have called Jerusalem, the Bride, Mount Sion, the Temple and Tent of God."[19] The task of virgins here below is to imitate this heavenly Mother, seeing her "like a virgin prepared for her wedding." In other words, the Ecclesia is given us as an icon of the heavenly type of womanhood. And women in history are progressively uplifted toward that image. "Mankind has been raised by degrees toward virginity through the impulses of God age after age."[20] There will come a time when marriage will no longer be practiced. This will be when fruits and animals are no longer made, "when the predetermined number of mankind has been reached."[21] Meantime, one may still enter marriage in order to fulfill the creator's injunction: "Increase and multiply." Yet the Christian newness resides precisely in the possibility of participating now in the heavenly life, of overcoming corruption and of growing the seeds of immortality.

The history of the Church, like the spiritual interpretation of Scripture, leads from the letter to the Spirit, from the shadows of the Old Testament to the reality of heaven, by way of the image of heaven now enshrined in the Ecclesia.[22] The ancients practiced polygamy and endogamy, including even incestual unions; then exogamy was adopted when women were chosen from outside the clan; then monogamy became the standard; later, adultery was rejected; later still, continence in marriage or in widowhood was accepted, and finally, the age of virginity has dawned. This process of history, which is by the same token a spiritualization of mankind, is summed up by Marcella, the virgin of Discourse 7: God "aimed at bringing mankind nearer to heaven by passing from one practice to another, until, having reached the supreme and ultimate teaching, that of virginity, it finds its fulfillment there."[23] At this level, the order to "increase and multiply" finds an application which is indeed higher than in Genesis: through her espousals with Christ, the virgin Ecclesia unites in the highest manner virginity and fruitfulness. Yet *The Banquet* never completely identifies virginity and spiritual perfection. Indeed it distinguishes between "the great mass of the faithful" and "the more perfect, who are progressively brought to become the person and the one body of the

Ecclesia."[24] In this we may recognize the theme of *gnosis* as developed in Alexandrian Christianity. The perfect chose virginity; but others, having already chosen marriage, may also grow spiritually to the perfection of Christian life.

By the fourth century, virginity has become the Christian ideal, to be lived in the various structures available for its protection, the home of one's parents, the Order of Virgins, the Order of Widows, the Wilderness, the monastic foundations. Yet, all in all, the Greek Fathers do not disparage marriage. Or, if they maintain that virginity is better, they still teach that marriage is good; and if they dwell on the drawbacks of married life in the conditions of the present world, they assert that, in its essence, marriage is good.

Marriage is often defended even in works written to promote virginity. *The Banquet* itself includes a discourse on marriage which defends it against its detractors. Basilius of Ancyra justifies it with more common sense than most as the choice of a legitimate way of life. It is good since it channels the God-given sex appeal of woman and "the power of love placed in man for woman."[25] There remains, however, a major difference between pagans and Christians. Pagans commonly enter marriage out of passion and in view of its pleasures, whereas Christians, as true philosophers, do it "with reflection, in order to organize their existence."[26] The treatises by Gregory of Nyssa and John Chrysostom carefully distinguish their love of virginity from the condemnation of marriage by the encratics or by some who show an excessive zeal for the ascetic life. The bishop of Nyssa places a defense of marriage in the middle of his dissertation on virginity (chapter 7). Chrysostom begins his on a similar note (chapters 2 and 3) and returns to the question at length in the course of his work (chapters 8 to 10).[27]

Chrysostom, himself enthused for virginity, describes marriage in general and analyzes some marital situations with traits that are caricatures of doubtful taste.[28] Even in regard to the very nature of marriage, Chrysostom's early works—written before his ordination to the priesthood (386) when, as a monk and a deacon, he was intent on promoting the monastic life—come near to Tertullian's excesses. Marriage, which did not exist in Paradise, was born of sin and is now permitted rather than willed by God.[29] His *Homilies on Genesis* trace back the practice of sex to the order of things which followed the fall of Adam and Eve; it resulted from the loss of the angelic life in Eden. God's wisdom invented this way of propagating the race as a consolation for mankind, which had lost its immortality. He "granted succession of children, thus somehow suggesting a shadow of the resurrection, making it possible that, for those who die, others would arise."[30] In this man finds "his greatest consolation after the introduction of death." At the beginning then, marriage had the positive purpose of propagating the race and the negative one of providing a lawful channel for the satisfaction of libido. But, as remarked in the *De virginitate* (written around 382), the world is already full, so that propagation can no longer be a useful purpose. Only the second need now persists, "the suppression of debauchery and licentiousness."[31] It is better to marry than to frequent prostitutes. In this sense Chrysostom speaks even of the "beauty" of marriage, but he cannot see it as a very high beauty: marriage is beautiful only in the abstract, insofar as it keeps the faithful from "becoming members of a prostitute."[32] Even so, marriage is not very effective, since all this can be accomplished, and much more thoroughly, through asceticism. As to the beauty of woman, Chrysostom writes to Theodoros, a young monk who is tempted to leave the ascetic life and marry: "Should you reflect about what is contained in beautiful eyes, in a straight nose, in a mouth, in cheeks, you will see that bodily beauty is only a white-washed tombstone, for inside it is full of filth."[33]

Though his first works show no understanding of the gifts of marriage when he refers to it in general, Chrysostom becomes much more human when he addresses himself to one particular person. His short letter "to a young widow" shows great understanding of the beauty of her past relationship with her husband. Chrysostom apparently knew both of them well and sincerely shares her sorrow. He recognizes all the solace they could find in each other and speaks with delicacy of the drama of sudden separation. He promises the young woman, a still more beautiful union with her husband after she joins him in heaven, at least if she enters no other marriage. For the unity of love need not end with death. It still joins the living and the dead. Her husband continues to protect her. As she should remain faithful to him in her continuing love, she should also look forward, in hope, to their future reunion: "After reaching the same degree of virtue, you will be admitted in the same tabernacle, again you will be able to be united to him for eternity, no longer in the harmony of marriage but in a higher one. Here below it only joins bodies; but then there will be unity of soul with soul, much more pleasurable and noble."[34] Gregory Nazianzen, in all things more sensitive then most of his contemporaries, speaks of marital unity with great tact and understanding, as witness the poem he addressed to Olympia on the occasion of her marriage in 384.[35]

Our authors dwell at length with the practical problems of marriage, Gregory of Nyssa and most others with more respect than John Chrysostom, who frequently falls into bad taste.[36] Chrysostom is particularly savage in his indictment of remarriage, to which he devotes an entire writing.[37] His argument is commonplace for his time: remarriage shows that one has not learnt one's lesson. The troubles of a first marriage ought to be enough for anybody. A person who tries again behaves like a fool. His "On the One Marriage" adds a more interesting reason taken from psychology, namely, the love of the male for his wife is jealous. Man does not want to love what has already been shared by others: "We are thus made, we, men: through jealousy, vainglory or what not, we like above all what nobody has owned and used before us and of which we are the first and only master."[38] Woman should know this, and not enter a marriage where she will not be truly appreciated. At this point the modern reader ought to remember that reflection on the sacramentality of matrimony came late in the history of Christian thought. As experienced in the first centuries, marriage was chiefly a family and civic affair. The Church entered the field mainly to promote the evangelical notion of permanent marriage, condemning divorce and, for a long time, frowning on remarriage. Gregory of Nyssa, who had himself been married, may speak for the others when, with a touch of humor, he explains that it is not necessary to encourage the faithful to marry: "Let no one believe that we reject the institution of marriage. We are not ignorant of the fact that it is not excluded from God's blessing. But it finds a sufficient advocate in the nature shared by all men, which has placed a natural inclination toward these pleasures in all those who come to existence through marriage. . . . It would be superfluous to compose a discourse of encouragement and exhortation to marriage."[39] The promotion of virginity has, on the contrary, been entrusted to the Ecclesia.

In his later years as archbishop of Constantinople, when Chrysostom reflects on marriage, he sees it, after Saint Paul, as "a great mystery." But the exact point where the mystery lies is the very possibility of love between man and wife. Chrysostom still speaks of the petty sides of matrimony and of its constant worries over health, or children, or mutual bickering. But he seems more aware than formerly of the fact that love does exist, and that it ties together for life partners who, in the current customs of Greek society, had never set eyes on each other before the day of their wedding: "How great is [this mystery], tell me: that a virgin who has always been kept inside, from the first day [of marriage] desires a husband whom she has never seen before, and loves him like her own body; that from the first day a man prefers to all others, to his friends, to those of his home and to his parents, a woman whom he has never seen and to whom he has never spoken."[40] Indeed, this is where the Apostles' injunction becomes important: man must love his wife as Christ loves the Church, regardless of her shortcomings. Thus John Chrysostom, mellowed by age and experience, is now willing to find beautiful relationships in marriage seen as a "*koinonia* of life"[41] and a sharing of complementary qualities and capacities for mutual assistance.

The virginity which is identified with perfection and the life of contemplation is spiritual rather than bodily. As is made clear in *The Banquet* we shall not be judged on the presence or absence of virginity, but on faith: "Let no one imagine that the rest of the crowd of the faithful is rejected and believe that we alone, the virgins, will see the fulfilment of the promises; this would misunderstand the fact that there will be tribes, families and ranks according to the measure of the faith of each."[42] Discourse 10 explains that bodily virginity accompanied by pride avails nothing to salvation.[43] In the eyes of Gregory of Nyssa, it is not bodily virginity that counts, but the spiritual elevation to which true virginity contributes. For him, virginity belongs among the attributes, energies or angels of God: "So great is the power of virginity that it dwells in heaven near the Father of spirits, that it dances in choir with the hypercosmic substances and that it devotes itself to man's salvation. For it brings God, through its mediation, to share human life here below."[44] In this context virginity is the unity of a human being totally oriented to God through all his powers. Only the eye that is pure of all corruption can see the light of God.[45] Gregory of Nyssa aims at spiritual marriage. As there are two men, corporal and spiritual, in each man, so there are two marriages, one with the other sex, the other with the True and the Beautiful. One may recognize in this neo-Platonism's concept of union to the One,[46] which in the Christian context becomes union with the God who has revealed himself as the One, the True, and the Beautiful. "When, according to the Apostle's words, there is neither male nor female and Christ is all and in all, truly the lover of wisdom possesses the divine aim of his desire, true Wisdom, and the soul, clinging to the incorruptible Bridegroom, possesses the love of the true Wisdom which is God."[47] For John Chrysostom, the ultimate justification of the virginal life lies in eschatological awareness: "If marriage does not reach beyond the present, if in the future life one neither marries nor is given in marriage, if the present time nears its end and the time of resurrection stands at the gate, this is no moment to think of marriage or of the goods of this world, but rather of our frailty and of all the other elements of wisdom that will help us in the next life."[48]

Of this virginity alone do the Fathers speak when they insist that its standard lies in the soul, not in the outward garments,[49] that it dwells inside the heart.[50] They relate it to the vision of God. They depict it as an icon of the divine blessedness,[51] as a share in the divine life.[52] They claim that it has already overcome death.[53] They see it as a liberation, as an epitome of the new order inaugurated or restored by the coming of the Lord into the flesh. It achieves among men the life of the angels,[54] as it already did in paradise.

Physical virginity alone is of so little value that according to its most forceful proponent, John Chrysostom, the gnostic heretics will gain deeper damnation through their practice of it.[55] For him too, a widow can rank higher than a virgin.[56] Married persons may even be called virginal if they are totally given to God.[57] Chrysostom insists: "Not to be married does not make a virgin; but there must be chastity in the soul."[58] Against all customs, he lets the widow Olympia, a deaconess, sit among the virgins in the Church of Constantinople.[59]

Only in the proper order of faith and life does bodily virginity count. Then it becomes an ascetic practice serving the higher purposes of virtue. It also provides convenient symbols to help the mind conceive of spiritual realities. Indeed, because the worries and the drudgery of married life, the dangers of pregnancy, the subservience of wife to husband, and the strenuous duties of a husband and father constitute such telling examples of the cares and troubles of the present life, encouragements to virginity frequently dwell on these, the celibate life standing in happy contrast. The qualities of spiritual virginity, which are identical with the higher degrees of the contemplative life, are rhetorically attributed to bodily virginity. But these are figures of speech, metaphoric appropriations, literary and pedagogic devices, which are to be understood as such. The mistake is ours if we take them literally.

The nature of womanhood not only raised the question of virginity and marriage. At a deeper level of discussion, the account of the creation of Adam and Eve posed problems which the theologians of the great patristic age attempted to solve as best they could. Of the various questions that could be asked, I will select two, which bring us to the heart of the theological concepts of woman that are reflected in the works of the Greek Fathers. Is Eve also, and not only Adam, created "in the image and likeness of God"? What is the function of woman as a "helpmate" for man?

The first question is briefly answered in the *Commentary of Genesis* of Diodoros of Tarsus (d. 390). Paul speaks of man as being the image of God. The word he uses is not *anthropos* (man in general) but *aner* (man as male). In 1 Corinthians 11:7, man is the "image and glory of God," whereas woman is only "the glory of man."[60] The "image of God" resides in the power given to man: as God has power over all, so has he granted man power over all the earth. Woman has received no such authority and, being also on earth, she has been placed, like everything else, under man's dominion.[61]

Diodoros of Tarsus is associated with the more literal interpretation of the Bible of what we call, with more or less accuracy, the school of Antioch. John Chrysostom is himself an Antiochian by birth and formation. His solution of the problem follows similar lines. Man is made in the image of God; woman is not. Yet John Chrysostom's explanation is of a more sophisticated coinage. The principle is clear and admits of no exception: "Man commands, woman obeys, as God said to her at the beginning: Your desire will be after your husband and he will lord it over you."[62] But is there nothing common in man and in woman? As Eve was built from a bone extracted from Adam's body, this would be astonishing indeed. What is common to them both, however, does not lie at the level of the "image" of God, for woman can only be the "image" of her husband. Yet man and woman have the same "form and structure": "Because man was made in the image though not in the structure by virtue of power, man dominates all and woman serves. For this reason Paul says that man is the image and glory of God, and woman the glory of man. Had he said this of their form, he would not have separated them so, for man and woman have the same model."[63]

The words which I translate as "form" and "model" are μορφή and τύπος. Μορφή refers both to the inner structure and to the external appearance, while τύπος refers to what later philosophy will call the prime analogue of a created reality. In other words, "image" and "glory" do not connote the structure of man and woman in themselves: at that level they are alike. They stress rather a function and a task. The "image" in man resides in his power, analogous to God's dominion over all. Chrysostom uses this to refute what he regards as an absurdity: because the *Logos* took "the form of man," he must have been female as well as male, for man and woman share the same form. We touch here on some of the problems that Platonism introduced into Christology. That mankind has one form is a commonplace of Platonic philosophy. Yet Scripture, as read by John Chrysostom, does not see the Incarnation at the level of the form but at that of the image.[64]

The question of the image of God has thus been raised as a historical, or prehistorical, problem concerning the first men, and as an ontological one concerning the nature of man. Many answers are then possible, for these two fields lie wide open to speculation. Diodoros or Chrysostom do not include woman in the natural image of God, since this image is one of power and dominion, of which woman has been deprived by God and society. In another perspective, Gregory of Nyssa, working along lines already pioneered by Origen, sets the image in the soul itself, beyond the distinction of male and female.[65] The image results from a first creation anterior to the fall: this made human nature "like God."[66] Made in the image, man before the fall had a natural beauty patterned on that of the archetype.[67] This image resides in all men, who all have their root in the divine prototype. As to sexual distinction, it is due to a second creation, which added the separation of sexes to the oneness of the image of God. Only after man's sin and exile from Paradise was "marriage invented to compensate for death."[68] Not all the Fathers, of course, follow this line of thinking. Yet, in the main, the Greek Fathers opted for a view of the secondary nature of sex. As God foresaw man's sin, his fall into corruption and mortality, and consequently his loss of the angelic mode of multiplication, he gave man in advance the means to perpetuate the race with the method used by the animals rather than by the angels. Accordingly, the present historical state of man depends on the two images that are in him:

that of God, which is common to all and by which all are one, and that of animality, whereby mankind is divided into men and women with diverse and complementary natural functions.

In such a view, sex has nothing to do with the image of God. Male and female are equal in their divine likeness. For at that level there is neither male nor female, even after the fall.

Whether proposed by Diodoros, by Gregory of Nyssa or by John Chrysostom, these speculations should not overshadow the deeper dimension of the doctrine of the image, which is found in the main trends of oriental theology. Whatever was given to Adam and Eve, and whether creation was in one or two steps, the image of God in man (to speak the usual language) or the form and structure of man (to use Chrysostom's distinction between image and form), though given, is still to be built up through the Christian sacraments and life. Men equally with women must grow in the response to the inspirations of the Spirit. To say that they are made in the likeness or in the form of God is not enough. For they must grow into the image, regain incorruption and immortality, develop their participation in the divine life, be elevated to deification. To borrow the vocabulary of Dietrich Ritschl, this is a *doxological* rather than an *ontological* doctrine.[69]

Precisely, the ascetic and the monastic movements from the third to the sixth century were a response to this challenge. The life of virginity was a prophetic anticipation of restored incorruptibility, a manifestation of the fullness of deification, of the final integrity of the image of God in man and in woman. Although still subject to the conventions of this world, the virgin was spiritually free. She experienced the fulness of baptismal restoration. In her, as in the martyr or in the holy man, the image of God beyond the distinction of male and female, or the form which is common to male and female, came to light. She was the equal, in the Ecclesia, of any man.

Coming now to the other problem of woman as helpmate of man, we will return to John Chrysostom, who, on this point, may stand for the Greek Fathers in general.

Writing against remarriage, around 383, John Chrysostom makes a fairly long and not unsympathetic description of the tasks of woman as man's helpmate. Although God gave man dominion over things, animals, and women, he did not intend to leave woman without dignity or responsibility. Rather, he divided mankind's capacities into two broad areas: to man the important things of social life, like politics, war, the acquisition of property; to woman the small things, like the care of the household, the protection of the patrimony. To man the glorious and public affairs; to woman the private concerns and the hidden chores. To man questions of principle and philosophy;

to woman practical problems. "Since private affairs are part of the human condition as well as public ones, God has doled them out: all that takes place outside, he has entrusted to man, all that is within the house, to women."[70] When she loses her husband, woman keeps the same tasks if she has been left with children: she must preserve their inheritance and defend their rights until they can take care of themselves. Even then, a widow should not attempt to increase the family wealth, for this is not a woman's job; her role is only to see that it is not wasted away. "To make money is man's function; all lucrative activity is forbidden to women."[71] Of course, Chrysostom can quote no biblical precedent for this line of thought. Indeed, one could well object that Proverbs 31 contradicts him. He simply relies on fairly common ideas among Greek philosophers, although this opposition to woman earning money was contrary to the mores of Greek society, where women often assisted their husbands in the family business. His ideas on the matter are a mere rendering of the classical Greek view that, in well-to-do society, women belong within the *thalamos* or *gyneceum,* the part of the house reserved to them.

What Chrysostom found in the type of civilization with which he was acquainted colored his understanding of the stable nature of men and women. The feminine activities of which he speaks at length in *On the One Marriage* and in his homilies on marriage have been forced on woman by society: "The one task of woman is to keep the acquisitions, to preserve the gains, to take care of the houses: God gave her for this purpose. . . ."[72] John Chrysostom willingly details the number of things that she may not do. She may not engage in sports, speak in the senate or obtain public office; but she can spin, decide family questions, educate children. From matters of fact in the world of John Chrysostom, these restrictions on women become in his mind eternal decrees enshrined by divine providence in the nature of things:

> This is an aspect of the divine providence and wisdom, that the one who can conduct great affairs is inadequate or inept in small things, so that the function of woman becomes necessary. For if he had made man able to fulfil the two functions, the feminine sex would have been contemptible. And if he had entrusted the important questions to woman, he would have filled women with mad pride. So, he gave the two functions, neither to the one, to avoid humiliating the other as being useless, nor to both in equal part, lest the two sexes, placed on the same level, should compete and fight, women refusing authority to men.[73]

It is therefore by God's act of creation itself that woman is, in society, subservient to man. She was created as man's helpmate. In the *De virginitate,* Chrysostom defines this assistance first of all in terms of sex and procreation,[74] although woman can make herself her husband's associate in the spiritual life, especially if she invites him to continence.[75] But this can be only a limited contribution to his ascetic development, for she may not refuse sex if he demands it.[76] But this is not all. In his letter to the "young widow," Chrysostom already spoke with sympathy of the assistance that man and wife find in each other. His *Homilies on Genesis* bring further lights to bear on the matter. By creation, woman is made *for* man, that is, "for his consolation." She is so constructed that "she may talk to him and bring him much comfort through a total communion." She is rational like him "in order to help him in the necessities and the utilities of life."[77] Yet she is not *under* man, except as a result of the fall and the curse. Acting on her own, woman, in the person of Eve, behaved irresponsibly. So God gave her a tutor. Henceforth she must obey, in order to walk straight. Subjection is imposed on her for her own sake: "It is better for you to be under him and to have him as your lord, than, that, living freely and on your own, you fall into the pits."[78]

After the fall, it is only through grace that woman can reach equality with man. This will depend on her charisms and therefore on the Spirit. Homilies for the commemoration of martyred women praise them for having reversed the customary order of nature. The martyrs overcame the frailties of soul and body. Some orators who pronounced panegyrics on their own mothers or sisters, like Gregory Nazianzen on his sister Gorgonia or Gregory of Nyssa on his sister Macrina, picture them as so filled with the Spirit that they were raised above the inferiority of their sex. Gorgonia took the best of marriage (a way of life which is "humble and secure") and the best of virginity ("sublime and divine, but hard and dangerous").[79] And Gregory Nazianzen wrote of his mother, in a poem *"On His Own Life"*: "In body she was a woman, in her behavior, higher than a man."[80] John Chrysostom thought that his mother Anthousa had been a model of feminine heroism through her courageous widowhood.[81] His homilies on the saints harp on these themes: of Saint Thecla, for instance, he shows that her virginity gave her the power to withstand torture.[82] Allowing for oratorical exaggerations and the use of rhetorical clichés, we may still admit that for the Fathers the fruits of the Spirit in woman entailed their uplifting above the condition of nature, into a realm of freedom unknown to natural women. With the recess of persecution in the fourth century and the growing rarity of martyrdom, virginity became the very type of a life that has overcome the limitations of nature.

A woman of the fourth century could also rise above her conditions through study, especially through the study of the Scriptures. Saint Jerome in Palestine animated a cluster of studious women.[83] One such circle gathered in Constantinople around Theodosia, sister of the bishop of Iconium, Amphilokos. Like Gregory Nazianzen, Chrysostom knew it personally and he wrote letters to several members of it. In his admiration for these women, Palladios (363–c. 431), in his *Laudiac History* (420), calls them "virile women"[84] at the same time betraying the male complex of superiority which had left its mark on language ("courageous" being one of the derived meanings of "vir-ile") and illustrating the Christian assumption that perfection implies a rever-sal of nature. Olympia (c. 368–after 408), who had been educated in this cir-cle, was widowed at eighteen years of age and worked from that time on as a deaconess in Constantinople. It was on the occasion of her wedding that Gregory Nazianzen composed his poem *Carmen ad Olympiaden.*[85] A touching sign of John Chrysostom's mellowing with experience is that, during his exile from 404 to 407, he wrote her long letters of friendship. These were meant to help Olympia, also victimized by the wave of opposition which caused Chrys-ostom's loss of favor at court. They were also letters of self-consolation. To this great woman who had worked closely with him, Chrysostom confessed that separation proved hard to bear: "Do you see the hard struggle of accept-ing with serenity the absence of the one we love? This is painful and bitter; it requires a courageous and noble soul. . . . To those who love each other, it is not enough to be linked at soul-level. This does not comfort them, but they need physical presence. And if this is not granted, a great deal of their happi-ness is taken away from them."[86] Thus in his old age Chrysostom came to un-derstand love, and to share it with a woman who had become spiritually free. In this sense, she had overcome nature while, as the letters show, she had also preserved the delicacy of cultured womanhood.

Even then, Chrysostom grants less dignity to woman as such than another great Antiochean, Theodoretos of Cyrrhos (393–c. 466). In his *Therapy of Hellenic Diseases,* Theodoretos approaches the question from the standpoint of the essential oneness of mankind: creation gives the principle of the essen-tial equality of man and woman. There is admittedly a touch of male superi-ority in the suggestion that Eve was extracted from Adam "so that woman, claiming to have another nature, would not go another way than that of the male." However, "God prescribes the same laws to men and to women, since their difference resides in the structure of the body, and not in the soul." At the level of nature woman has the same intelligence, the sense of duty, the knowledge of good that man has; sometimes she even shows better judgment. As for the level of the Ecclesia, Theodoretos says:

> Not only men, but women also must be admitted to the divine Temples; and the law which permits the former to take part in the divine mysteries does not forbid the latter, and even orders them, like the men, to be initi-ated to the divine mysteries and to take part in them.[87]

The principle is clearly stated. Yet it is understandable that possible appli-cation of it beyond the practice of the Church of his time do not enter Theo-doretos's horizon. Even so, his thought is well in advance of that of his con-temporaries.

On the equality of men and women, no other Greek Father seems to have reached the forcefulness of Gregory Nazianzen. His *Homily 37 on Matthew*, preached in 380 in Constantinople, condemns the legal injustice by which civil law permits a husband to be unfaithful to his wife and punishes the wife who is unfaithful to her husband. "I do not accept this legislation; I do not approve this custom. The law was made by men, and for that reason it is directed against women." By contrast, God makes no distinction between sexes. "There is only one Creator of man and of woman, one dust from which both have come, one image [of God], one law, one death, one resurrection."[88] Thus, men and women must be equal in the Ecclesia, just as they are equal in God's sight.

The equality of woman with man is also affirmed, at least as a spiritual ideal, in other circles. In the *Life of Saint Melany*, written by her disciple and friend, the priest Gerontios, Empress Serena—a woman of considerable importance, as she was the niece of Emperor Theodosius, the wife of Emperor Stilicho, and the legal guardian of Emperor Honorius—praises Melany (383-439), who is no more than twenty-one at the time, for proving herself the equal of men: "Having mastered nature, she has undergone death daily, showing evidently to all through her works that, as regards godly virtue, the female sex is not inferior to the male sex when its purpose is steady."[89] Melany herself appears through her *Life* as a perfect example of a free woman. Belonging to a wealthy and aristocratic Roman family, herself the granddaughter of another famous lady, Melany the Elder (c. 345-410), she persuades her husband, Pinianus, to lead the ascetic life with her. She is received at court and known to the greatest personages in Rome and Constantinople. Consulting with learned and holy men, she travels in Africa and settles down in Palestine. She acts as a true spiritual director to her chaplain and biographer, the priest Gerontios, on whom she herself bestows the monastic habit. She establishes two monasteries, one for women and one for men.

We might also mention Etheria. This lady, presumably a native of Galacia, travelled extensively at the beginning of the fifth century in a pilgrimage on the traces of the Old Testament and left us the account of her journeys. Totally immersed in biblical culture, she visited the Sinai, Mount Nebo, Idumea, and Palestine, returning home by way of Constantinople. Her piety was more liturgical than ascetic. And she faithfully recorded descriptions and impressions of liturgical ceremonies as well as of the sites and buildings she visited. This is another, very attractive type of Christian woman who meets bishops and monks on terms of equality and manifests the greatest freedom even from social conventions.[90]

The peregrinations of Etheria bring in a question, which, I suspect, greatly influenced the practical and theoretical status of woman in the Church.

Church buildings often included a hospitality house for pilgrims and travellers. Monastic foundations were open to visitors. Etheria herself was freely received by male monasteries, who set her and her companions in their guest house. Bishops invited her to share their meals and to rest in their residences.

How far could such hospitality go? Once a woman entered the way of life of virginity, was counted among the ascetics, frequented the sacred liturgy assiduously, and conversed on biblical matters, what difference remained between her and a monk? Could the equality of souls, included in the common doctrine of the image of God and practically achieved through asceticism and the sacramental deification of the faithful, sufficiently transform persons so that differences of sex could safely be ignored? There were some who thought so. The extensive literature against the *agapetai*,—or, as they were called in the West, *virgines subintroductae*,—proves that this optimistic view was fairly widespread. There were unmarried deacons, priests, monks, and even bishops who shared their living quarters and perhaps—this at least seems to have been the case with some Africans about whom Cyprian was consulted by a puzzled bishop—their beds, with women consecrated to virginity. The old idea of some apocryphal writings and of the *Second Epistle of Clement* had not fallen on deaf ears: the Kingdom will come "when the two are one, and the outside like the inside, the male like the female, that is, neither male nor female." In the *Epistle*, this means: "when a brother seeing a sister does not think of her as a woman, and when a sister seeing a brother does not think of him as a man."[91] If this provides a valid eschatological sign, there is no intrinsic reason why those who have reached the eschatological awareness of overcoming sex should not live accordingly. Once this was granted, there could develop beautiful friendships. But the door was also open to abuses. Paul of Samosata, who became bishop of Antioch in 260, lived with several *virgines subintroductae*. The fact that he favored an adoptianist Christology and that he was suspect in other areas of behavior, did not help the cause of these unconventional women in the eyes of the orthodox. Likewise, the influence of women in the Montanist movement helped to discredit women prophets and those who claimed Christian freedom outside of the usual regulations concerning virgins and widows.

At any rate, strenuous opposition grew against the practice of chaste promiscuity. The two *Epistles* of Pseudo-Clement; an unknown author of the third century (around 270); John Chrysostom in two treatises; Cyprian in Africa (Letter 62), who dealt with a case involving a deacon and a virgin; in the West, Ambrose of Milan—all condemned the movement, in spite of the venerable eschatological tradition that could support it. In the words of Charles Williams, this was a "great experiment," "dangerous, but dangerous with a kind of heavenly daring."[92]

I suspect that the final settlement of the status of woman in the Church proceeded from a reaction against the fear of scandal, that is, ultimately, from acquiescence to social conventions, rather than from theological principles. The advocates of the eradication of sex in anticipation of the Kingdom could rest their case on the theological ground of their very opponents: were they not reaping the fruits of the movement for the reversal of nature of which all the promoters of virginity spoke? What can be the good of a program of life if we are immediately told that it is unattainable? But, the writings that lambast the *virgines subintroductae* and their protectors do not argue from theology. They adduce considerations of social conventions and of ethics: it becomes a matter of avoiding scandal and of not falling into sin by presumption. John Chrysostom admits the validity of the purpose, but realistically postpones its achievement until we have entered heaven: "When bodily passions have been removed and the tyranny of concupiscence is extinct, there is no objection: man and woman can be together"; but this is reserved to "those who have been introduced into the Kingdom of heaven";[93] it is the life of the angels. Here below we remain in the conditions of the world. Christian freedom must be, at least at this level, a hope. Such a reaction could be valid only to the extent that the virginal ideal had been utopian; but nobody seemed to realize this. The Council of Antioch, which condemned Paul of Samosata, confessed: "We are aware how many, through taking spiritual brides, have fallen, while others have become suspect. Even if we grant that [Paul of Samosata] does nothing licentious, he should at least have taken care to avoid the suspicion to which such practices give rise. . . ."[94]

On the face of it, the opposition to *virgines subintroductae* was ethically and psychologically the only sane attitude. But it could not be theologically satisfactory as long as the emancipation of woman from man was necessarily tied to virginity and to an ascetic reversal of nature. Not only did this amount to separating some Christian women into a small elite (John Chrysostom, for one, was well aware of this); it furthermore removed Christian freedom from the sacramental experience of baptism to a program of self-education and effort throughout life. Admittedly, this asceticism was kept in balance by insistence on the Eucharist as the sacrament of immortality and incorruptibility and by the experience of the Holy Liturgy as the event in which the deification of the Christian is manifested. Thanks to this, asceticism in the East did not turn into pelagianism. Christian liberation was given not achieved.

Meanwhile, the average Christian woman remained at the place which society, that is, Greek paganism, had assigned to her. Equality with men was claimed only for the small number of the ascetic elite. And the reaction against gnosticism, Montanism, and the *virgines subintroductae* curtailed the freedom even of those, as it restricted the behavior of bishops, priests, and deacons in their dealings with women.

This last point may be illustrated with a brief look at Church institutions.

The Order of Widows, never very successful, declined in the fourth century and practically disappeared by the year 400. The Order of Virgins continued, to be eventually incorporated into monastic institutions for women. The Order of Deaconesses seems to have grown out of the Order of Widows, the widows really interested in Church service often being given recognition and responsibility as deaconesses. There is evidence that in some areas deaconesses were created through an imposition of hands which, in the *Apostolic Tradition* of Hippolytus (c. 170-235) is identical with the ceremony for the male diaconate:[95] in other words, they received a real ordination and not simply a blessing. The Councils of Nicaea (canon 19) and of Chalcedon (canon 15) allude to this ordination, which the latter regulates (no ordination of a woman under forty years of age). Throughout the fourth and fifth centuries the institution of deaconesses thrived in the East. Deaconesses had to remain unmarried.

At the same time, a trend toward separating Orders from womanhood developed.[96] The third canon of the Council of Nicaea forbade bishops, priests, and all members of the clergy to have an *agapeta*. Yet this was not too rigid, for exceptions were made in favor of relatives (mother, sister, aunt) and even of "persons beyond suspicion."[97]

In his *Ecclesiastical History*, book 1, chapter 11, the historian Socrates reports that several bishops urged the Council of Nicaea to forbid bishops, priests, and deacons to have intercourse with their wives any time after their ordination.[98] This custom was then spreading in Thessaly, Macedonia, and Greece, counter to the common practice of Egypt and Syria. After the intervention of an Egyptian bishop, Paphnutius, the Council dropped the matter. In 400, Synesius, bishop of Ptolemais in Egypt, clearly refused to repudiate his wife and expressed the fond hope of having many more children still.[99] In Cappadocia, Gregory Nazianzen was himself the son of the bishop of Nazianzen, born while his father was effectively bishop.

Around 340, the Council of Gangra had specified that no distinction must be made between a married and a celibate priest and blamed the faithful who attended only the liturgy celebrated by a celibate.[100] At Nicaea, Paphnutius, who was himself unmarried, had argued that it was quite enough to forbid single priests to marry and widowed priests to remarry; those who were already married should not be restricted.[101] And, according to the tenth canon of the Council of Ancyra (314), a deacon may marry even after his ordination if he had expressed this intention beforehand and the bishop had agreed to ordain him with this proviso.[102]

Thus, until well into the fourth century there were diverse practices and customs in the East, yet no clear or final legislation. But the trend to bring further separations between the service of the altar and women was growing. By the end of the fourth century, the canonical compilation known as *Apos-*

tolic Constitutions formulated rules that have remained basic to the Eastern Church. Bishops, priests, and deacons, if they are celibate at their ordination, may not marry; if already married they may continue in marriage. Except as concerns bishops, this has remained the discipline to this day. Concerning women, the *Apostolic Constitutions* specify that women must obey their husbands "for the man is the head of the woman."[103] They should keep away from the mores of pagan women and avoid going to the public baths.[104] Not only is woman forbidden to teach in church, moreover she may not usurp any priestly function. To ordain a woman would be against the natural order, for woman may not yield authority over man. The creation of priestesses is a pagan impiety. A woman may not even baptize, for Christ, as creator of nature and lawgiver of the Church, has given her no such power.[105] Neither virgins nor widows receive an ordination.[106] As for deaconesses, the eighth book of the *Apostolic Constitutions* records that they receive the imposition of hands from the bishop, "in the presence of the presbyterium, the deacons and the deaconesses." The prayer is the following:

> Eternal God, Father of our Lord Jesus Christ, Creator of man and woman, who filled Mary, Debora, Anna and Holda with the Spirit, who let your only Son be born of a woman, who instituted women-guardians for the holy gates of the Trent of Witness and of the Temple: look now upon this your servant who has been elected for your ministry; give her the Holy Spirit and purify her from all sin of body and of soul, that she may worthily fulfil the function assigned to her, to your glory and to the praise of your Christ—with Whom be to You glory and worship, and to the Holy Spirit for ever. Amen.[107]

It is difficult to read this text as implying less than an ordination to a sacred order of the ministry. Thus, the *Apostolic Constitutions* have preserved a testimony that in the fourth century and at least in Syria women could be ordained to the diaconate. In the practice of later centuries, however, the legislative sections of the *Constitutions* which outlawed women from sacred functions, won the day over the liturgical sections.

In another area the canonical legislation of the East is much harsher on woman. The second chapter of the *Canonical Epistle* of Dionysius of Alexandria (190-264), a former disciple of Origen, forbids women to enter a church building at the time of their period, which is understood to imply a spiritual as well as a corporeal impurity: "The one who is not entirely pure in soul and body must be stopped from entering the Holy of Holies."[108] Such women should stay outside the gate and must abstain from communion.

After the chaotic contrasts of the second and third centuries, the Greek tradition has now taken a definite orientation. The liberation achieved by Redemption, communicated in baptism and nurtured through the Eucharist, provides the basis of the theological tradition on womanhood, even though the situation of woman in society makes it impossible for a new type of sex relationship to be effectively established. The tendency to stress the essential identity of man and woman is clear. Their differences and the ensuing subordination of woman to man are seen as elements belonging to the curse. The progress of Christian life should wear away the sequels of the fall, now that the fall itself has been overcome in baptism. The image of God will shine through more and more as the charisms of the Spirit become more active in the Church, carrying the faithful from glory to glory. Everything that divides man from himself will go. Sex and marriage belong to the order of the fall, and they will progressively disappear. Thus, whatever their social inequalities, physiological differences, and psychological diversities, man and woman, as νοῦς and πνεῦμα are theologically one. The life of virginity testifies to this oneness. Even though the servitudes of marriage will help to promote, by contrast, the ascetic ideal, the expectation of the parousia and the desire to live like the angels of heaven will continue to provide the main justification for the central place of the charism of virginity in the life of the Ecclesia. The eschatological sense will never disappear, although its form will change: the expectation will not be that the end may soon burst on us, but that heaven may come down and make its presence felt in the Holy Liturgy.

The ethical concerns of John Chrysostom's homilies added to the conservative structure of Byzantine society, will slow down and even, to all practical purposes, halt the emancipation of woman which should logically have followed the proclamation of her spiritual freedom. A number of excesses had the same effect. The *agapetai* threw a veil of suspicion on relations between men and women in the Church. The overenthusiastic promotion of virginity over against the decadent sexual mores of society made marriage a second-rate vocation. The former freedom of the clergy to be married was drastically reduced. And the feminine diaconate, at one time an option that could have gathered strength and, in the long run, genuinely altered the very tone of clerical life, was on the way out.

Yet in all this, the sense of eschatological participation in the freedom of God through the Sacred Liturgy and the sacraments kept the balance from tipping over into excessively ethical concerns and even secular considerations and motivations. John Chrysostom well illustrates the actual status of woman as in fact it persisted for centuries. Yet Gregory of Nyssa provides a more adequate instance of the theology at work in the Greek conception of woman.

5

Liberation through the Ecclesia

As on all matters of Christian faith and life, the Latin tradition on womanhood emerged from the older Greek tradition. During the third century, mainly with the appearance of Tertullian on the intellectual scene, Latin displaced Greek as the theological language of the West. Yet fruitful exchanges of thought continued to multiply between Greeks and Latins, who formed one world until well into the Middle Ages. Travel was fairly easy within the boundaries of the empire, especially for those who were allowed to use the official postal services, as, after Constantine, bishops commonly did when journeying to and from Councils. Melany the Younger herself frequently travelled with the post. After the Council of Nicaea, imperial policy wavered between the many interpretations of, and opposition to, the formula ὁμοούσιος, thus occasioning discussions and exchanges that might not otherwise have taken place. In 343, Latin bishops attended the Council of Sardica (Sofia today) in strength. Athanasius (295-373), "pope" of Alexandria and the most ardent supporter of the Nicene formulation, sojourned in the West for years during his exiles. He lived at Treves from 336 to 337 and in 342, in Rome from 339 to 342, in Aquileia from 344 to 346. According to Jerome,[1] he became familiar with the ascetic circle that met on the Aventine hill in the house of Marcella, thereby exercising a direct influence on the Roman concept and practice of virginity. Conversely, Hilary of Poitiers (313-367) spent several years in Phrygia, exiled from Gaul because of his orthodox convictions. Jerome of course had travelled extensively in Gaul, Italy, Palestine and Egypt, had studied in Constantinople under Gregory Nazianzen, had known Gregory of Nyssa in the same city, and had acted as secretary to Pope Damasus in Rome before settling down as an ascete near Bethlehem around 386.

Above all, perhaps, the land of Jesus held a peculiar fascination for the Westerners. Melany's and Etheria's examples have been cited. Melany's grandmother, called Melany the Elder (c. 346-410) had left an influential situation in Rome for the neighborhood of Jerusalem, followed later by the holy women of Jerome's circle (Paula, her daughter Eustachium and their epigones) and

97

by those who followed Rufinus of Aquileia on Mount Olivet. Rufinus himself (c. 345-410) had studied in Alexandria for six years under the great teacher Didymos the Blind.

In spite of this cross-fertilization of Greek and Latin thought in the great patristic period, the Western approach to womanhood developed some features of its own which distinguish it both from previous Greek writing of the West and also, by and large, from contemporary Greek emphases. Some tural factors influenced this specific development.

The laws of Roman society were more generous to women than those of the Greek lands, although the language knew no such thing as a feminine name.[2] By the third century after Christ, Latin women normally could marry whom they wished or, in the decadent mores of the last decades of the Republic, live maritally with anyone and leave him when they had enough. True, the basic concept of the early Romans had given women the status of children, to be kept always under a man's guardianship: a woman passed from her father's *potestas* to her husband's *manus*, falling back under her father's *potestas* when her husband died. Thus, the law of the Twelve Tables (451-449 B.C.) specified:

> Women, even though they are of full age [that is, twenty-five years old], because of their levity of mind, shall be under guardianship . . . except vestal virgins, who . . . shall be free from guardianship. . . .[3]

In case a woman had no natural guardian (father or husband), a male, not necessarily of her own kin, was appointed to be officially responsible for her. The initiation of this legislation is credited to Romulus himself.[4] On this legal status of women, there was no fundamental difference between the older, Roman and the Greek customs.

Roman life and religion were focused on the home and its gods (*lares*), whereas Greek life gave all importance to the city as the unit of religion and of politics. In politics man dominates, since public order rests on power, and power rests on wealth and on military might. Woman, however, rules the home, even when, as in Rome, all authority officially lies in the hands of the husband. Even under a guardian, the Roman woman can own property. Soon the evolution of Roman legal thinking, necessitated by the growth of the mother city into a potential world empire, led to the progressive disappearance of the right of life and death over his children hitherto accorded to the *paterfamilias*.[5] Likewise, the *manus* over his wife relaxed. The status of woman, who was thus gaining freedom little by little, remained affected by the laws which forbade legal union between persons of different castes, thus leading to widespread concubinage. A married woman could obtain a divorce. By the end of the Republic, licentiousness had become universal and marriage was held in little esteem, concubinage being much more common. The matrimonial laws of Augustus at the start of the empire attempted to restore marriage. They exempted mothers of three legitimate children from the tutelage of their legal guardians, an exemption which Hadrian extended to all married women, thus ending the husband's *manus*. They also imposed heavy taxes on all legal celibates, many of whom in fact lived with a concubine, Augustus, however, involved as he was in a scandalous divorce and remarriage with Livia, who had herself divorced her first husband to marry him, could hardly set a good example. The outcome of his reform was catastrophic: instead of settling down in one legal marriage, men and women commonly passed through a succession of marriages and divorces.

Roman religion went very far toward giving at least some women unique influence and honor. The institution of the vestal virgins, which goes back at least to Numa Pompilius (716-673 B.C.), placed a group of distinguished women at the very apex of sacred hierarchy.[6] Entrusted with the care of the holy fire symbolizing the continuity and divinity of Rome, the vestals belonged to the highest circles of public and social life. Selected from the most noble ranks of society at an early age (between six and ten), they lived a celibate life in their palace on the forum. The few who broke their vow of virginity were buried alive. After thirty years in the vestal order, they were released from their obligations. They then returned to the world and could marry if they so wished. Most of them apparently continued in a celibate life, covered with honors and wielding great influence.[7] To the considerable annoyance of Ambrose, bishop of Milan, their virginity took the edge off the doubtful apologetical argument which Christians borrowed from the beauty of consecrated celibacy. This may be surmised from the savage attack on the vestals contained in a letter of 384 to Emperor Valentinian.[8] The bishop of Milan supported a decision of the Roman senate removing a statue of the Goddess Victory from the senate hall and cancelling the immunities of the vestals and of all pagan priests. This naturally provoked much resistance from the pagan aristocracy, and Ambrose refuted the objections raised against the senatorial decree. The vestals, he pointed out, number only seven; they live in luxury in a palatial residence on the forum; they have enjoyed extravagant privileges; they are paid substantial stipends; they follow the most expensive and decadent fashions of society women. In other words, they are false virgins, for true virginity, which is of the heart and not only of the body, implies simplicity and poverty. Be that as it may, by the time the vestals lost their status, Christian virgins were numerous and influential. The vestals went down with the old religion which they incarnated. Their demise implied nothing about womanhood as such.

Moreover, a "feminist" movement agitated the empire, leading Latin women, pale imitations of the Spartans, to compete with men in many fields, including the national sport of *palaestra*. The satirist Juvenal (c. 55-135) took the emancipated women of his time as a choice and easy target for his irony.

The Latin Fathers had to take account of the temper of their society which, at least in Rome and the larger cities, allowed to women whatever licence they wished. Latin women had gained freedom at the very moment when the mores of society reached an all-time low. It is more than a coincidence that Tertullian, the first Latin author to write on women, strongly reacted against his times, considerably restricting the freedom and the activities of Christian women in contrast with the licence of the secular women of those days. His reaction may have been inspired by personal misogynism, but it was also prompted by disgust at the prevailing decadence of society.

A major influence on the Latin Fathers' conception of womanhood is tied to the name of Tertullian. The African priest, who had created the very vocabulary of Latin theology, continued to wield a tremendous influence in spite of his later Montanism. Indeed, the bishop of Carthage, Cyprian, belonged in the tradition of Tertullian. Augustine, the greatest Latin Father, bishop of Hippo in Numidia, lived and worked at a time when the thinking of Tertullian and Cyprian on woman and virginity was still vivid. But Augustine cannot be explained only by Tertullian and Cyprian. He had been a Manichee before turning to neo-Platonism and, later, to Christianity. Certainly, his views were tainted by his own history, even when he refuted the dualism between spirit and flesh, good and evil, which the Manichees still taught. Furthermore, Ambrose of Milan had helped him to arrive at an understanding of Christianity when he was seeking for a better way to God than neo-Platonism. Ambrose was not only an enthusiastic promoter of the virginal life; he had also put forward what may well constitute the only profound theology of womanhood of the Latin world. It also happened that Augustine wrote about virginity and marriage in order to soften the tone of some of Jerome's blasts against those who questioned the value of consecrated virginity. We will therefore read Cyprian, Ambrose, and Jerome before reaching Augustine, who fixed Latin thought on our topic for centuries.

Tertullian died some time after 213. Cyprian must have been born around 200. Converted and baptized around 245, he was soon ordained and became bishop of Carthage shortly before the Decian persecution (250-251), which he spent in voluntary exile. He died in September, 258, a victim of the persecution of Valerian.

If Cyprian did not teach any original theology on the problem of woman in the Church, he shows himself to be, in this as in most other matters, a good witness of the African tradition. A short work, *On the Dress of Virgins*, probably written in 248 or 249, before the persecution, is largely dependent on Tertullian. Cyprian presents the voluntary virgins as forming the highest order in the Church: "That is the flower of church-seed, the beauty and ornament of spiritual grace, the joyful youth, the perfect and immaculate work of praise and honor, the image of God reflecting the Lord's holiness, the better part of Christ's flock. The glorious fecundity of Mother Ecclesia rejoices through them and flourishes abundantly in them."[9] These lines refer to the charismatic order, at the apex of which are the virgins. According to the letters sent to Carthaginian Christians during his exile, and as the biography written by his deacon Pontius testifies, Cyprian himself had several visions which helped him determine his conduct in the difficult problem of the reconciliation of those who had lapsed from the faith during the persecution. In other words, although Cyprian was by no means a Montanist, he still lived in the eschatological, apocalyptic atmosphere that we have already illustrated with the *Acts of Martyrs*. This was a time when the Spirit showed himself, establishing an order of values which neither was that of the world nor entirely coincided with the hierarchy of government in the Church. The confessors who considerably annoyed Cyprian by claiming the right to demand the reconciliation of their lapsed friends were arguing on ground that was not unknown to Cyprian himself. The charismatic order has rights that the government of the Ecclesia should recognize. Cyprian, too, was a man of the Spirit. Yet it is significant that, previous to the persecution, Cyprian did not place martyrs and confessors, but virgins, at the summit of the charismatic order.

As he understood it, virginity included, besides a gift from the Spirit, recognition by the Ecclesia: "A virgin should not only be, but be known as, and believed to be, a virgin."[10] Hence the virgin's obligation to dress with recognizable simplicity. Should she be herself wealthy, still she ought to avoid ostentation, giving up the luxury of the pagan world, shunning the arts of make-up formerly taught by "the sinful and apostate angels," keeping away from the licentiousness of wedding feasts, not going to the baths where, even though she herself would remain pure when showing herself nude, she would be lusted after by men.[11] In all things, she must remember that "continence follows Christ, and virginity is destined to the kingdom of God."[12]

In his *Letter LXII*, also written before the Decian persecution, Cyprian answers questions asked by Pomponius, bishop of Dionysiana in Byzantium, concerning virgins who have been living with men, among them a deacon, even to the point of sharing their beds. According to Pomponius's letter, no sexual intercourse took place. In other words, this was a case of ascetic cohabitation. Cyprian handles the matter with common sense, if not with theological profundity: the virgins and the men must be separated while they are still innocent. Pomponius acted properly when he excommunicated the men involved, "the deacon who often stayed with a virgin, and the others who used to sleep with virgins."[13] The women may be received to communion after doing penance, but they should be examined by midwives and their penance must be greater in case they had lost their virginity after all. The letter ends with the remark that spiritual charisms and the institutional hierarchy ultimately must work together in unity: "Those who have made themselves eunuchs for the kingdom of heaven should please God in all things, should not offend the priests of God and the Church of the Lord with the scandal of their depravity."[14]

Like Tertullian himself, Cyprian is able to speak of married love with delicacy. In 253, barbarian tribes raided some towns of the province of Numidia, kidnapping a number of Christians, among whom were married women and virgins. Cyprian organized a collection in Carthage to contribute to their ransom. He was considerably worried over the fate of the virgins, fearing that "members consecrated to God and devoted to the cult of perpetual continence in asceticism" be desecrated.[15] He also alludes to the married women who have been kidnapped: "Who, remembering his humanity and moved by mutual love . . . does not, if he is married, imagine his wife held captive there, in the sorrow and the fear of her matrimonial estate?"[16] For the bishop of Carthage, Christian love shares the sorrows of all; and these in turn strengthen the joys of each, for those who thus empathize with the suffering members of the Church will better love their own wives.

Nearly one century separates the death of Cyprian (258) at Carthage from the birth of Augustine (354) in neighboring Numidia. During this period, some of the problems that Cyprian met in his episcopal career grew out of proportion. The strict moralism of the Novatianists, which Cyprian had fought, spread to Africa, where it found an unexpected ally in what remained of Cyprian's own notion of the episcopal structure of the Ecclesia, thus giving birth to the Donatist schism. The Peace of Constantine finalized the Church's compromise with a morality for the average man, already made possible by the overcoming of Novatianism. Meanwhile, the ascetic movement grew, in opposition to the increasing mediocrity of the majority of the faithful. Out of the ascetic circles of Rome there will eventually arise Pelagianism. Augustine's stand on virginity and marriage, and by implication on womanhood, will depend on, and react against, the Pelagian interpretation of asceticism.

. Ambrosius (333-397) was proclaimed bishop of Milan by the people in 374. Early the following year, he explained many of his ideas about women in a series of commentaries on Scripture. Throughout his episcopate he preached and wrote on the virginal life, of which he made himself an eloquent champion, leaving us several important treatises. And some of his letters contain material which illustrates his views.

Ambrose is the first of our authors who presents a real typology of womanhood. Although he is immediately concerned about all the women in his care as belonging to the people of his diocese and about those who have recourse to his advice and help (and such requests came from all over northern Italy), Ambrose sees also the feminine as a principle at work in mankind at large and extending beyond the social or physical boundaries of the female sex. The creation of woman shows her to have been adapted to procreation and the reproduction of the human race. Instead of reading this only in terms of biological necessity, Ambrose concludes that within mankind woman represents the principle of universality. Not before the creation of Eve did God proclaim the goodness of mankind. After making Adam, God even remarked: "Man alone is not good."[17] It was better to make mankind twofold, with the possibility of sin but also of reproduction and therefore of universality, than single, sinless but sterile. If sin entered through her, Eve also carried the principle of Redemption, since the Savior would be born from the possibility of multiplication which she brought to mankind. Should woman be deemed to be no more than an inferior member, her gift to mankind was good, necessary to the human race, and made her an integral part of the body of mankind: "Not in vain . . . was woman made from the rib of Adam himself, that we might know that there is only one nature of the body in man and woman, one source of the human race."[18] Woman represents universality within the unity signified by the identical origin of man and woman. As Ambrosiaster says more succinctly, "The one Adam sinned,—that is Eve, for woman is also Adam."[19] And the *De institutione virginis* (c. 392) states: "Without woman, man receives no congratulation, but he is praised in woman. For when he [God] says that it is not good for man to be alone, he implies indeed that mankind is good if the female sex is added to the male sex."[20]

As the principle of completion and perfection for the very structure of mankind, woman is also the principle of life, in the twofold sense of the term: biological life will bring mankind to its full quantitative stature; spiritual life will lead mankind, through redemption by Christ, to eternity. "Through woman the heavenly mystery of the Church has been fulfilled; in her grace has been typified, for which Christ came down and completed the eternal work of human Redemption. For this reason Adam called his wife Life: the line and the descent of human succession pass through woman, and eternal life is given through the Ecclesia."[21] On the basis of this typology, Ambrose does not hesitate to identify Eve with the holy women of the Old and the New Testament: Eve is Sara; she is Mary, sister of Aaron; she is Mary, the Mother of Emmanuel, the Mother of God.[22] What Scripture says in the story of the woman judge Deborah applies to a woman when it is read as "history," and to the Church when it is understood as "mystery": "In the history, and in order to enthuse the souls of women, a woman judged, a woman decided, a woman prophesied, a woman triumphed and, in the midst of the fighting troops, taught men the art of war under feminine command. In the mystery, however, the struggle of faith is the Church's victory."[23]

Ambrose is also familiar with another kind of feminine typology, which Tertullian had exploited with particular eloquence: woman is the type of evil. Under his pen however, this is considerably toned down and the accent has shifted. Ambrose does not see the typology of evil in relation to a supposed congenital inferiority which would make woman prone to sin, but rather in relation to what he considered a fact recorded in Genesis: sin came through Eve before it reached Adam and was then communicated to mankind. When he explains the historical meaning of the fall, Ambrose does not put the blame on Eve's shoulders, but finds many excuses for her and judges Adam's crime greater. The *De paradiso* notes that, for "several" interpreters, the sin responsible for the fall was Adam's not the woman's. "For we know that Adam, and not Eve, had received the commandment from God. Woman had not yet been made."[24] With what words Adam communicated the rule to her we cannot know. Ambrose, however, admits that the sin started indeed with Eve. Confronted with her behavior, Adam found himself less free to decide than he would otherwise have been.[25]

The *De paradiso* was written in 375. In the *Commentary on Luke*, composed over the years between 377 and 389, Ambrose briefly says: "As sin began with women, so the good also begins with women, so that women too, leaving aside female doings, abandon their weakness, and the soul, which has no sex, like Mary who makes no mistake, devotes itself to the religious care of chastity."[26] In the *De institutione virginis*, however, written about 392, Ambrose has shifted his position. "Woman," he now writes, "may find an excuse in sin; man cannot."[27] For the serpent was "the wisest of all," a "superior creature," whereas she was "inferior." Deceived by "an angel," even though an evil one, how could she have resisted his superior intelligence, when man did not resist even her? Besides, the curse of woman is milder than the one on man: Eve will simply fulfill her function of motherhood and be dominated by man, but man will revert to the earth. This difference in punishment is just. For Adam had personally received God's command not to eat of the tree, whereas Eve, having heard it only second-hand, could not truly assess its gravity. How could she endorse a human word, when Adam did not even endorse the word of God?[28] Again, after his sin, Adam throws the blame on Eve, whereas Eve states the fact that she had been tempted, confessing her sin without looking for excuses or seeking even to blame the serpent. She thus becomes the model of Christian penance.[29] Finally, the woman's punishment implies also her liberation, for she will devote herself to those she will bring into the world in sorrow: "Woman struggles for you in her pains, and finds reward in her punishment; she will be saved through the sons who afflict her."[30]

At another level of interpretation, the three protagonists of the tragedy of Eden rank in ascending sequence. The serpent symbolizes lust (*delectatio cor-*

poralis); woman represents sense perception (*sensus*); man is intelligence (*mens*).[31] That is, temptation proceeds from the body through the psyche to the mind. This implies that Eve, transmitting temptation, cannot be held responsible for falling: it is the mind that sins—in this case, Adam, man—by assenting to what perception has handed over to it. If man and woman act as co-principles of the soul, both have their share of temptation and both together bring sin about, but the endorsement of sin comes only from the higher principle, the *mens*. The appropriation of evil actions to the feminine aspect of the soul and of good actions to the masculine is far from accurate. Although Ambrose does it, this is in a context where the female function of parturition has been attributed to the masculine part of man: "As the soul has no sex, it represents the attributes of both sexes; it receives, conceives and gives birth." Thus the soul has in itself a spiritual womb from which thoughts and intentions proceed. Some of these products are female: all the bad thoughts "by which the virility of our soul is weakened." Others are male: the holy thoughts which "strengthen our mind and our body."[32] Thus Ambrose cannot consistently espouse the identification of the female with the evil principle. In his typology of the soul, the male principle itself (*mens*) fulfills the procreative function of the female. There is actually in his works a double typology of womanhood. Most Church Fathers, borrowing from neo-Platonist, Pythagorean, and Stoic models, equate the female with various degrees of evil, imperfection, or congenital weakness. Ambrose discovers in the Bible that the female represents both biological and spiritual fruitfulness. On this basis, the Ecclesia is female. So is the soul, which, through the practice of the Christian life, learns to seek God like a bride in search of her husband.

Not inappropriately, this is the theme on which the *De institutione virginis* ends: Ambrose prays to God, "the Father of love and glory,"[33] to come to the virgin as to his bride. The *Exhortatio virginitatis* (c. 393) applies the image to the soul, which is asexual: "When the Bridegroom finds [the Christian virtues], he passes by. And the soul must follow him, rise from its bed, leave its house . . . that is, start on a pilgrimage out of the body in order to be united to God, for in the body we are on pilgrimage away from Christ."[34] Those who thus follow the Bridegroom receive the wounds of love from him. Ambrose cites some of those who have received these wounds: Job, Jeremias, Stephen, the Apostles, all masculine instances of a feminine pursuit and adventure.[35] The *De virginitate* describes at length the search of the soul after her bridegroom.[36]

This interchange of feminine qualities and masculine identity is grounded on Ambrose's belief that the soul itself, *mens,* escaping the polarity of the sexes, may be seen as either male or female. It is male in relation to the lower activities of man, female in connection with the superior activities of God, though in itself it is beyond the male and the female. In his *In hexaëmeron*

(375), Ambrose equates the image of God in man with the soul's fundamental freedom from time and space. The soul is not bound to the limitations of the body and can, being physically in Italy, think of what is in the East or the West, in Persia or Africa: "We follow those who go, we are with travelers, we join the absent, we speak with those who are far away, we raise up the dead to converse with them, we see and hold them as though they were alive. . . ."[37] The image of God resides in this freedom and power. Such a description of the image makes it, in our terms, "natural" rather than "supernatural." The natural image, which comes from creation, already implies the presence of God in the soul, who could not be his image without him.[38] There is continuity between this and the image that is built up through grace, as Paul suggests: "All of us, reflecting the glory of God face to face, are reformed into his image, from glory to glory, as by the Spirit of the Lord" (2 Cor. 3:18). "What is richer than to be in the image and likeness of God?" Ambrose wonders in the *De institutione virginis.* His answer insists on the interiority of the image, which dwells in the soul and not in the body: "The inner man, not this exterior one, is in the image; the one who is guessed at through perception but not comprehended by the eyes."[39]

At this interior level, men and women are equal in grace; both are in the image, sharing the same spiritual structure. In his *De virginibus,* Ambrose tells the story of a soldier who freed a Christian girl from her captivity in a brothel by giving her his clothes and wearing hers. Eventually, however, both were condemned to death. Exteriorly they were as different as a soldier can be from a consecrated virgin. Yet inside they were alike: "Add the persons, the soldier and the virgin, different by nature, but similar by the mercy of God; and the oracle is fulfilled: At that time wolves and lambs will graze together. There you have the female lamb and the wolf, who not only graze together, but are immolated together."[40] At this level of the interior man, the curse has already been lifted. "Come, Eve," Ambrose calls, "not as excluded from paradise, but already as raised to heaven." In Sara, Eve has overcome her condemnation: "Come, Eve, already Sara who begets sons not in pain but in joy, not in sorrow but in laughter."[41] At that interior level, Eve is also Mary "who brought us not only the example of virginity, but God."[42]

Man and woman are equally able to lead the angelic life by choosing the state of virginity. The reward has been promised: "A kingdom is obtained and the kingdom of heaven shows the life of angels. Let me persuade you that nothing is more beautiful than to be angels among men, unfettered by nuptial ties. For those who neither marry nor are taken in marriage are like angels on earth: they do not feel the trials of the flesh, they do not know slavery, they are freed from the contagion of worldly thought, they are turned to divine realities. As though liberated from the weakness of the body, they think thoughts of God and not of man."[43] At this point Ambrose willingly dwells on the inconveniences of matrimony, although he does so more freely when he addresses his discourse to widows who have experienced what he now talks about, when he speaks to virgins.[44] For him also, the virginal life manifests the fundamental Christian freedom by gaining now what others will obtain only in heaven. The theme of virginity as anticipation of heaven recurs with him as often as with the other authors, although Ambrose treats it with infinitely more tact.[45]

By freeing the faithful from the limitations of being tied to another person for life, virginity manifests the equality of male and female as souls rather than bodies and their identity as images of God. It is curious that Ambrose's *In hexaemëron* should end with descriptions of the soul and of the body where hardly any distinction appears between man and woman.[46] For Ambrose the soul is nonsexual. And the body as made on the sixth day, that is, before the fall, appears to have no sexual characteristics. Ambrose barely mentions that men wear short hair and women long hair;[47] but this is of course a social, not a natural, characteristic. Had Ambrose described Adam and Eve on the eighth day, after the fall, he would have described sex. Augustine will react strongly against the view which excludes sex from Paradise, fearing that this ties in with some form of Manichean dualism.

Nonetheless, for Ambrose the choice of marriage remains good and holy. For it is grounded in the state in which mankind finds itself, whatever one may think of the absence of sex in Paradise. Marriage is founded on the complementarity of man and woman. "Grace is not only for men, while woman would be alien to sanctification; and the nature of the two sexes is distinct so that bodies are not confused in procreation. Men have their tasks, and women have the precise functions of their sex. The generation of human succession belongs to woman; it is impossible to man."[48]

The differences of bodily functions entail a series of psychological consequences which Ambrose explains in a letter to a certain Irenaeus, apparently a young man who had asked for advice concerning clothes: May men dress like women, or women wear men's garments? Ambrose notes that the law of Deuteronomy condemns it severely. It is also against nature, for it implies a lie: why should a man want to be seen as what he is not? Why should a woman want to lie about herself? "Nature has clothed each sex with its own dress. The male and the female differ by their customs, their color, their motions, their pose, their strength, their voice."[49] Granted, the Greek fashion makes women wear short skirts like men. But if Greek women wish to imitate the "nature of the nobler sex," why should men do the opposite? Granted, in pagan Temples "it is considered holy for men to wear feminine vestments and to make feminine gestures." Yet why be surprised at that? After all, it is normal that "where one lies to faith, one should also lie to nature."[50] The most important point, however, regards behavior rather than dress. If men "curl their hair like women, let them conceive and bear children." It may be excusable to follow the customs of one's country, but all such customs derive from the barbarians, Persians, Goths, or Armenians, and "nature counts for more than fatherland."[51] Little need be said of those who exploit these fashions for their own mercantile purposes. The conclusion is clear: "Chastity is not kept when the distinction of the sexes is not observed."[52]

As a result of the difference of sex, marriage is not only in keeping with nature, but also good. Ambrose wants the adepts of both states of life to respect the other.

> Let no one who has chosen marriage despise virginity, or one who has chosen virginity condemn marriage. . . . A field has many fruits, but the best is filled with both fruits and flowers. The field of the Church is fecund with diverse riches. Here you see germs of virginity blossoming; there, in the woods, venerable widowhood; yonder, the harvest of the Church filling the barns of the world with the fruit of the womb, and, so to say, the presses of the Lord Jesus in which the fruit of faithful marriage abounds, overflowing with the products of the marital vine."[53]

Chastity is not univocal and reserved to virgins, but each calling—of marriage, of widowhood, of virginity—has a chastity of its own.[54]

In keeping with the human generosity which underlies all his treatment of our theme, Ambrose does not associate marriage with procreation only. He speaks frequently of the "grace of mutual love,"[55] which is good, though it does not do away with the servitude of marriage; of "the good chains of marriage," which are yet chains; of "the good wounds of love," which are, however, to be distinguished from, and preferred to, kisses, for Peter, after wounding the Lord, bound the wound with his tears, but Judas condemned himself with the kiss of betrayal.[56] "Divine law joins together married persons by heavenly authority, and mutual love remains difficult. He took a rib from man, and formed woman in order to couple them together for himself: And they will be two in one flesh."[57]

When he writes for the benefit of those who are not married, Ambrose mentions and even dwells, however slightly, on the subservience of woman to man, the difficulties of living together and of bearing one another's burdens, the pains of pregnancy, the worries of education. Yet, writing to Eusebius, bishop of Verceil, he recommends dignity and spiritual freedom within marriage. "Woman must respect her husband, not be a slave to him; she consents to be ruled, not to be forced. The one whom a yoke would fit is not fit for the yoke of marriage. As to man, he should guide his wife like a pilot, honor her as his partner in life, share with her as a co-heir of grace."[58] In other words, married persons should also participate in Christian freedom. They are not destined to live like pagans in the bonds of matrimony, the male dominating the female by strength and she in turn capturing him through lust. In Christian marriage the partners are tied together by mutual love, which entails "a greater service." Marriage is not only sex, but service. "How great is the power of marriage, that the stronger is also at the service of the other!"[59] Admittedly, Ambrose writes this to widows, at the same time suggesting that one such experience ought to be enough and that they should not marry again. Still, it shows his appreciation of the bonds of love which in Christian marriage become bonds of mutual obedience and service.

As for man, he should not complain that temptation originates in woman. Ambrose is prepared to grant this as regards Adam and Eve, since, whatever excuses one may find in Eve's favor, Adam was still tempted through her. He then adds, with a touch of irony: "Indeed, if she is beautiful, this is another temptation." But, he asks, "Why should you seek beauty of face in a wife, rather than of conduct?" In other words, if a woman's beauty is for man temptation, this is the man's fault: "A wife should please by her honesty more than by her beauty. . . . It is no crime for a woman to be what birth has made her; but it is a crime for a man to seek in a wife that which is likely to tempt him. . . . We may not blame the work of the divine Artist; but the one who delights in corporal beauty should rather delight in the charm of the image of God inside, not in that which appears outside."[60]

Ambrose's doctrine is fairly complete and very balanced. Men and women do not differ in their souls but only in their bodies, destined to diverse biological functions which in turn specify them socially and psychologically. The Christian order, however, allows them to recover their ontologically pristine oneness, since the practice of the virginal life, made possible through asceticism, lifts them up to the angelic level, which will characterize the next world. Even those who choose marriage should live, not like pagans abandoned to wanton lust, but with the freedom of those who have been redeemed, finding in mutual love the strength to give themselves to each other in mutual service. Furthermore, the female sex, which has been given the harder place in society, is raised through symbolism to a position of universal superiority in the Christian order: it becomes the very image of the Ecclesia and of all mankind in relation to the eternal Bridegroom.

Even when presented with the unequalled delicacy and balance of Ambrose, the problems of this approach are patent. By stressing man's efforts, asceticism will soon lead, with the career of Pelagius, to the heresy that bears his name, Pelagianism. The emphasis on virginity, considered to be of heaven while marriage remains of the earth, radically separates an elite, which is no longer defined by knowledge (*gnosis*) but by ethical standards, from the majority entangled in the bonds of matrimony.

Is it by accident that the first protest historically registered against this theological interpretation of man's condition originated in a layman? Helvidius, by birth a Milanese, lived in Rome. He was in some ways a follower of Ambrose's predecessor in Milan, Bishop Auxentius, whose leanings toward Arianism were notorious. He published a pamphlet against a certain Carterius, a priest who had argued in favor of the monastic life and virginity on the basis of the perpetual virginity of Mary. This Marian doctrine was not yet universally held, although it was widely accepted. Helvidius claimed that Mary bore children to Joseph after the birth of Jesus, and he denied the moral superiority of virginity over marriage. Jerome's refutation of Helvidius was written in Rome in 383.[61] Helvidius was obviously not alone in his thinking. In 389 or 390, Pope Siricius condemned the ideas of a Roman monk, Jovinian, who also downgraded virginity.[62] Ambrose and a Council of Northern Italy took a similar stand shortly after.[53] And Jerome, then living in Palestine, published a long and fierce refutation of Jovinian in 393.[64]

Jovinian's writing has not survived unfortunately. From the refutation of it, it seems that, like Helvidius, Jovinian denied the perpetual virginity of Mary. This point in particular drew the attention of Ambrose, although neither Siricius nor Jerome mentioned it. Jovinian tried to establish four propositions which Jerome quotes or summarizes as follows:

He says that virgins, widows and married women, once they have been washed in Christ, are of equal merit if they do not differ in their other works. He wants to prove that those who have been baptized with full faith cannot be changed by the devil. Thirdly, he teaches that there is no difference between abstaining from food and receiving it with thanksgiving. Fourthly and finally, that for those who have been faithful to their baptism there is only one reward in the kingdom of heaven.[65]

In other words, baptism alone defines Christianity. The status of a Christian in relation to marriage entails no spiritual value. The other points pursue the same principle in other fields of "works." Baptism makes all the faithful equal in the eyes of God, all being redeemed through the blood of Christ: accordingly, distinctions among Christians are meaningless. Neither continence nor fasting has any special values. Differences between marriage and celibacy, asceticism and ordinary human weaknesses become matters of indifference. Jovinian can therefore write: "I do you no wrong, virgin. You have chosen a life of chastity on account of the present distress. You determined on the course in order to be holy in body and spirit. Do not be proud: you and your married sisters are members of the same Ecclesia."[66] Jovinian's volume was successful enough in Rome to convince a number of virgins that they should leave their way of life to embrace matrimony. At least this is reported by the

Retractions of Augustine.[67] For this reason the authorities tried to protect the virgins by obtaining a powerful refutation of Jovinian. The book was sent to Jerome by his friend Pammachius, in the hope that his powerful pen would silence Jovinian and bring back peace to the Roman virgins.

A little later, Vigilantius, a priest from southern Gaul who had spent some time with Jerome in Bethlehem, published an attack against monks, whom he accused of laziness. At the same time, he denounced the cult of relics, prayer to the saints, and the commoration of the martyrs. He objected to clerical celibacy, which was then spreading in the West and in some parts of the East. He denounced asceticism as a heresy. The tract seemed to have been aimed mainly at Palestinian monks, but it also condemned many well-received practices and doctrines. Jerome refuted it in 406 with a biting pamphlet against Vigilantius.[68]

The importance of these writings should not be stressed; only Jovinian's essay seems to have had theological value. All certainly reflected some of the conflicts that occasionally arose between priests and monks and some of the rumors that could start about persons who had given up wealth and situation to seek holiness in the desert. The important effect of these writings was that they triggered Jerome's responses. For the unchastened language of Jerome's long refutation of Jovinian brought him into immediate disrepute, especially in Roman circles. One of the reasons why Augustine eventually entered the fray was precisely that Jerome's excesses had caused scandal and needed to be corrected.

Jerome's oppositions to Jovinian illustrates a period of transition. There were still churchmen who lived within an eschatological perspective. With the expectation of the Kingdom, marriage, though good when seen in the abstract, becomes a frivolity which draws a man and a woman away from thinking about the End. Others however, like Helvidius, Jovinian or Vigilantius, no longer sensitive to the parousiac expectation, could see no difference of spiritual quality between married and unmarried persons.

In his nonpolemical writings, as in his admirable letter to Eustochium, Jerome speaks highly of virginity without despising marriage. He shares the position that has by now become traditional in both Greek and Latin Christianity. Marriage is good, as instituted by God for the management of this world; voluntary virginity is better as anticipatory of the Kingdom. Between them, accepted widowhood partakes of both. Yet for those who have entered marriage, a holy life remains entirely possible. These points are carefully explained to Eustochium, the second daughter of Paula, who has, under Jerome's guidance, embraced the life of virginity. Already her mother has consecrated her widowhood to God; her sister Bresilla, married for only a short time when her husband died, had also chosen widowhood but passed away a little while later, to the great embarrassment of Jerome, accused by malicious tongues of killing her through fast and penance.

Now Jerome writes to the younger girl, whom he calls "my Eustochium, daughter, lady, fellow servant, sister," for, as he explains, "one name suits your age, another your rank, another your religion, another your love."[69] He advises her on how to live as a virgin, abstaining from wine and taking only simple food, renouncing the luxuries to which her wealth and social rank entitle her, staying away from men and married women, whose worries and concerns she cannot share. Jerome moans about the modern fashions, warns against false virgins, expresses disgust at the lingering unofficial institution of *agapetae*: "How has this pest of *agapetae* come into the Church? Whence this other name of 'wives' for the unmarried? Worse, whence this new kind of concubine? I will go further: whence these one-man prostitutes? They use one house, one bedroom, often even one bed—and they call us suspicious if we infer anything!"[70] Certainly the great project of virginity is not easy. The devil often attacks men through sex: "All the strength of the devil against men is in the loins, all his force against women is in the naval," loins and naval being, as he has explained, metaphors for the sexual organs.[71] The ascetic life cannot be understood indeed by those who do not know Christ. "Let her turn to her husband, she who is not married to Christ. And at the end, 'you shall die the death', that is, the end of marriage." Virginity aims higher: "My goal lies outside of sex. Let married women have their time and title. To me, virginity is given in Mary and in Christ."[72]

Although difficult in the present condition, the continent life is not only possible, but also natural. On this point, Jerome alludes to the theology of Gregory of Nyssa whom he had known in Constantinople: "Eve was a virgin in Paradise. After the garments of skin her marriage began. . . . Virginity, belongs to nature; marriage comes after the offense."[73] Creation originally made human beings virgin and destined them to a virginal life. The "garments of skin"—that is, sex—were made later after the first sin, in what Gregory depicts as the second moment of creation. But the Christian, who is aware of his origin and looks toward his destiny, still belongs in Paradise. As an illustration of this, Jerome points out that all children are born with "virgin flesh": in the proper order of nature, "what was lost in the root is restored in the fruit."[74] Thus the faithful one who has chosen the continent life exemplifies in himself both the original order of creation and the restored order of the Kingdom.

There is nothing in the letter to Eustochium that even suggests a contempt for woman. But if his doctrine remains traditional, Jerome cannot always control his pen or his amazingly bad temper. The letter to Eustochium, prompted by love, rings more neatly than the three writings against Helvidius, Jovinian, and Vigilantius, in which Jerome's indignation leads him to unedifying excesses of language.

As soon as the *Adversus Jovinianum* was out, Jerome found himself deep in hot water. He had scandalized a good part of the public, especially in Rome, by his disparaging references to marriage and to women. He had so much emphasized the beauty of virginity that readers understood marriage to be ugly. His careful interpretation of Saint Paul's treatment of marriage had led him to conclusions that made virginity excellent and marriage imperfect: "Between the good and the better, the reward is not the same; and where the reward is not the same, the gifts are different. The difference between marriage and virginity is as great as between not sinning and doing good; rather, to speak more gently, as between the good and the better."[75] The trouble is that "not sinning and doing good" do not amount to "good and better," but to "mediocre and good." As now presented, marriage corresponds to the goodness of the Old Testament, and asceticism to that of the New. "Let us, who served marriage under the Law, serve virginity under the Gospel."[76] Virgins understand mysteries that others cannot fathom:

Peter is an apostle, and John is an apostle. The married man and the virgin. But Peter is only apostle; John is apostle, evangelist, and prophet. . . . Virginity explained what marriage could not know. . . . [77]

This is extravagant enough, but Jerome oversteps all bounds of taste and decency when he musters help from pagan authors, not only to show that the heathens appreciated the beauty of virginal life, but furthermore to describe married life as a hopeless entanglement with a shrew, into which no man would ever enter if he had any common sense.[78]

Jerome was puzzled by the outburst in Roman society. Never had he meant to disparage marriage! Yet he had written: "All love for another man's wife is shameful, and so is excessive love for one's own," thus practically equating marriage with adultery.[79] Those who did not know Jerome well could be pardoned for concluding that he was a foe of marriage; even his friends could be worried about his doctrine and annoyed at his language.

One gathers from the *Retractationes* that Augustine's main writings on marriage and virginity were occasioned by the continuing influence of Jovinian's ideas and, partly at least, by the ineptitude of Jerome's answer.[80] Augustine recoiled from excesses. In one passage at least he even contradicted Tertullian by name.[81] For he was appalled at defenses of the virginal life which directly or indirectly discouraged the faithful from marrying. With the bishop of Hippo, the promotion of virginity need not entail a lesser esteem for marriage. There is no question any longer of dwelling on the practical inconveniences of matrimony, still less of describing awkward or disgusting marital situations. The virginal life must not be entered into as an escape from the duties and concerns of marriage: "Those who decide to remain unmarried should not flee from marriage as from a snare of sin. They should rise above the hill of smaller good to rest on the mountain of greater continence."[82] Augustine therefore fights the neoencratic orientation of Tertullian and Jerome, as well as the trend represented by Jovinian, who finds no spiritual differences among the various forms of life recognized by the Church and sanctified by the experience of three centuries.

This second concern is clear from the dates of Augustine's chief writings on the question: *De continentia* in 395 or 396, some five years after Jovinian's treatise and two after Jerome's refutation; *De opere monachorum* in 400, prompted by a request from Aurelius, bishop of Carthage, worried over monks who refuse to do menial work; *De bono conjugali,* followed by *De sancta Virginitate,* in 401: both of these openly refute Jovinian and implicitly rebuke Jerome (though Jerome is not named). Much later, in 414, Augustine writes *De bono viduitatis* as a long letter to a widow named Juliana.

Augustine's approach is also dominated by another perhaps more important fact, relating to the history of Christian doctrine. Tertullian's eschatology is still "imminentist," tainted by the experience that the Spirit is now manifesting himself and inaugurating the last age of the world, and Jerome, with his enthusiastic endorsement of asceticism, still presents the angelic life as a genuine alternative for the cares and troubles of this world. Augustine, however, has accepted a compromise with the realities of the human condition. Even the sack of Rome by Alaric, which inspired the most somber pages of *The City of God,* did not suggest to him that the end was around the corner. The motivation for the virginal life cannot derive from a belief that the angelic life is truly possible here below. Augustine knows too much about human libido and is too pessimistic about the present state of human nature to accept this. A virgin should not think she can live on earth better than a married person; she only aims at a higher reward in heaven.[83] Virginity will allow her (or him) to "follow the Lamb wheresoever he goes."[84] It relates to life in the world to come, not to the sublimation of the present condition. Eschatology has become individual: the eternal life is life with Christ after death.

If Augustine is pessimistic about mankind's condition, his understanding of creation, Paradise, and the proposed place of woman in it is quite generous. Unlike Gregory of Nyssa, he does not believe in two creations and he denies that sex was created only in view of, or after, the fall.[85] The first creation story of Genesis refers to *informatio,* the formation of man and woman as human beings related to God and equal to each other in this relationship; the second, to *conformatio,* the formation of man and woman as beings related to each other for the purpose of procreation and unequal at that level, the one being active and dominating, the other passive and subordinate. In the first, Adam is made "male and female." That is he contains in himself the "seminal reasons" which, being later activated, will give rise to woman and to the whole race. In the second takes place the actual elaboration of Eve out of the humus already inserted in Adam.

As souls, both man and woman are equally the image of God. As bodies, however, only the man is made in the image, for only he expresses in his body the power and superiority of God, the female body expressing, on the contrary, passivity and inferiority. Thus, man experiences no conflict between his soul and his body from the point of view of being God's image, whereas woman is caught in a permanent squeeze between her soul—image of God—and her body, which cannot image God. For this reason, woman was, in Paradise itself, nearer to Satan than Adam could be. In the Augustinian logic, this makes her somehow loathesome to a Christian: "In her the good Christian . . . likes what is human [*quod homo est*], loathes what is feminine [*quod uxor est*]."[86]

As thus made by *informatio* and *conformatio*, man and woman are sexed. Sex was destined to function in Paradise for the multiplication of the human race.[87] It would not then be prompted by passion; the flesh would not draw man and woman to one another; no sexual motion would anticipate the utterly spiritual and free decision to procreate. Sexual intercourse would entail no feeling of shame or embarassment,[88] or cause any deterioration or loss of virginity. There would be a virginal intercourse.[89] As a point of fact, however, Augustine does not think that Adam and Eve had sexual intercourse in Paradise. He "does not find" the meaning of "Man will leave his father and his mother and will cling to his wife," in its literal sense or historia: it must be a prophecy for the time after the fall.[90]

This at least is the version of the matter proposed in the *De Genesi ad litteram* and in *De civitate Dei*. It is his mature position. In earlier works Augustine wavered. In *De Genesi contra Manichaeos* he had explained away the union of man and woman in Paradise as being purely spiritual, ending in immaterial fruits of an intellectual and moral order. This allegorical interpretation was not unusual among the Greek Fathers. In *De bono conjugali*,[91] he proposed another view: procreation could take place in Paradise, though in a mysterious non-sexual way. The beginning of this book lists several possibilities about paradisiac procreation, among which Augustine finds himself unable to decide. At that time he had discovered no way to separate sexual union from the unlawful libido which, because it followed upon sin, could not be experienced in Paradise. The later position could be adopted only after Augustine concluded that sexual desire, being a disorder engendered by sin, does not belong to the essential structure of procreation.

However this may be, woman's role and only purpose is to help man in this work of procreation. She is compared to the earth, which receives the seed that will grow into trees. Augustine repeats this often, adding that in all other matters a male friend is a more efficient helper than a woman.[92] Sex is

to the survival of the race what food is to that of the individual.[93] On this basis, Augustine makes the surprising statement that polygamy is not against nature, for it serves the purpose of marriage and respects the procreative function of man and woman.[94] Since marriage is good, Augustine does not share
Tertullian's distaste for remarriage; he will not even condemn subsequent re-
marriages. In themselves these are good, as long as they serve the purpose and
intention for which marriage was made, whatever reservation one may have
concerning the subjective motivations of the marriage partners.[95] The New
Testament admittedly outlawed polygamy, but this is law rather than nature.
It is in this context that Augustine ascribes three goods (*bona*) to Christian
marriage: procreation (*proles*), mutual bond (*fides*), sacrament (*sacramen-
tum*.[96] The first fulfills the purpose of marriage; the second excludes adultery; the third condemns divorce and polygamy.[97] Procreation is the basic
natural purpose; loyalty corresponds to the experience of marriage as good;
monogamy is required by Christian ethics.

In the present order of the world, however, marriage and sex have been
vitiated by original sin. As soon as they disobeyed, Adam and Eve discovered
that they were nude. Not that they did not know it before, but whereas they
had known it without feelings of shame, they now are ashamed of their nakedness. In the Augustinian analysis of emotions, shame arises from the experience by the mind of not mastering its body. In Paradise, grace had hidden the
possibility for the body to revolt against the mind. All of a sudden, grace
being removed, "the motions of their body released the shocking news of their
indecent nakedness, made them notice it, and gave them shame."[98] The continuing experience of sexual emotions is the outcome and the sign of original
sin. The experience of sex, even in marriage, is inseparable from this sense of
shame.[99] The wise man therefore wishes that he could obtain children without it.[100] And true Christians try to mitigate this shame by using marriage
solely for its original purpose of procreation and by being as moderate as they
can in this experience of sex.[101]

The pessimism of Augustine's concerning man's lot dictates his analysis of
the feminine condition. At the symbolic level, Augustine speaks of three
unions that are revealed in Scripture: between Christ and the Ecclesia, between man and woman, between spirit and flesh.[102] In each of them the second term is both inferior and feminine. The fight in man between spirit and
flesh is therefore symbolized in mankind by the man-woman polarity. Writing
against the Manichees, Augustine even interprets the biblical statement, "Man
and woman he created them," allegorically: in Paradise the male and the female are principles within man, expressing the domination of the body by the
mind.[103] Only after sin was this also expressed in the carnal unity of man and
woman. While this is contradicted in the *De Genesi ad litteram* and retracted
in the *Retractationes*,[104] nonetheless it shows that the spiritualizing tendency

which Augustine had learned from neo-Platonism occasionally surfaced in his writings. Thus, the analogy Christ-Ecclesia, man-woman, spirit-flesh, has become, in the *De opere monachorum*, man-woman, mind-concupiscence.[105] Concupiscence or libido, as Augustine also calls it, includes for him more than sexual desire. It is the conglomeration of all the bent tendencies awakened in man by the fall, in which the revolt of the flesh against the spirit vents itself. But the union of man and woman in sex is directly connected with this libidinal revolt in the recesses of human nature. Woman herself and her status in the Church and society are affected by it.

In Paradise, as depicted by the bishop of Hippo, man and woman were to cooperate (primarily for the purpose of procreation), but without any inferiority of the female, or any submission of woman to man. They were called to oneness (*conjunctio*), not to domination and obedience. They were going to walk side by side. Of course, the feminine body was the same as now. In a sense. Eve was to be below her husband and she would serve him. But this would be a service of love (*dilectio*), not of slavery. The subservience imposed on woman by the curse "corresponds to necessity rather than to love; what originated in punishment is the sort of service by which men later became slaves of other men." The present condition of woman does not come "from nature, but from sin." The historical woman is not in the same situation as the natural woman. Admittedly, the order of Redemption has changed this slightly, for the Christian woman is not a slave. "Saint Paul says: Serve each other in love. He would never say: Dominate each other." In Christian marriage, the partners can serve each other with love. Yet woman is never allowed to give orders to a man. The man carries power. And Augustine sees no escape from this law of the curse: "Unless this is followed, nature will be more completely distorted and sin will increase."[106]

In this context, Augustine recommends the virginal life as best ensuring the growth and the spiritual liberation of Christian women. In the hierarchy of values that may be embodied in a feminine life, the unmarried girl ranks lowest. Destined to marry, she already suffers from all the problems of marriage, wondering how to please her husband and to raise her children, without even knowing who this husband will be and without yet having any children. The married woman comes next. She is divided between God and her secular responsibilities, for she must please her husband, bear and raise her children. The married woman belongs to her husband as his own property. On this point, the bishop of Hippo goes much further than the texts of Roman law of his time. The official references to marriage contracts (*tabulae matrimoniales*) no longer mention any subordination of wife to husband. Augustine reacts against the progressive emancipation of women in society. He also takes his mother's principles and practice as the absolute standard of feminine behavior in marriage. According to the *Confessions,* Monica considered herself to have freely chosen to become her husband's slave.[107]

Be that as it may, as seen by Augustine, the Christian wife has at least the satisfaction of being a slave out of Christian love. For her, marriage and sex are not goods to be enjoyed for their own value; but they become good by virtue of their purpose. At his best moments Augustine equates this purpose with "friendship" (*amicitia*):[108] it makes friendship possible through the creation and development of a society. In his sterner moods, friendship is not mentioned and only procreation remains, a purpose that has now lost much of its goodness from the fact that the world is already populated.[109] Finally, the consecrated virgin ranks highest. She prepares the glories of the next life exclusively, not being divided between God and the cares of this world.

When he reflects on Eve herself, Augustine abandons the lenient position taken by Ambrose and returns to the tradition of Tertullian and to what Augustine thought was the position of Saint Paul as illustrated in 1 Timothy 2: 14. Sin really began with Eve; she is therefore chiefly responsible for the fall. Furthermore, Eve and Adam become truly hardened sinners through their refusal, not only to repent, but even to acknowledge their fault. Each makes a mere statement, putting all the blame on the tempter. Eve accuses the serpent while Adam accuses her.[110]

Yet Augustine continues to waver between his prefall optimism and his postfall pessimism. Where does the Christian woman stand? She is not, as with Tertullian, Eve the eternal temptress. Yet she cannot profit from Eve's example of immediate repentance since there was no such contrition. She should seek her model in the symbolic woman which is the Ecclesia. Through the flourishing of their virtues, consecrated virgins become "mothers of Christ," like the Ecclesia. And as virtues are not reserved to virgins, all faithful women, even married, can also become "mothers of Christ."[111] But virtues are not even the privilege of women: all Christians, men and women, married or virgins, may be "mothers of Christ":

He who does the will of my Father in heaven, is to me brother, sister and mother. He brings to light these relationships in the people he has redeemed: his brothers and sisters are the holy men and holy women, for these inherit the heavenly legacy. The entire Church is his mother, by the grace of God, for she gives birth to his members, that is, to the faithful. Likewise, every religious soul is a mother to him when she does the will of his Father with most fruitful charity in the actions she gives birth to, until Christ is himself formed in them. Mary, doing the will of God, is the mother of Christ only corporally; spiritually she is his sister and his mother.[112]

As developed by its greatest representatives, the Western patristic tradition on woman did not only, like the Eastern one, promote the life of consecrated virginity; it also tended to separate, much more than was ever the case in the East, the liturgical service of the Lord from contact with women. As early as the beginning of the fourth century, the Council of Elvira, which grouped nineteen bishops and twenty-four priests from all over Spain, unequivocally forbade married bishops, priests, and deacons, ever to have intercourse with their wives. The penalty was expulsion from the clerical order (canon 33). Canon 27, which permitted the consecrated sister or daughter of a bishop or of any cleric to live in the same house, implicitly forbade his wife to live there.[113] The legislation passed in Spain was harsher than anywhere else. Italy started in the same direction a little later. Pope Siricius and the Council of Rome in 386 outlawed the cohabitation of priests and deacons with their wives (canon 7);[114] and Siricius, supported by Ambrose of Milan, endeavored to have this decision implemented, not only in Italy, but also in Spain and Africa. Similar decrees were passed by several African Councils (Carthage, 390 and 401).[115] The Council of Toledo in 400 reiterated the Elviran legislation. A Council of Tours in 460 endorsed a similar decision for Gaul. Ordination did not become an impediment which nullified marriage before 1123, when the First Council of the Lateran (canons 3 and 21)[116] marked the crowning point of the papacy's efforts since Leo IX in 1050 to abolish completely the marriage of priests—a practice which, instead of dying out, spread considerably during the tenth century. An unexpected result of this legislation was the spread of clerical concubinage in the fourteenth and fifteenth centuries, when the desire of priests to marry reappeared. The Council of Trent reinforced the prohibition of clerical marriage with a great deal of success.[117]

My topic is not clerical celibacy, but womanhood. Yet it is unavoidable that the theology of womanhood which is accepted by the larger part of the Church should depend partly on the type of relationship which obtains between women and those who build theological systems. In the West at least, theology has always been a specialty of the clergy or, one had rather say, of a section of the clergy. This means that it has reached fruition in the cogitations of celibate persons. For this reason, a brief glance at the history of clerical celibacy belongs in our study. The separation between priests and women is bound to entail a one-sided theology of womanhood, to which woman remains alien and from which she is likely to find herself alienated.

The universal patristic tradition endorsed the ascetic ideal of virginity, on the Pauline ground that "the time is short": marriage impedes Christians from seeking the advent of the Kingdom wholeheartedly because it divides their heart between God and their partner in marriage and their work between the contemplation of the divine realities and the responsibility of their family.

Woman, who was created primarily to be man's partner in procreation, need no longer consecrate herself to this task, for the world is already populated. The life of virginal consecration presents her with an alternative: through it she can free herself from her subjection to man by becoming spiritually his equal. In the course of the first few centuries, however, the accent shifted from the Pauline concept of liberation through baptism, by which "there is neither male nor female," to liberation through asceticism and consecrated virginity. Estimates of woman herself varied. For some, she could never be man's equal partner in anything, for the curse that subjects Eve to Adam had not been lifted. For others, the curse was lifted in principle through baptism and in fact through asceticism. For others still, every faithful woman, virgin or married, would accede to this Christian freedom. Some assimilated woman to Eve, the first human being who sinned, whereas others thought that Adam's sin was greater. All considered the ideal womanhood to be achieved symbolically in the Ecclesia, and found types of her in the soul and in Mary.

This does not constitute a systematic theology of womanhood. Yet it enables us to see the focal point of any attempt at such a synthesis: In what way is Christian freedom, clearly affirmed in Scripture and maintained—though considerably toned down—by the Fathers, attainable to woman? As long as the sense of the imminent return of the Lord was vivid, the ideal of virginity constituted a perfectly valid answer to the question. And this answer had the additional advantage of not distinguishing between men and women: both were called to virginity in anticipation of the Kingdom. However, the problem arises when the sense of the nearness of the End is waning. Although he could pay lip service to the older concept, Augustine justified the superiority of the virginal life on other grounds, namely the desire for a greater reward in heaven. This carried no Pelagian implications with it, but the danger of Pelagianism was patent: the Pelagian movement itself grew in ascetic circles. With the loss of an imminent eschatology, marriage was bound to become the normal way of life for most Christians, and the bishops had to speak of it with more understanding than before. This is clear in the career of John Chrysostom and in the contrast between the tone of Augustine's writings with those of his African predecessors. Ambrose himself, whose own orientation was profoundly eschatological, spoke of marriage with much delicacy as a community of love.

Although the Greek and the Latin traditions are at one on most points, we can distinguish two distinct orientations. The main bulk of Greek thought is primarily dogmatic and only secondarily ethical. That is, the chief considerations remain always of the order of Revelation, even with a man like John Chrysostom, who has to deal with the practical problems of the people of Constantinople. The Latin approach, however, was set by Tertullian on a definitely ethical course, which has persisted through all his successors with the notable exception of Ambrose of Milan. Although Ambrose, like all bishops, is also concerned with practical and ethical questions, the focus of his thought remains theological: it is centered on the revelation of, and participation in, the angelic life. As for Augustine, his world is now too far removed from the expectation of the proximate return of the Lord for him to be deeply interested in the angelic life. The problem is how to live in this world and determine the tasks that need to be done by Christians. Most will enter marriage, trying, if they are spiritually sensitive, to avoid the pitfalls of the human libido; others, aiming at a higher reward in heaven, will give up thoughts of marriage and consecrate themselves to the service of the Church in the priesthood and to the contemplation of God in male and female monasteries.

This then would seem to be the state of the question toward the middle of the fifth century. The older view that feminine freedom **is achieved** through a spiritual ascent to the angelic life in preparation for the imminent parousia is being abandoned. There are no signs any longer that the world is coming to an end. The time of the Ecclesia has been prolonged beyond all expectation. The Church now defines her function, as in Augustine's *De civitate Dei*, in relation to this world.

PART TWO

The Recent Tradition

6

Catholic Models

Contemporary Catholic attitudes toward woman may be traced back, in their basic principles, to Saint Augustine. Yet few of the authors that will be mentioned in this chapter have known the thought of Augustine directly without the mediation of Thomas Aquinas, since Thomism, rather than the older Augustinianism, has shaped Catholic thought and sensibility. From Augustine to Thomas significant differences arise, due to the philosophical presupposition of Aquinas's reflection rather than to his specifically theological positions. In her valuable comparison of these Doctors of the Church on the topic of womanhood, Kari Elisabeth Borresen summarizes their common doctrine in terms of "subordination" and "equivalence": men and women are equivalent in the Gospel, yet woman is subordinate to man in history.[1] She explains the differences between Augustine and Thomas in terms of two anthropologies, the first being neo-Platonic and the second, Aristotelian, and their unanimity in terms of an "androcentrism" borrowed from society and from what they believed to be the Christian tradition. With his personal experience of feminine relationships, Augustine could treat the problem with deep existential involvement, whereas Thomas, who always remained at a safe distance from women, examined the question as an interesting intellectual exercise. The major differences between the two touch on the soul and its origin. Because for an Aristotelian the soul is the form of the body, in Thomas's eyes, the female soul must be different from the male soul. And as the female body, is the biology of Aristotle-Aquinas, is a freak of nature, definitely inferior to the physical perfection of the male body, the feminine soul must also be less perfect than the male soul. Although Thomas is far less pessimistic than Augustine as to the effects of sin and does not see a causality, but only an instrumentality, between concupiscence and the transmission of original sin, the overall impact of his thought has been more devasting for the Christian conception of womanhood. Both agree that woman is made only for procreation; she is a helpmate for man in the only area where he cannot be served better by a male. But while Augustine finds no inferiority of woman at the level of her soul, Thomas extends to her soul the inferiority of her body.

The theological background of the question has not changed substantially since the days of Augustine of Hippo and Thomas Aquinas. Although the world of the twentieth century has passed through a series of catastrophes, modern men have not recovered the primitive Christian vision of, and wish for, the swift return of the Lord. Far from longing for the end, they dread it. And recurrent dissatisfaction with material progress is not such as to send them to solitude in whatever deserts are left by the population explosion; on the contrary, it has inspired an ever more strenuous search for earthly happiness. The intellectual world did not change in depth between the end of the Roman empire and the beginning of the modern world in the sixteenth and seventeenth centuries. Moreover, since religious institutions are generally of a more conservative bent than secular organizations, the theological mind has evolved more slowly than its secular counterpart. For these reasons, the contemporary ideas about women that are assumed in Catholic theology have preserved substantially the same principles as the theology of Augustine and of Thomas Aquinas. The Church still defines itself in relation to the world and the tasks of man in the world, rather than in terms of contemplating God and the transmission of Revelation and grace. Preaching and teaching continue to be practiced; and one finds theological tractates, encyclicals, pastoral letters, and spiritual books in which the search for contemplation still dominates. By and large, however, the primary point of view has become that of doing with faith the task that modern man has assigned to himself: to transform the world into a better one (with all the ambiguities that go with the appreciation of what is better).

It would be pointless at this moment of our reflection to show how this evolution, which is indeed amazing to a student of the early Church, was able to take place. The principle was set in the works of Augustine, with whom the collective hope of the faithful in a parousiac transformation of the universe gave way to an individual orientation, through faith and good works, toward a heavenly reward. With the advent of the modern world and the technological explosion of the last century and a half, the problematic of sanctification through detachment, which the Middle Ages had maintained, has become one of sanctification through involvement. The contemporary Catholic is no longer called upon to live in the city of this world like one who actually belongs to the invisible city of God. He is, instead, invited to share the concerns and projects of the men who try to change this world. The last major event where this problematic was clear was the Second Vatican Council. Beginning in 1962 with a beautiful and very traditional elaboration of the liturgical life, which did justice to both the corporate-eschatological dimension and the individual-holiness emphasis of recent times, it ended, in 1965, with a treatise on "the Church in the modern world" which attempted to counterbalance its previous accent with a theology of involvement and world transformation.

Among the dilemmas that this modern world puts in front of the Church, the question of womanhood is not negligible. For the position of woman has changed and is still changing considerably in society. Should her position in the Church change accordingly, adjusting itself to the newly won freedoms that modern men like to guarantee to modern women? If so, what theological basis can there be for a new position of woman? Is it possible to discard completely the old rationale which, even though it undoubtedly was influenced by the secular questions of former times, gained sufficient status over the centuries to have become part of the Christian patrimony?

As a point of fact, contemporary Catholicism has not given one answer to this type of question, but several. Or perhaps, instead of speaking of answers——a term which implies an aspect of finality that could hardly be claimed by any of the present assessments of woman in the Church and in society——we may introduce the notion of models: contemporary Catholic thought operates with several models of womanhood in mind. All of them can, I believe, be related to the theology of the Fathers in some ways; yet they do not all reflect the same point of departure, and accordingly they do not all end up with the same view of the being and function of woman and of the meaning of womanhood. Our present task lies therefore in a description and, if possible, an assessment of these models.

We will find our first models in the debates of the Second Vatican Council.

In October, 1965, while the Council debated the proposed Constitution on the Church in the Modern World, two American bishops submitted to the relevant commission some remarks about the position of women in the Church and in the world of today. The suggestions made by the late Archbishop Paul Hallinan of Atlanta include the confession that "the Church has been slow in denouncing the degradation of women in slavery and in claiming for them the right of suffrage and economic equality."[2] Then, regretting that women have not yet achieved equality with men in the secular world, even in areas where they would be perfectly competent, Archbishop Hallinan made four constructive proposals:

That the Church define the liturgical functions of women so that they could serve as lectors and acolytes, and, when properly prepared, also, as they once did, in the Apostolic office of deaconess. They could thus, as Deacons do, administer certain sacraments.

That the schema should include them in the instruments to be set up after the Council to further the lay apostolate.

That women religious should have representation in those matters which concern their interests, especially in the present and post-conciliar agencies.

That every opportunity should be given to women, both as sisters and as laywomen, to offer their special talents to the ministry of the Church. Mention should also be made of women who are not married. Because of the universal call to women (in *De Ecclesia*), they also promote family values by witnessing in their own way to this universal vocation.

The ideal of equality between men and women undergirds this short statement of goals. The four points assume that women enjoy a basic, natural right to do what men themselves do. Men fulfill liturgical functions; men will undoubtedly be among the instruments of application of the conciliar decisions; men are represented in the Congregation of Religious; men have opportunities to offer their talents to the ministry of the Church. Thus the one point of reference for the status and role of women in the Church is implicitly defined as men. Woman herself is not described, her needs are not analyzed, her wishes and aspirations are not mentioned for what they are in themselves. Rather, man provides the standard for feminine behavior in the Church. To the "secular" sources of this standard we will return later. But here runs an old undercurrent. If we have sensitive ears, we can hear a remote echo—which, I am sure, was not at all in Archbishop Hallinan's intention—of the saying which the *Gospel of Thomas* attributed to Jesus:

Lo, I will draw her
so that I will make her a man
so that she too may become a living spirit
which is like you men;
for every woman who makes herself a man
will enter into the kingdom of heaven.[3]

Another American bishop came forward at the same time in favor of a statement on the rights of women. Once again this was not in a public speech, but in a written communication to the appropriate commission. Bishop Fulton Sheen's approach was very different from Archbishop Hallinan's. "It was to a woman," his text began, "that the promise of salvation was given. The news of the Incarnation was given to a woman. Christ first appeared to a woman after his resurrection. A woman spoke for humanity when humble Mary's *fiat* responded to the creative *fiat* of the heavenly Father. . . ."[4] We can recognize here allusions to Eve, to Mary, to Mary Magdalen, and again to Mary. Fulton Sheen goes on citing more evidence of the actions of women as recorded in the New Testament. He then formulates his understanding of the specific qualities that are proper to women: "These can be characterized as purity, protection of the weak, sacrifice, procreation, the sustaining and caring of human life." In his mind, these qualities correspond to the general nature and function of motherhood. Yet motherhood should not be interpreted only in the physiological sense. Rather, if motherhood can be physical, it may also be spiritual and social. Finally, on the basis of a concept of social motherhood, Sheen comes out strongly in favor of the social involvement of women and of their freedom to fulfill themselves through social action by entering on a career in the secular world. "In the economic, civil, social and cultural order she will be associated with men, and she should exercise prudence, tenderness and the motherly instinct which is so necessary to compensate for administrative rigidity." After citing other possibilities of fulfillment in "the sphere of law," in "the area of communication, radio and television," and "in the search for peace," Bishop Sheen concludes: "Every woman without exception is morally obligated according to her capacity and conditions in life to realize one of these forms of motherhood."

Unlike Archbishop Hallinan's statement, Bishop Sheen's does not start from man, taken as the standard that women should equal. It rests on the underlying conviction that woman's specific role and function is motherhood; and this of course cannot be patterned on male behavior. This role clearly originates in nature and is given to woman by her physiological and psychological structure. Yet Bishop Sheen advances much further than a mere determination of the dictates of human nature. By extending the concept of motherhood to the spiritual, economic, civil, social, and cultural fields, he takes for granted the philosophical view that we may associate with scholastic thought, that women can be adequately defined as a prospective mother, all other aspects of womanhood being ancillary to this. Theologically, he gives this philosophy increased status by finding it exemplified in the actions of women recorded in the New Testament. Ethically, he concludes to the moral duty, on the part of all women, of fulfilling themselves through motherhood, of "realizing one of these forms of motherhood."

Comparing the suggestions of these two bishops, we see that one and the same concern—namely, the promotion of woman in the Church and the world —has been inspired by radically diverging principles. In one case, the principle is borrowed from the modern democratic concept of equality; in the other, from a philosophical-theological doctrine about motherhood. In the first case, the ideal is the legal enjoyment by women of all the liberties of men; in the second, it is the attainment of a certain and purely feminine status, that of a mother. In the first model, mankind is ultimately made of only one sex, the male, whom the female ought to imitate; in the second, mankind is made of two sexes, men and mothers. Insofar as she is not, or not yet, or not only, or even cannot be, a mother, woman has been left out of account.

I have not introduced the discussion of these two episcopal statements in order to indulge in the currently fashionable criticism of bishops, but because they provide us with convenient and authorized examples of two main contemporary Catholic points of view. They should by the same token help us to determine where the problem lies today. This is not, in my view, in deciding whether women should be allowed to become cardinals, or priests, or bishops, or to hold important administrative functions in ecclesiastical organizations. These are secondary issues. The preliminary problem is to discover the proper categories of thought within which to envision the role of woman. These categories ought to be theological. Yet the theological dictionary of such a reportedly "progressive" theologian as Karl Rahner does not contain one line on "woman," whereas it gives more than one page to "man."[5] Admittedly, it is mankind (the human being as such) which is considered under "man"; what is said there also applies to woman, but only to the extent of what she shares with man, not on the basis of what she is in herself, in her own feminine existence.

Our historical investigation has shown that a large amount of early writing considered some aspects of woman's life, particularly in the ethical dimension. With many authors, the subject of fashion and make-up has been a favorite. From the considerations of Tertullian on "female dress" to the recent lucubrations of the late Father Francis Connell and other moralists about the amount of female flesh that may be bared without sin, theologians have wasted a great deal of time writing against the current fashions of their times. Yet this has not been sheer stupidity. They did so only because they saw Eve the temptress within every woman. They worked on the hypothesis that Eve, being herself deluded, still approaches Adam with an illegal fruit to be shared, the fruit now being her own body. And being themselves Adam, they took measures to avoid being tempted by Eve. Woman, in this case, is perceived as evil, not the absolute evil of hell, but the relative evil of falling and fallen mankind. (In its crudeness, this approach is not frequently upheld today, although I am afraid we have not seen the last of the ethical columnists who are called on to regulate the length of skirts. Tertullian at least had the excuse that much of his writing was addressed to his own wife.)

A variant of this model presents woman as being not evil, but weak: the weaker sex, as even some Catholic liturgical prayers say. To give a harmless instance, the following collect for the feast of a virgin-martyr illustrates the male triumphalism of some of our official texts: *Deus, qui inter cetera potentiae tuae miracula etiam in sexu fragili victoriam martyrii contulisti . . .* (O God, who among other miracles of your powers, gave the victory of martyrdom even to the weaker sex . . .). The fidelity of a woman unto death seems to be a greater miracle than that of a man. This is to be compared with the liturgy for the feast of a holy woman, focused on the passage from Proverbs on "the vigorous woman" who is the last to retire at night and the first to get up in the morning and who never ceases working while her husband "sits at the gate with the elders of the land" in a leisurely palaver. Whatever may have been the original purpose of this biblical description, no doubt persists about its meaning in the liturgical context: the vigorous woman whose toil makes it possible for her husband to sit at the city gate is presented as an ideal, as the ideal of feminine holiness. But such an ideal cannot be attained through nature alone; it is the fruit of grace. What is, on the feast of a woman martyr, the weaker sex, remains so; yet grace can make of her a paragon of strength. In the two cases of martyrdom and of daily toil, grace rather than nature provides frail woman with her amazing power. What nature cannot reach, grace gives abundantly. The natural woman is weak, weaker than man, but the holy woman is strong, stronger than the natural man. The strength in question is primarily moral, since our authors are concerned chiefly with holiness; yet is shows itself also through physical strength, as in the two examples of martyrdom and of endless drudgery.

Apart from the absence of an eschatological reference, this is still the Tertullianist model for womanhood. One might object to lumping together the benevolent outlook of men who are aware of the frailty of woman with the excesses of Tertullian writing to his wife: "You are the gate of the devil. It is because of you that Christ died. . . ."[6] Yet the perspective remains truly the same in both cases. For what makes woman frail and what, in Tertullian's mind, defines her as the gate of the devil, is lack of divine grace. God chose neither to give her strength by the normal process of nature, nor did he assist her out of the serpent's temptation. Frailty is not sinful; but sin derives from an original frailty, the traces of which can still be discerned in woman.

Such a perspective has a long tradition behind it. Coming from Judaism and from the Fathers, it dominated medieval thought. The Scholastics agreed that woman is a misfit, a freak of nature. For Thomas Aquinas, there is in her "something deficient or accidental. For the active power of the male seed intends to produce a perfect likeness of itself with male sex. If a female is conceived, this is due to lack of strength in the active power, to a defect in the mother, or to some external influence like that of a humid wind from the South. . . ."[7] Granted, the image of God is in the soul, "where there is no distinction of sex."[8] But in the concrete, every woman results from a disruption of the processes of conception and pregnancy.

The sources of these ideas are to be found in Aristotle's anthropology and biology, especially in the *De generatione animalium,* where the philosopher applies his hylomorphic theory to the process of generation. Whereas woman acts as receptive matter, man acts as active form. But the efficiency of the form depends on the balance of docility and resistance in the recipient matter. When there is no resistance, the outcome perfectly reflects the form, and the child is male; where matter—that is, the woman—resists, the outcome is unlike the form and the child is female. In milder cases, the sex is still male although the face looks like the mother's.[9] The Scholastic explanations are variants of this theory. If all things are made of two coprinciples, matter and form, there must also be in mankind a pole of activity, corresponding to form, and one of passivity, corresponding to matter. Given the function of the form, the being which fulfills that function should be considered the more perfect, the head of the other, whereas the one who stands at the passive pole of mankind should be called less perfect, the servant of man. In this Hellenic-Scholastic tradition, the yin and the yang are essentially interrelated, but not coequal. Their sum total does not trace the perfect circle of the oriental tradition. Rather, the male principle is perfect, and the other fulfills itself by cooperating with that perfection. Perfection is not seen in the whole, but in its dominant part.

This has already brought us to a third form of this basic model for womanhood, expressed around the central idea that womanhood is essentially receptive. This again is a Greek notion, transmitted to the Middle Ages by the works of Aristotle. It is expressed by Thomas Aquinas in the following terms: "In the most perfect animals, the active power of generation belongs to the male sex, the passive to the female sex."[10] This is in keeping with the fundamental purpose of woman, created "to help man, not indeed to help him in everything, as some have said, for in any other field man is better assisted by another man than by a woman, but only for the purpose of generation." This passivity extends to the civic and social order, where woman has been made subject to man by nature, "for nature has given man more intelligence," and "good order would not be preserved in human society if some were not governed by those who are wiser."[11]

In taking this position, Aquinas followed his master Albertus Magnus (d. 1280), who had taken his cue from Aristotle. However, the Greeks were themselves divided on the issue of the passivity of woman, and so were the Scholastics. Whatever philosophers would say about the matter, medical science, as illustrated by Hippocrates or by Claudius Galenus,[12] already taught that woman actively participates in the conception of the child and is not a mere recipient and nutritionist of the seed received from the male. Supported by the Moslem philosopher Avicenna, who was also a medical doctor, this position was defended by the Franciscan school of theology, from its early representative Alexander of Hales to Bonaventure and John Duns Scot. For Bonaventure, two seeds contribute to generation, one coming from the father's body and one from the mother's. The former acts as "efficient" cause of conception, the latter as "material" cause. Both are endowed with the "power and the seminal reason of the propagation of the body."[13] Yet for Bonaventure too, "the male sex is in itself more perfect than the female,"[14] for the generation of a male corresponds to the full strength of the seed. Only when the seed—for complicated reasons that Bonaventure, following ancient medical science, analyzes minutely—lacks its full strength does it evolve into a female.[15] In Paradise, if mankind had not sinned, man would have himself chosen the strength of his seed and would have fathered at will a male or a female child. In the fallen order of nature, this escapes the control of the will, so that men and women are conceived haphazardly. Nonetheless, the birth of a woman is not, Bonaventure gracefully concedes, against nature or outside of it; it follows the order of nature, which makes it possible for the full strength of the seed to be impeded by interior dispositions of the man or the woman, as well as by external circumstances which themselves affect the dispositions of man and woman.[16] However, whatever superiority may accrue to men in society or in the Church does not originate in their sexual functions. Bonaventure finds the principle of this factual superiority in his belief that all mankind originates, through Eve, in Adam.[17] He sees it at work in the fact that man is oriented to action, while woman bears suffering better; but in human life leadership belongs to action rather than to suffering. Finally, he accepts the Apostle Paul's statement that "the head of the woman is man" (1 Cor. 11:3), interpreting it as an expression of the will of God over his creatures.[18]

In more recent thought it is the Thomistic rather than the Bonaventurian concept which has prevailed in theological circles. And in our century, the Thomistic opinion on the question of woman's participation in conception has been extended by some authors to the entire realm of feminine existence. Woman's very nature is essentially receptive. A woman gives herself only by receiving—no matter what she receives: the male seed, or commands, or a husband, or children, or God's inspiration, or the Church's sacraments. Her fulfillment is reached, not through agressive self-development, but through self-opening to others. She sanctifies herself by making herself available to those in need. And the difference between the saint and the prostitute does not lie in the objective structure of feminine self-offering, but in its direction: the saint gives herself for the greatest good and the prostitute for evil. Simone de Beauvoir and Gertrude Von Le Fort agree that this is womanhood.[19] But Simone de Beauvoir sees it as an aberration that has been bred into woman by male dominance and is maintained by education, whereas Gertrude Von Le Fort rejoices in the providential and universal mission of feminine availability.

For Gertrude Von Le Fort, the most eloquent exponent of this view of womanhood, woman is just as favored as man by nature and providence; yet "this does not benefit woman herself, but her offspring. The meaning of her qualities is not narrowly personal; it reaches much further. . . . Man represents one moment in history, woman the succession of generations; man embodies the eternal value of the instant, woman the infinity of the race. . . . Personality belongs to man, universality to woman. . . . Woman is not primarily personality, but the gift of it. . . ."[20] Woman is not life, but she transmits life. She is the passive instrument of nature and of mankind. This gives her a second paramount quality, that of anonymity. In most civilizations, she loses her name through marriage. This is a token of the fact that woman fulfills her function "under the veil."[21] Modern theater has given her an image in the figure of *la jeune fille Violaine* of Paul Claudel's famous play, *The Tidings Brought to Mary*. It is Violaine who, hidden by her leper's veil, declares: "The male is a priest, but it is not forbidden to woman to be a victim."[22] At the end of the play, while she is dying, her father Anne Vercors praises the beauty of the feminine vocation:

> ... I was shocked because the face of the Church was darkened and because it seemed about to crumble when everyone deserted her. I wanted to press again the empty tomb, and put my hand in the hole of the hands and the feet and the heart. Violaine was wiser. The purpose of life is not to live. The feet of the children of God are not bound to this wretched earth. It is not a question of living but of dying. Not a question of building the cross, but hanging from it and giving what we have joyfully. This is what is meant by joy and freedom, by grace and eternal youth. . . . Why be tormented when it is so simple to obey and the order is clear? That is how Violaine immediately follows the hand which takes her. . . .[23]

Here, as in the works of Gertrude Von Le Fort, a reversal of value has actually taken place. Priority in the order of creation does not belong to action, to man, but rather to the reception of God's creative and redemptive grace—to woman. Of the two vocations—that of the male, who leads and transforms the world by his deeds, and that of the female, who transmits and protects the permanent wisdom of the race—the female vocation is spiritually greater. It is the very vocation of the Church. Thus Gertrude Von Le Fort sums up her conception of "woman according to the Christian idea":

> Woman according to the Christian idea is not just woman, but woman as subject to the great divine laws that rule her. Each of these laws has its own full value, but each also implies a relation to the common pattern where they find their inspiration. The function of every woman in life is first to separate the virtualities of this pattern, to achieve it partially in virginity or in motherhood. But this function is also, finally, to construct the eternal image in its unity: The virgin must arrive at spiritual motherhood and the mother must recover spiritual virginity. If she fails to achieve this close union of contraries, there is no salvation for her, and no end to the two tragedies of virginity or of motherhood. This is tantamount to saying that salvation, for all women, is inseparably linked to the acceptance of Mary's mission, as also to the imitation of Mary's image. . . .[24]

This Christian model for woman has been endorsed by several contemporary authors, for example, F. X. Arnold, J. Galot, Willi Moll.[25] It corresponds in our period to the charism of Thérèse of the Child Jesus. Weakness and receptivity form a wedge for the insertion of spiritual strength. The weakness of woman dialectically symbolizes the power of God. Woman is no longer an instrument of evil and an image of sin; she symbolizes the littleness and the spirit of childhood which open the gate of heaven. "Blessed are the meek, for they shall possess the earth" (Matt. 5:4). The same model has been echoed in the writings of another great Carmelite, Edith Stein (1891-1942), although Edith Stein treats her topic with too much philosophical sophistication simply to follow a theological thought pattern.[26] For her, as for phenomenologists in general, woman is not a given nature, but a human being who lives through the experience of specific vocations. Or, femininity is a vocation in the light of which woman experiences the human nature, common to man and woman, which specifies mankind among the animal world. But, and this is the point that interests me here, this vocation is related to the "feminine" virtues glorified by the present model of womanhood. The feminine experience is focused on them.

Another theological model for womanhood is frequently proposed by Catholic authors. It may be abundantly illustrated from various speeches made by Pope Paul VI. At the close of the Second Vatican Council, Pope Paul solemnly addressed himself to the women of the world, to "woman of all conditions, daughters, wives, mothers and widows . . . consecrated virgins and single women," whom he identified with "one half of the immense human family." He reminded them that "the Church is proud to have magnified and freed woman, to have made to shine through the centuries her basic equality with man in the diversity of their temperaments." Even though Pope Paul might have been embarrassed had he been asked for details about when and where the Church has done this for woman, he voiced the general yet somehow vague feeling, which is shared, I believe, by the majority of Christians, that the Christian Gospel (and therefore, in Catholic context, the Church as preacher and promoter of the Gospel) entails the principle of the liberation of womanhood. The Pope then recognized the modern context of the feminine question: "The time is coming, and has come, when the feminine vocation may be fulfilled in its plenitude, when woman may obtain in society an influence, a scope, a power, never reached before." This is part of a "profound mutation" now undergone by mankind, and it provides Christian women with a unique opportunity to "help mankind not to fall."[27]

As seen by Paul VI in the modern context, the feminine vocation is essentially connected with the home and the family. Although it reaches further, even to the very dimensions of mankind, it still resides in an extension of the "home" virtues of woman as mother of the family and keeper of life. "You, women, you always have for yourselves the guardianship of the home, the love

of sources, the sense of the cradle. You are present at the mystery of the beginning of life. You bring consolation in the separation of death." As nurse of
mankind, woman should play a negative function in relation to the fundamental tendency of men, which she should moderate. For men develop technology, and technology may destroy civilization. "Our technique runs the risk of
becoming inhuman. Reconcile men with life. And especially watch, we beg
you, over the future of our species. Stop the hand of the man, who, in a moment of madness, would try to destroy human civilization." Woman also enjoys a positive role in education, for mothers are "the first educators of mankind." The Pope tells them: "Transmit the traditions of your fathers to your
sons and daughters, while you prepare them for the unknowable future. Remember always that, through her children, a mother belongs to the future,
which she herself perhaps will not see."[28]

It is therefore in the light of motherhood that Pope Paul sees the vocation
of the single woman and of the consecrated virgin: their vocation of "self-giving" still hinges on the family, for "even the families cannot live without the
help of those who are without a family" As for consecrated virginity, its
meaning lies also in "the infinite love and the service of all"; those who have
chosen it become "the keepers of purity, disinterestedness, piety."

The same central message is more especially addressed to the women who
suffer, "standing straight under the Cross like Mary." These ought to witness,
for the benefit of men, that one can fight to the end: "Help them once again
to persevere in the boldness of great endeavors, together with patience and the
sense of humble beginnings." Finally, turning once again to all women, ("O
you, who know how to make the truth sweet, tender, accessible.... You to
whom life has been entrusted ...") the Pope urges them to make the spirit of
the Vatican Council known and effective, and "to save the peace of the
world."[29]

In this short but important passage of the most solemn discourse of the
Second Vatican Council, Pope Paul clearly asserts one basic notion about
woman: all her tasks, all her achievements, all her virtues, all her dreams are
derived from her call to motherhood. Everything that woman can do is affected by this fundamental orientation of her being and can best be expressed in
terms of, and in relation to, motherhood. Woman thus appears as a fugitive
figure symbolic of life, hyphening in between the fathers with their traditions
and the sons and daughters of the future. All her consistency lies in making
herself evanescent, disappearing in her service of the species. Her ambition is
to be a guardian, conservative of the wisdom of the past which she transmits
to her children and to those of others. Thus, woman does not really exist. She
is, but she does not stand out (*ex-istere*) in her personality. She hides behind
a generic vocation which reaches her in whatever she tries to do or not to do,
and which stands over her as both an appeal and a judgment.

This analysis, with its tendency toward nonpersonality as the characteristic of womankind is confirmed by a later speech, in which Paul VI explained at length his conception of womanhood and his understanding of the Catholic tradition on this matter.

In a little-known address given on October 29, 1966, Paul VI painted a profound and profoundly moving vision of womanhood. Speaking to a congress of Italian gynecologists, he did not, as Pius XII might have done, describe their delicate art and discuss medical problems. Instead he contrasted two views of woman. One, by method, considers her as an object of scientific study; this is necessary to arrive at a better knowledge of the problems and processes of female physiology. There is also another view, to which the Pope drew attention in these terms: "At this moment it is not so much your knowledge and your art which prompts our thinking, as the ideal value, the symbolic significance, the sacred and lofty vision that our religious doctrine and our humanistic training attribute to the feminine creature, to woman."[30] As contrasted with the first, this theology, which is also a philosophy of woman, dwells in the realm of symbolism. But the previous symbolism has been reversed; far from looking at woman in the perspective of evil (of Eve, the tempted turned temptress, of the wiles which male psychology attributes to womanhood), it turns in the opposite direction, toward a perception of goodness, beauty and oneness. The Pope enters this horizon with full awareness of its symbolic structure, as he admits from the start: "It may also be that our perspective is deeply steeped in feelings and poetry, and expressed in the manifold language of supra-sensory values which belong to the anthropology of faith as well as to a metaphysical and deontological conception of human life."[31]

Having thus introduced his point of view and indicated its limits, Paul VI continues:

For us, woman is a reflection of a beauty greater than herself, the sign of a goodness that appears to us as having no bounds, the mirror of the ideal human being as conceived by God in his own image and likeness. For us, woman is a vision of virginal purity, which restores the most lofty affective and moral feelings of the human heart. For us, she is, in man's loneliness, the arrival of his companion who knows the supreme gift of love, the value of cooperation and help, the strength of fidelity and diligence, the common heroism of sacrifice. For us, she is the Mother—let us bow our heads—the mysterious source of human life, where nature still receives the breath of God, the creator of the immortal soul. For us, she is the creature who is the most docile to education, and therefore she is equipped for all cultural and social functions, especially for those which are most congenial with her moral and spiritual sensibility. For us, she is mankind as adopting the best attitude facing the attraction of the sacred, mankind which, when it wisely follows this attraction, elevates and sublimates itself in the most authentic expression of womanhood; mankind which, whether it sings, prays, sighs or weeps, seems thus naturally to converge toward a unique and supreme, spotless and sorrowful figure, the privileged woman, blessed among all women, the Virgin, Mother of Christ, Mary. Such is, gentlemen, the level at which we encounter woman.[32]

This very interesting text opens up a perspective rather different from that of Bishop Sheen's idealization of womanhood. Sheen started from the scriptural exemplifications of womanhood in the Virgin Mary, in whose light he looked at the tasks and functions of women in society. The Pope's speech, on the contrary, begins with womanhood perceived in its terrestial embodiment through the light of faith, in an anthropology which is theocentric before being philosophical, ending with the Virgin Mary as the highest concretization of womanhood.

Analyzing this text we can distinguish in it several distinct and complementary strata in its vision of woman:

First, woman as exemplifying the goodness of the creator and specifically the true meaning of creation in God's image and likeness.

Second, woman as insight into ultimate moral and spiritual purity.

Third, woman as man's companion, who is not just a comrade, but brings with her the true meaning of self-gift.

Fourth, woman as source of life and as ultimately united to God's creative act in her own conception of human life.

Fifth, woman as disciple and student, especially suited to the pursuit of cultural and social values.

Sixth, woman as embodying the human religious aspirations. At this level the orientation of womanhood toward an ideal, yet real, woman, the Virgin Mary, is clear.

The Pope thus unfolds before our eyes a sixfold vision of woman which, for him, sums up both Christian insights and the highest human desires. We may wonder at this point, what man, the male becomes in such a vision, in which the very best of mankind as a whole is symbolized in and through the feminine sex. Obviously, man is called upon to look at the vision, to follow woman where she leads, to give thanks for the goodness of the creator, for the perception of the moral order, for the reception of the gift of love, for the source of life, for the cultural and social capacities and contributions of woman, for entering into a religious universe focused on the blessed vision of peace. Yet, it is fair to add, the Pope depicts a symbol rather than an achieved reality; his categories ring true in the realm of typology, not in that of the down-to-earth embodiments of womanhood that one may meet. What he describes is an exemplar, an archetype, a divine idea, which women of flesh and blood can only approximate.

One may find this description unreal. It is a dream, or perhaps a myth, with very little relation to actual women and to the tasks of womankind. Mary, whatever devotion one may feel toward her, is only Mary. Not all women are called to be the same. And it requires a good deal of imagination to see Gertrude Von Le Fort's "eternal woman" embodied in what she calls "woman in time." Nor is the Christian woman of today likely to become the "woman outside of time" in which Gertrude Von Le Fort sees the meeting point of the eternal feminine and the daily experience of womanhood.

More critically, one can note that, as in the concluding conciliar address, the very orientation of feminine life lies away from herself: she "reflects"; as a "vision," she shows something other than herself; she accompanies man, driving away his loneliness and comforting him; she is the source of life; in her social activities she places herself at the service of society and of culture. Once again, what she can be in herself gives way to what she is for others. Her personality is not hers, but mankind's.

Here, too, a long theological tradition stands behind this address of Pope Paul. The idealized vision of woman derives from the Old Testament descriptions of divine wisdom. It inspired Methodius of Olympia, Ambrose, and even Augustine with pages that stand in happy contrast with the strictures of Tertullian and of Jerome on the dangers inherent in womanhood. It flourished above all in the Middle Ages. Denis de Rougement has studied some of its manifestations in medieval literature and especially in the poetry of the troubadours.[33] It reached its acme in Dante's *Divine Comedy,* where the feminine figure of Beatrice—a real girl who had walked the streets of Florence and who, after dying very young, remained the muse who guided Dante's poetic genius—introduces the poet into Paradise and accompanies him there until he leaves. This has remained one of the recurrent themes of Western poetry, even with poets who were not exclusively religious and were hardly theological, like Goethe ("Das Ewig-Weibliche zieht uns hinan")[34] or Baudelaire ("Je veux bâtir pour toi, Madonne, ma maîtresse, / Un autel souterrain au fond de ma détresse . . .").[35] Above all, it was familiar to the medieval theologians who developed the theme, already formulated by Ambrose of Milan, of the intrinsic correspondence between four terms, the Ecclesia, Mary, the soul, woman. Originating with Justin of Rome, who suggested a parallel between Eve, the original woman, and Mary, this theme gained prominence, still in this double form, with Irenaeus of Lyon. Ambrose of Milan exploited it in a threefold and a fourfold form: Ecclesia, Mary, the virgin woman, the virgin soul.[36] The Middle Ages used it, varying from the two to the four points of the comparison. Best known is a passage from a sermon by the Cistercian abbot Isaac of Stella (c. 1100-1169), where the three terms, Ecclesia, Mary, the soul coincide in their being bride, mother, and virgin, that is, in the qualities of the fourth term. This famous text deserves quoting at this point:

> Mary and the *Ecclesia* are two, yet one single mother, two virgins and yet one. Each is mother; each is virgin. Both conceived by the same Spirit without human seed. Both bore to God the Father a spotless child. The one, without sin, gave birth to Christ's body, the other restored his body through the power of the forgiveness of sins. Both are the Mother of Christ, but neither can bring him to birth without the other. Thus in the inspired Scriptures what is said in the widest sense of the Virgin Mother the *Ecclesia* is said in a special sense of the Virgin Mary. And what is spoken of the Virgin Mother Mary in a personal way can rightly be applied in a general way to the Virgin Mother the *Ecclesia*. But every faithful soul is in a sense the bride of the Word of God, the Mother of Christ, his daughter and his sister, virgin yet mother. And moreover what is said of God's eternal Wisdom itself can be applied in a wide sense to the *Ecclesia*, in a narrower sense to Mary, in a special sense to every faithful soul.[37]

Perhaps the most intriguing recent exploitation of this theme has been made by Teilhard de Chardin in a prose poem entitled, "l'éternel Féminin," which Henri de Lubac has considered important enough to write an entire book about.[38] Teilhard's vision of the Feminine is far from simple. He does not idealize woman in the sense of removing her from an existence of flesh and blood. She does not descend from heaven, a celestial type proposed to this vale of tears as a dream, a model to imitate, and a saint to pray to. Here, the Feminine emerges from below, with the self-evident proviso that, the entire cosmos being created by the hand of God, it is from the hand of God that the Feminine originates. In the dynamic universe of Teilhard, the Feminine takes many forms; it is a common principle with universal applications diversified in their forms and gradually ascending from latency in the world of matter to total and perfect explicitness in the spiritual world, where it becomes the Church and the Virgin Mary. In between, the Feminine individualizes itself, passing from the stage of universal principle to that of concrete human feminine being. Here, again, the Feminine takes many forms. It is recognized by man in the faces of concrete women. Yet even there it is more than concrete: in each woman there hides the essential and universal magnetic presence of the Feminine, so that the man who associates himself with a woman in love enters a realm which is far deeper and wider than the two persons concerned. "Soon he is astonished by the violences of the forces unleashed in him at my approach, and trembles to realize that he can not be united with me without inevitably becoming enslaved to a universal work of creation."[39] Woman has many faces and many tasks. Man sees her as "the Temptation,"[40] not because she would be evil, but as a result of the sin of mankind. If indeed the expression "original sin" does not appear in the poem, the reality is very much present. The sin of mankind consisted precisely in misreading woman:

> When he saw that I was *for him the universe,* he thought that he could encompass me in his arms.
>
> He wished to shut himself up with me in a *closed* world, the two of us, where each would be sufficient to the other.
>
> At that very moment I fell apart in his hands.[41]

What saved woman from being taken as, and remaining, the gate of evil, was no other than the coming of Christ. The Incarnation redeemed womanhood, to which a new dimension was then assigned. It can no longer be only the "feminine essence,"[42] underlying all created being and placing in it a nisus toward life; or the "feminine universality,"[43] activating each and every "monad" of being as well as the general orientation of the universe. It cannot be only what the feminine metamorphoses through history have progressively unveiled: the "feminine attraction,"[44] which animates the vegetal and the animal worlds, "the Gateway of the Earth, the Initiation,"[45] which reveals to man the face of glory of the universe and of life. And it cannot flounder for ever in the tragedy of mankind: it cannot become, as it could indeed have become had it not been for Christ, "forever evil."[46]

A critical remark should be made here about the problem of translating Teilhard's prose poem into English. The translation of *Writings in Times of War* (New York, 1968) by René Hague, systematically makes the Feminine into a substantive: "I am the essential Feminine . . . the universal Feminine . . . the magnetism of the Feminine . . . the ideal Feminine . . . the eternal Feminine." However, in Teilhard's text, "feminine" is not the noun, but the adjective ("l'essentiel Féminin . . . l'universel Féminin . . . l'attrait Féminin . . . ., l'idéal Féminin . . . l'éternel Féminin"). That is, it is never a substance, always a quality. Its consistency does not reside in itself; it comes from another, from a personalization of Essence, Universality, Ideal, Eternity. In final analysis, the Feminine qualifies an aspect of the Universe as God's work.

Henceforth, then, Woman, after revealing to man the Earth, will reveal to him God. She is "set between himself [Christ] and men as a halo of glory." The Feminine is the very halo in which Christ shows himself. It is "changing" its "form," yet "without impairing" its "former nature." Hence one must distinguish between the "deceptive image" of the Feminine as it may be seen on the face of a woman, and the "reality" which "floats between the Christian and God."[47] At this stage of its development, the Feminine acquires a new name: "I am now Virginity."[48] In other words, if the feminine function—to bring mankind to unity and to fertility—remains, its sign has changed; its orientation is entirely new, although it was already present in some way, latently, in all the metamorphoses of the Feminine. From now on, the Feminine leads, not to slavery in the enmeshment of man in the tasks of this material world, but to freedom.

Freedom is not escape. Teilhard insists that "the voice of Christ is not the signal for a rupture, for an emancipation, as though the elect of God. rejecting the law of the flesh, could break the bonds that tie them to the destiny of their race, and escape from the cosmic current in which they came to birth." But "Christ has left me all my jewels,"[49] and he has given an impetus to the natural functions and tasks of woman. The Feminine continues, but it also evolves. Indeed, woman will still be wife and mother, for new generations are to come. She will still—in analogy with the experience of Dante—harvest the fruits of art and science in her task as "Beatrix." Yet through all this the Feminine becomes something greater still than those great achievements: "I am the unfading beauty of the times to come—the Feminine ideal." As nisus toward the future, as hope, the Feminine calls its lovers to change with itself, for it leads more and more toward the Spirit. "It is God who awaits you in me."[50]

At this point of its avatars, the Feminine becomes, as so often in the experience of men, a concrete being; but this concretization faces the entire human race. The Feminine is the Church, which Teilhard, in keeping with the old tradition that has been mentioned, associates with Mary:

I am the Church, the bride of Jesus.
I am Mary the Virgin, mother of all human kind.[51]

This leads to the climax of the poem. The Feminine is of the earth, of creation; yet it will change again into an eternal form. "The Cosmos, when divinized, will not expel the attraction of my influence." It keeps in store an eschatological significance and function. "Even in the rapture of the divine touch I shall subsist, entire, with all my past." And one aspect, at least, of eternal life will consist in the progressive discovery of the deeper layers and of the highest points of the Feminine, "an inexhaustible in my development as the infinite beauties of which I am always, even if unseen, the raiment, the form and the gateway.... I am the Feminine eternity."[52]

In the meantime, the Feminine leads men to his cosmic and transcendent fulfillment. Though forgotten by man, Eve attracts him higher. In a reminiscence from Hopkins's poem on "the Blessed Virgin compared to the air we breathe," the Feminine is shown as "the air of your lungs and the light of your eyes."[53] These elements are so near to man that he is hardly aware of them, yet he could not live in their absence.

Thus, Teilhard places, in the substratum of creation, a Feminine principle which takes higher and more spiritual forms as we pass from the realms of matter to those of the Spirit. It is the same principle throughout, and the highest form is already latent in the lowest, although it is only through the highest that the lowest acquires its full meaning. In all its epiphanies and in all its avatars, this is the principle of life; it is a drive with positive orientation; it is the Call, the Dream, the Inspiration, the Appeal toward self-transcendence. Degraded by man, it can appear as a call to sin, for even when distorted it continues to function according to its inner structure, namely, to allure and to attract. As embodied in mankind, it takes the form of woman, who can herself consciously seek to function in one or in several of the forms of the Feminine: woman can make herself all that the Feminine can be. (This, at least, is my way of reading the poem, for Teilhard does not apply this to any woman other than the two he mentions by name, Beatrix, the inspirer of art and of science, and Mary, the woman who is twice feminine, for she is the inspirer of the Church, who is herself the bride of Christ.)

The symbol of womanhood, which examplifies goodness and devotion, has undergone a double transformation under Teilhard's pen. First, it has reached a deeper level than the moral qualities which it represents, say, in Pope Paul's address. The Feminine is now a cosmic quality affecting everything in the universe. It is the inner dynamism which leads the universe as a whole and its component parts separately toward spiritualization. Second, the symbol has attained to the dimensions of a myth. The essence of the prose poem is precisely to indicate the successive transformations of the Feminine from the lowest layer of matter to the highest degree of spirituality. It is an ascending myth, tantamount to the myth of creation, with a major difference: in the myth of creation which Christian theology developed by drastically altering the neo-Platonic myth of descent and ascent, of emanation and return the universe comes down from the Father until, at the turning point of the redemptive Incarnation, it starts the ascent which will effect its return to the Father. With Teilhard, all in the universe is laid out on an ascending scale, occasionally interrupted by failure or sin. Thus, the evolution of the Feminine, while it carries the universe in its ascent toward union with God, undergoes crises and dramas, when the possibility of warping the entire scheme of life raises immediate dangers that call for drastic options. Only through the direct intervention of Christ is the Feminine able to pursue the ascending effort of mankind and of the cosmos toward God, until the moment when what was hitherto "essential," "universal," personal as in "Beatrix," transpersonal as in the Church, again personal (but at a higher level of personality) in Mary is finally haloed into the eternal Feminine.

Can we aim further than Teilhard de Chardin? Is it possible, remaining within the context of the Catholic tradition, to place the "eternal feminine" beyond the realm of creatureliness, however privileged, and to set it in God himself? After all, it is to a Catholic mystic of the most certain orthodoxy that we owe profound insights into the "motherhood of Christ." The *Revelations of Divine Love* of Dame Julian, the twelfth century English recluse, refers to the savior as being "our very Mother, in whom we be endlessly borne, and never shall come out of him."[54] Not only is Jesus our Mother in his humanity, which somehow enwombs all the elect; his divine Personality, too, exhibits the qualities of pregnant womanhood: "In our making, God, Almighty, is our kindly Father; and God, all-Wisdom, our kindly Mother; with the Love and the Goodness of the Holy Ghost: which is all one God, one Lord." "I beheld," Dame Julian adds, "the working of all the blessed Trinity . . . the property of the Fatherhood, the property of the Motherhood, and the property of the Lordhood. . . . And in the Same Person in wit and wisdom we have our keeping as anent our Sensuality: our restoring and our saving; for he is our Mother, Brother and Savior. . . ."[55]

Thus, in the Trinitarian relationships, insofar at least as they relate to creation, the Word is Mother, the Father being Father and the Spirit Lord. From the Mother as "Mercy" we draw our "increasing," as we obtain our Being from the Father, who is "Kind" and our "Fulfilling" from the Spirit, who is "Grace." While the Trinity as Power entails Fatherhood, it implies Motherhood as Wisdom and Lordship as Love.

The Divine Motherhood affects our substance or being. By taking on our "Sensuality" in the Incarnation, it becomes also our Mother in Mercy: "And thus our Mother is to us in diverse manners working: in whom our parts are kept undisparted. For in our Mother Christ we profit and increase, and in Mercy he reforms us and restores, and by the virtue of his Passion and his Death and Uprising, ones us to our substance. Thus works our Mother in Mercy to all his children which are to him buxom and obedient."[56] In keeping with traditional Trinitarian thought, the Motherhood of Wisdom, the Second Person, belongs to the whole Trinity and the mutual relations of the Three are reflected in it. Thus Julian of Norwich can explain: "I understood three manners of beholding of Motherhood in God: the first is grounded in our kind making; the second is taking of our kind—and there begins the Motherhood of grace; the third is Motherhood of working—and therein is a forth-spreading by the same Grace, of length and breadth and of height and of deepness without end. And all is one love."[57] Julian does not rest here. Having obviously borrowed her analogy of Motherhood from human experience, she now affirms that the word "Mother" can properly be applied only to "our tender Mother, Jesus."[58] All other applications are deficient and secondary:

This fair lovely word, Mother, it is so sweet and so kind itself that it may not verily be said of none but of him; and of her that is very Mother of him and of all. To the property of Motherhood belongs kind love, wisdom, and knowing; and it is good: for though it be so that our bodily forthbringing be but little, low and simple in regard of our ghostly forthbringing, yet it is he that does it in the creatures by whom it is done.[59]

Thus, motherhood is achieved in God in its fullness. It is manifested next in the Virgin Mary, the human mother of our heavenly Mother. Finally it is embodied in ordinary human motherhood, a distant image of our inclusion and nurture in divine Wisdom.

Critically examined, the insights of Julian of Norwich into the motherhood of the divine Wisdom (the Word) and of its incarnate manifestation, Jesus, fall short of assigning femaleness to God himself. For Julian takes account only of one aspect of femininity, motherhood. Yet woman is not only mother; and the feminine principle as embodied in the lives of women is not tantamount to the principle of motherhood. The task therefore remains of looking for the divine archetype, if there is one, of other aspects of the feminine.

Motherhood comes last in the human experience. Woman is first of all virgin, rich with possibilities that are both precise and indefinite, a ground waiting for preparing, and seeking the activating force that will make it pass from the innocence of expectation to the experience of fulfillment, a closed garden (to borrow a biblical metaphor) some of whose charm derives from its internal debate whether and to whom to open the gates and from its dream of the male figure who, knight or savior, will lead the passage to the second type of womanhood, woman fulfilled in relationship.

At this second stage of development, woman is related to another person in the human, spiritual, and sexual relationship of married love. If the virgin may be called *agapè* on account of her universal yet indefinite availability, the wife is *philia,* friendship, working its way through *eros.* Related to a man in a stable relationship, she shares her personality with him and she mutually shares in his. It is only as a consequence of this that woman can reach the third stage of her development, where, becoming mother, she experiences another level of *agapè*: her agapic love is no longer the indefinite and protected availability of the virgin; it is the poured out giving of her own substance to their child.

The problem of the femaleness of God does not reside primarily in the virginity of the creator, whose divine actuality implies the potentiality of the universe. Nor does it refer with any great mystery to the motherhood of the creator and the savior, who project their image into creation and who incessantly nurture the created child of the eternal womb. Julian of Norwich rightly expressed this motherhood of God as Creator and redeemer; and the virginity of God is clearly attested in Bonaventure's insistence on the "unbornness" of the Father, understood as a positive principle. The crucial question regards the relatedness of God. Is there a transcendent nuptiality of which human nuptials can be no more than shadowy evocations?

In two chapters of his book *Soul and Psyche* (1960), the late Victor White, drawing on the psychology of Jung, suggested that Catholic thought ought to recover the dimension of the divine femaleness.[60] Using Dame Julian's texts, which he related to the patristic and medieval statements about the Church and Mary, he also referred to the notion, which is to be found in some Catholic mystics, and mainly in those of the Rhineland school, that the divine Essence in the Father has the feminine characteristic of encompassing all in itself. It is not only being and act, but also abyss. Blessed John Ruysbroeck describes it as "an abyss so dark and unconditioned that it swallows up every divine process and activity and all the attributes of the Persons within the rich compass of the essential Unity. . . ."[61] There, it would seem, the eternal feminine is, beyond all created images of it, the Essence of the divine Oneness, which encompasses in itself the Word and the Spirit and, in the Word, the eternal types of all created forms. This line of thought could be related to the "exemplarist" doctrine of medieval authors, particularly of Bonaventure and the Franciscan school.

Trying another line of thought, Victor White suggested also that the image of the virgin-mother, as presented in Catholic dogma and experienced in Catholic Marian devotion, constitutes an icon of the feminine dimension of God. Of the people of God praying to Mary he asked: "Can they be finding in her image less than a true theophany, a manifestation of something truly divine, and which they do not find in other images?"[62] In other words, Mariology would really mean that our traditional presentations of God as one-and-three fail to reveal to us a dimension of the divinity which is nonetheless true, the feminine dimension: this is communicated to us, instead, through the created embodiment of it in Mary the Virgin.

Valuable as these suggestions are, they do not take us further than Dame Julian's insight into the motherhood of God and of Jesus. Woman as virginal womb and woman as fruitful womb, as virgin and as mother, have their eternal image in the all-encompassing wisdom of God arising in all eternity out of the silence of the Father. Woman as relatedness to another is not yet accounted for.

The preceding pages have studied two "good" models of womanhood as presented in contemporary Catholic thought, followed by suggestions for an unfinished third model. The third model, which has few witnesses, will not detain us at this point, as we will consider it again in the next chapter. In the first two, the feminine is seen as essentially good, yet their accents are rather different, stressing as they do woman as the handmaid, or woman as the eternal ideal. There is of course no contradiction between the two, insofar as the way of the handmaid leads to the ideal, and the most telling image of the woman begins, in the Gospels, as the handmaid of the Lord. For this reason, the basic problem of Catholic thinking and practice in this matter does not arise from this plurality of models. It arises from a real dichotomy between these types of the feminine and the remnants of that section of the patristic, especially the Latin, tradition which viewed woman as a symbol of evil and temptation.

The tradition to which Paul VI and Teilhard have, each in his own way, witnessed and the tradition of Gertrude Von Le Fort are not the only ones. The problem cannot be simply of reconciling two views that are neither identical nor contradictory (as would be the case between woman as handmaid, and woman as cosmic force). It arises from the fact that one form of the tradition that sees the female vocation as that of a servant actually constitutes a countertradition. Servanthood (patterned on the songs of Isaiah and their image of the Servant of Yahweh) is translated as slavery (on the social patterns of Helleno-Latin civilization). Woman must always be a slave, because she is radically evil. Whether this corresponds to their actual purpose or not, the names of Tertullian and of Jerome have remained attached to this view. Certainly, these did not consider woman as entirely evil, but as dangerous on account of her potential for evil. This thought was infinitely more complex than most accounts would lead the reader to believe, and we shall see that the most antifeminist statements of modern times have not been made by Catholics or Christians, but by pagans. Yet a misogynist strain that may be called Tertullianist has existed within the Catholic Church; and it is difficult to escape the impression that it has tainted much popular pious literature and a certain amount of educational policy. Woman is not evil, yet many Christians, including theologians, have seen her as a symbol of temptation, to be kept at arm's length—or even as a symbol of evil. Must we choose between these two traditions? Are they exclusive of each other? On what basis, other than one's own experiential preconditioning, should we choose between them? And when we choose, how can we explain the existence of the contrary tradition?

It will not be out of place to insist that these traditions be taken seriously, even if we eventually decide that they are not adequate or even that they are seriously misleading. Much contemporary theological journalism behaves as though we could now interpret the Gospel for our times without paying any attention to the insights of those who lived before us. If Catholicism has meant something clear and constant, this has been indeed continuity with the past no less than anticipation of the future. Tradition grows and increases, thus preparing for the future, but it also derives from antecedents that cannot be ignored without impoverishing our thoughts, our understanding of Christianity, and our effectiveness as witnesses to the Christian faith. The good news of salvation cannot be recovered anew every morning as though it had not been lived and announced the day before.

In the context of Catholic theology, this is all the more serious, as Catholic thought has always been deeply sacramental. It cannot be satisfied with preaching a nude Gospel, with proclaiming an absolute Word from God for our situation, with discerning the way of the Spirit in the circumstances in which we have been individually and corporately placed. It is also concerned with the specific forms of approach that God himself has endowed with numinous power among his manifold creative mercies. God does not only come to man. He comes to man in Christ, that is, in an enfleshed situation as one man among a multitude of men. And since the ascension and pentecost, Christ reaches men through the innumerable lanes of the Spirit, who also becomes, though in a different manner, a Spirit incarnate. One may speak of the esthetics of Revelation because the Spirit uses the creative material like an artist who selects the proper medium for the effect he seeks. Thus, the sacraments confront us with realities from this world, bread, wine, water, oil, gestures, words, actions, which channel divine grace and through which the Spirit activates the presence of the Lord in us. But the sacramentality of creation and of the Church does not end with seven sacraments. Men and women also are imbued with sacramental power, as is clear in the sacrament of marriage, in the lives and activities of the prophetic personalities whom we call saints, in the sense of the sacred which should be inspired by the liturgical actions of the People of God, in the sense of peace and serenity which some persons radiate. In this sacramental universe we do not look at things whose meaning ends and dies with themselves, but at symbols whose scope extends indefinitely, and which open up vistas on the invisible world. What can be the meaning of man being male and female in such a world? What symbolic implications are carried by the person who, as he passes from childhood to adolescence, discovers that he has been made not just man, but precisely this type of man, that he or she is man or woman, that manhood is experienced along two distinct, if related, lines by persons who are called men and those who are called women? Does this last word, *woman,* imply an addition to man, or (as medieval authors thought) a subtraction from man? And suppose it should imply neither addition nor subtraction but simply otherness, what kind of otherness is this and what meaning should it convey? Above all, manhood (in the limited sense) and womanhood are not objective data alien to the life that meets them; rather, they themselves are experiences in which the human being is subjectively involved to a greater extent than one could suspect before the advent of Freud.

This series of questions points to the urgency of elaborating a Christian anthropology that has been updated from what it was with the Schoolmen. Pope Paul's speech to the gynecologists mentions in passing the existence of an anthropology of faith. But if there is one, it still remains largely embryonic, and, as I think I have shown, it is still too ambiguous to be entirely satisfactory. There are several anthropologies, which imply diverse evaluations of sex, diverse understandings of the purposes of marriage, diverse moral judgments on some activities related to sex (as, for instance, on birth control and its methods), diverse opinions as to the advisability of introducing women into the governing offices of the Church, diverse positions on the possibility of ordaining women to the priesthood, diverse spiritualities also, which adversely appreciate the nature and role of the male-female relationship in love and friendship. These divergences do not remain academic, for they inspire opposite philosophies relating to the education of girls, to coeducation, to dating, different understandings of the authority of parents over their unmarried daughters; and the generation gap is caused not so much by differences in age as by differing philosophies of life, that is, it rests on, and betrays, anthropologies with incompatible orientations and assumptions.

Much of the recent literature on womanhood keeps a veil of silence on what I would identify as the central problem of the recent Catholic tradition in this area, namely its open schizophrenia: contradictory streams of thought to see woman as weak and as symbol of temptation and to idealize her as symbol of transcendent goodness. At first sight, the inferior place effectively assigned to woman in the organization of the Catholic Church reflects the Tertullianist-Scholastic concept of woman's submission to man because of her native incapacity to cooperate with him in anything but procreation. Encomiums of the feminine ideal and praises of the Virgin Mary notwithstanding, the position of woman reflects the idea of her debility rather than any other of the elements of the total Catholic tradition. The fact that the misogynic tradition has seldom been as violent as its adversaries have formulated it need have no special significance, besides showing once again that the necessary theological groundwork has seldom been done. Yet, in the absence of this groundwork, most recent critics of the status quo have borrowed from other sources than the Christian past. Thus it happens that Catholics who wish to promote the rights of women today confront us with the humanistic tradition of Simone de Beauvoir, with Freudian reconstructions or, at a lower level of sophistication, with statistical data on women in and out of wedlock. The theological picture is clouded by the fact that, whatever model of womanhood has been favored by speculative theologians or spiritual authors, the practical life of women and their participation in the Church's activity have been regulated, since at least the end of the Middle Ages, by the Tertullianist view rather than by the more generous assessments of womanhood that have always existed in the Church. Thus a view that may well be of lesser theological value has gained dominance over canonical legislation. And it is a practical question of great importance whether theology or law should have pride of place in the Ecclesia.

If we are thus faced with basically two theological models, one of these corresponds to the canonical model in existence: woman as the handmaid of man, physically weak except for what pertains to pregnancy, receptive, and finding her salvation in extending this receptivity to the whole realm of her spiritual being. The other model idealizes woman, seeing her as the proposed embodiment of holiness; but this seems to have no effect on the status of woman in the Church militant, whatever it may imply concerning the Church triumphant. Misogyny has often been appended to the first view; woman has then become so weak that she is evil embodied, the eternal temptress. Mariology has come to the support of the second view: woman finds the very type of her existence in the emergence of "the eternal woman," "the eternal feminine," the Virgin Mary. The most sophisticated exponents of the first view relate it to the Holy Spirit. For, in the words of Willi Moll (these are the titles of several chapters of his book), "The Holy Spirit and the woman are receivers," "The Holy Spirit and the woman are God's great 'and,' " "The Holy Spirit and the woman are life-givers." The introduction of the Spirit into the discussion of womanhood brings in our unfinished third model, in which some form of the feminine is attributed to God himself. Perhaps Pneumatology will provide, next to Mariology, a workable model of womanhood.

7

Orthodox Models

Greek patristic theology, the subsequent Byzantine developments both before and after the separation of the eleventh century between Rome and Byzantium, and some of the more recent theology of Greek and Russian Orthodoxy stand in homogeneous continuity. Within the limits of this volume, however, there can be no question of tracing the historical curve of reflection on womanhood through this long period of Christian thought. Yet the Western world, especially in its American form, has unfortunately remained estranged from the spiritual and theological realities of Orthodoxy. Recent Orthodox theology is not easily understandable to readers who are not themselves familiar with Greek patristics and with the continuous stream which links modern authors to the Greek Fathers. Since I have treated the Fathers in Part One, I will now make a brief survey of some of the stepping-stones over which the oriental tradition passed between the career of John Chrysostom and twentieth century speculations on the eternal principle of womanhood.

As a rule, the Hellenic structure of society was still less permissive for woman than were the Latin norms of social behavior, even though the first centuries of the Christian era coincided with a progressive movement of feminine emancipation in Greece. In its perennial struggle with the pagan elements of Hellenism, the Church helped toward the spiritual emancipation of woman by freeing her from the obligation of entering marriage and by making it possible for her to live as a virgin, spiritually free and legally protected. At least in some regions, particularly in Syria, women were admitted early to ecclesiastical office as deaconesses. Everywhere a new ideal of womanhood was promoted through the image of the Virgin, the All-Holy (*Pan-agia*), the highest creature in the order of redemption, the first fruit of deification, in whom human nature has been—much more than restored to its primordial status—raised to a state higher than the first through the process of deification. By looking upon sex as a second creation logically, if not chronologically, following upon sin, Greek theology avoided the pitfall of Latin theology where mankind was commonly equated with Adam the male, and therefore womanhood viewed as an adjunct to him. Instead, both sexes were judged to be accidental accretions on the original oneness of mankind. In this

151

case, the superiority of man over woman remains merely social or legal and can never become spiritually normative.

Gregory of Nyssa summed up the matter in these words:

> Having regarded or rather having foreseen in advance by the power of his anticipatory knowledge in which direction the movement of man's free and independent choice would incline, and having thus seen what would happen, [God] added to the image a division into male and female: a division which has no relation to the divine Archetype, but which, as we have seen, is in agreement with irrational nature.[1]

Mankind as the image of God is not sexed. Sex was superimposed upon the image which alone is properly constitutive of mankind. Separation and dividedness, opposition and polarity, dialectic and contradictories are not primordial but have resulted from man's choice in sin. Yet the spiritual man, the true "gnostic," recovers oneness in the very state in which human nature is now shared and experienced: reunion can arise out of the separation of the sexes. The theology of the Byzantine Middle Ages as well as that of recent Orthodoxy has insisted that sacramental marriage, no less than the transcendence of sex through the monastic or the virginal life, belongs to the way of deification, the restoration of the image of God to its intended fullness.

The praises which oriental hymnody likes to shower on both the Church and on the All-Holy Virgin, the *Theotokos,* are not therefore to be understood as tokens of a "high" ecclesiology or of a more or less extravagant cult of Mary: they actually express visions of, and insights into, the state of mankind as deified. Through the Church in her glory and through Mary in her elevation to heavenly power, one perceives mankind as set in the harmony of a restored cosmos in which God is all in all. Thus, the *Acathistos Hymn,* written by an unknown poet toward the beginning of the seventh century, addresses the *Theotokos:*

> Hail, through whom creation is renewed. . . .
> Hail, atonement for the whole cosmos!
> Hail, God's kindness to mortals!
> Hail, trust of the mortals in God![2]

Likewise, Romanos (d. 556), the great hymnwriter of Byzantium, frequently speaks of the *Theotokos* as the privileged instrument and medium of God's action. Romanos's testimony is particularly relevant. For his many hymns do not only extol Mary; they also depict the specific function of woman as such in the divine economy. Though antithetic, the images of Eve and of Mary are nonetheless in many ways similar. Mary corrects what Eve did. Yet it is Eve, rather than Adam, who understands redemption. A hymn on the nativity shows Adam and Eve talking together, Adam reluctant to believe Eve's contention that redemption is being effected through a woman:

Eve: Look at the wonders: see the virgin who knows no man heal our wound with the fruit of her conception. . . .

Adam: . . . The voice of the singer does not charm me this time, for that is a woman, and I fear her voice; taught by experience, I fear the female sex. I like the sound, but the instrument worries me: will she mislead me as of old, and bring me shame, the woman full of grace?

Eve: . . . You will never again find me a dispenser of bitter advice. The past is gone, and all is new, thanks to the son of Mary, the Christ.[3]

Echoing older traditions, the poet Romanos sees Eve as the initiator of the fall and Mary as the instrument of the Incarnation; yet he also identifies Eve, and through her, woman, as the one who believes first. Mary is both the counterpart and the daughter of Eve: "A woman has destroyed, a woman has restored, a virgin from a virgin."[4] But the feminine function in the economy does not end with Mary the *Theotokos*. Mary Magdalen witnessed the resurrection before the Apostles. And Romanos has her say to these: "What has happened was providential, that women, having fallen first, should first see the one who has resurrected."[5] Within the renewed order of the universe according to the economy of salvation, woman is first in faith and highest in the hierarchy of the restored image of God.

As used in the poetic visions of Romanos, the feminine typology does not end with the exaltation of Mary and the restoration of Eve. His rendering of the parable of the ten drachmas (Luke 15:8-10), in his sixth hymn on the resurrection, identifies the woman of the story with Christ. This was not entirely new, and Romanos could have been inspired to do so by Cyril of Alexandria.[6] Drawing on the Old Testament texts on wisdom, Romanos establishes an equation between the three terms, woman (specifically the woman of the parable), wisdom, and Christ, who is, according to Paul, the wisdom of God:

The number of the drachmas is clear to all: ten, that is, the sum total of all the possessions of the Lord who created the universe in Wisdom. The woman is, according to Scripture, the Virtue and the Wisdom of the Creator, that is, Christ, the Wisdom and Power of God. The ten drachmas are the Principalities, Powers, Virtues, Thrones, Dominations, Angels, Archangels, Cherubim and Seraphim, and the First-Born whom Life and Resurrection lost, sought and found fallen.[7]

Thus creation takes place in Christ, the wisdom of God, who therefore encompasses in himself all creatures, the invisible world of the angelic spirits and the world of man, fallen and restored. But the English language fails to express this properly, for wisdom, *Sophia,* is a feminine term both in Greek and Hebrew. We ought to say, were it linguistically possible: Christ, the Wisdom of God, encompasses in *herself.*

One may see a relationship between Romanos's vision of Sophia and that which another poet, Saint Ephrem of Syria (c. 303-373) had spun, two centuries before, around another feminine image. I am not arguing a historical influence, although Romanos himself had travelled to Byzantium, where he lived during his mature years, from his native Syria. Ephrem, in any case, was Semitic and wrote in Syriac, while Romanos was a Greek. The point, however, is that for both poets a feminine activity presides over the world.

One can easily perceive the rich poetic possibilities of this line of thinking. The poems of Ephrem of Syria present the interesting characteristic that they are purely Semitic and totally innocent of Hellenism. In them the great Syrian poet vividly paints the picture of a world which is somehow around God, in which God dwells and is to be found, and which is quite distinct from the present world: that is the world of Paradise. Ephrem describes it in physical terms that are not unlike the coranic descriptions, yet he makes it abundantly clear that such analogies are to be understood spiritually rather than materially. As seen by him, the entire created universe is encompassed by the "air" of Paradise, which acts like the great mother of the world:

> Learn from the fire
> that the breath of the air supports all:
> when fire is shut in
> in an airless space
> its flame wanes,
> its breath weakens.
> Who has ever seen a mother nursing
> with her entire body!
> The whole Universe
> hanging on to her,
> while she herself hangs on to the One
> who is the feeding power of the Universe![8]

In the Syriac language used by Ephrem, the word "air" is feminine, which renders the image plausible: the feminine air is the mother of the universe and is itself sustained and fed by the One, by God. In Paradise, the divine air carries in itself the nutritious power of the Eucharist: "The scent of Paradise / acts like bread, / and this breath of life / like drink. . . ."[9] Thus Paradise, in Hymn XI, is a banquet where man feeds on divine food: "The air of Paradise / is the delightful source / which Adam sucked / when he was young. / Like a breast, this air / nourished his childhood. . . ."[10] Paradise is the first creature of God; it is the all-encompassing mother of the universe. The fall has estranged man from this mother, but the Christian aspires to return to Paradise and to eat again at "the Table of the Kingdom,"[11] where one feeds on the air of Eden.

With Ephrem, as with Romanos and the *Acathistos Hymn,* these views were poetic images of great evocative power. Undoubtedly they also express-ed theological convictions, although these, especially as they appear in the perspective of Ephrem, maybe difficult to put in the relatively clear terms of speculative theology. However, enough ingredients were available in the theology of the Greek Fathers to open the way to a theology of the feminine in God.

The oriental authors tend to see God and the world in less sharp an opposition than appears to the Latin mind. Or, granted that the essence of the Divinity remains ultimately unknowable, that it must ever escape inspection by a created mind, that even Revelation cannot allow us to fathom the hiddenness of God, God nonetheless makes himself known in his actions and activities, which are like a halo around the core of the divine Abyss. Classical Western theology will handle the problem by distinguishing between God in himself and God in his works, between the inner life of God and the created effects of his acts. What is directly known of God is only a created effect, either in the world of nature where God is known through his visible works, or in the soul where he is known through the gift of his grace. Even the highest mystical states will be understood by most Western mystics and theologians as man's awareness of God's action in the recesses of his soul rather than as an immediate encounter between God and man. While acknowledging the fundamental difference between God and his works, Eastern thought tends to distinguish between the works of God as they are posited outside of himself and the divine activity or "energy" by which God posits them: this activity is identical neither (as in some Asian forms of pantheism) with the works it creates, nor (as in Latin theology) with the essence of God. To participate in the divine nature (2 Peter 1:4) implies not a reception of created grace as Latin theology will see it, but a deification (*theosis*) by union to the divine "energies" which are God's own action. The Cappadocian Fathers already alluded to the distinction between God's *Ousia* and his *energeiai,* although this remained unsystematic and there was no hint of anything feminine about the activities of God.[12]

This fundamental orientation of Greek soteriology raised a major problem when Origenism (that is, the ideas of Origen's work on *The Principles,* as spread and developed after his death) threatened to alter the very structure of the Christian faith. The question concerned the nature of the created world and its relationship to God. The Origenists were hellenizing, neo-Platonist Christians strongly influenced by the neo-Platonism of the Alexandrian philosophers Iamblichus (312-337) and Proclus (411-485). For them man was not created in time; he was an eternal soul who, after living in God for countless ages, had fallen by sin into a material body. After living in the world of the divine Ideas, in God, he had been thrown temporarily into the present world. The process of Christian life is a return to the Father, to the world in God, by way of asceticism and mystical contemplation.

Although this theology nearly won over to its side the monastic movement, it was systematically fought by the Councils (mainly the Fifth Ecumenical Council, 553) and by many theologians.

At the theological level, the problem was to assign an acceptable status to the Platonic world of Ideas, which could hardly be ignored in the context of Greek culture. The unknown author called Dionysius or Pseudo-Dionysius, a Syrian monk of the fifth or early sixth century,[13] elaborated an impressive theology of the invisible world, which he equated with the world of angels: created by God, it is distinct from, although actively related to, the world of men. The utter transcendence of God is affirmed; yet intelligent creatures (angels and men) participate in the divine nature, being illuminated down the celestial hierarchy of angels, to which the Church's hierarchy corresponds on earth. Although Dionysius wielded considerable influence over later theology, the common answer of Greek Orthodoxy to the allurements of neo-Platonic philosophy was provided by Saint Maxim the Confessor[14] (c. 580-662): it is in the divine *Logos,* and not among angels, that the heavenly counterpart of the present world dwells. The *Logos* enfolds in himself the model (*logos*) of all created beings. Man is not this *logos,* although he participates in it, and his participation is properly constitutive of his being. Man himself is created as a microcosm, an epitome of the whole world. The dividedness which he now experiences in himself as spirit and flesh, and in mankind as male and female, is not primitive. Man was created in oneness but fell into estrangement through sin. As forcefully expressed in the text quoted at the beginning of this chapter, sex is "a division which has no relation to the divine Archetype." But the divine economy will not allow man to remain estranged and divided forever. The entelechy deposited in him longs for his return to unity. Monasticism is the model for all Christian life, for it witnesses to, and constitutes an education for, the reintegration of man in unity. Already sex has been overcome. "By his birth of the Virgin, [Christ] suppressed the division of human nature into male and female."[15] In those somewhat cryptic words, Vladimir Lossky sums up Saint Maxim's conception of the beginning of overcoming human dividedness.

With this view of sex as accidental to human nature, Maxim could not possibly suggest any hint of a male-female polarity in God. The heavenly world of the *logoi* lies in the *Logos,* in God, who can never be seen as a feminine figure, even when the biblical image of Sophia is applied to him.

Yet the question is now clearly posited: if God encompasses a world of "energies," if there is in the *Logos* a world of *logoi,* the eternal patterns for all creatures, or if there is around God a radiation of the divine light, is it not likely that this divine world will be seen as a feminine image of God, as a divine Sophia related to, yet somehow distinguished from, the divine *Ousia,* the unknowable, ineffable essence of the Divinity? Or, to express the matter differently, if, in the process of creation, God may be seen as the Father of man (which is a commonplace of all theology), can be not also be seen somehow as the Mother? As long as the dangers of Origenism and its sequel, Messalianism, persisted, the point could hardly be raised. But it was bound to become a live theological possibility as soon as that threat had vanished. It is certainly not by accident that Justinian (483-565), the emperor who condemned Origenism at the Council of Constantinople (553), also built the great Church dedicated to Holy Sophia, the divine wisdom manifested in Christ. Inaugurated in 538, the church was not erected as a monument to victory over Greek philosophy; yet the condemnation of 553 was the logical outcome of a christology which placed wisdom in God himself rather than in an eternal world emanating from God.

As long as the theological vocabulary about the divine "energies" was clearly metaphorical, the question of the divine Sophia could also be handled and answered at the level of metaphors. In himself, in his eternal and hidden essence, God is ultimately unknowable, and the theology called "apophatic" attempts to approach his inaccessible light by renouncing what he is not, without being ever able to grasp what he is. God is known in his activities because these activities are experienced: man is created, redeemed, and progressively deified. If the wisdom of God is that which has been made known of him, wisdom and essence are really one and the same, although conceptually distinguished: Sophia is the essence of God entering human life through his activities. The activities of God, his "energies," are God as active outside of himself, as positing and creating effects the sum of which constitutes the created world. The difference between God as unknowable *Ousia* and as manifested and shared *"energeia"* is relevant to man's situation as participant in the divine nature, yet unable to fathom the depths of this divine nature; but it is not relevant to God himself, who is utterly simple despite being both at rest in himself and active outside of himself. At this level, there is no danger of personalizing or hypostatizing the divine "energies" and no threat to the traditional concept of God as Three and One.

During the fourteenth century, however, Saint Gregory Palamas (c. 1296-1359), archbishop of Salonica, followed by several Councils of Constantinople (June and August, 1341, 1351, 1368), was led to affirm a real distinction in

God between the divine "energies" and the divine essence or *Ousia.* The deification of the Christian implies a participation in the "energies," but not in the *Ousia;* likewise, the knowledge of God reaches the "energies" alone, not the *Ousia.* Although the essence and the "energies" are really distinct in relation to us, each is nonetheless adequate to the totality of God: "What is manifested, what makes itself accessible to knowledge and to participation, is not a part of God, lest God be divided because of us: but the whole of God shows itself and does not show itself, the whole is known and is unknown, the whole is participated in and cannot be participated in."[16] Palamas affirms the paradox of all Christian dogma: God is transcendent and incarnate; he is in himself and he is also in man; inexhaustible, he shares his life with his creatures.

The theology of Gregory Palamas bears relevance to our study in one of its possible consequences: if the "energies" of God are proclaimed to be really distinct from the divine essence, we are not far from the temptation to identify the energies with the divine Sophia understood as an eternal feminine principle. Palamas himself does not seem to have envisaged this possibility. His problem was still the old concern of Greek theology: to defend the Fathers and the monks against attacks inspired by a philosophical Hellenism embodied in the works of **Barlaam** the Calabrian (d.c. 1348). His concern was not directly to investigate, and still less to systematize, a Trinitarian theology. But in terms that appear strangely germane to those of Mother Julian in England at approximately the same time, Palamas did **allude to the motherhood of** Christ:

> Christ has become our *brother* by union to our flesh and our blood; and he has in this way assimilated himself to us. . . . He has bonded and adapted us to himself, as the *bridegroom* does with the bride, by becoming one flesh with us through communion to the Blood; he has also become our *father* through the holy baptism which makes us like to him, and he nurses us from his own breast, as a *mother*, filled with tenderness, does with her babies. . . .[17]

It is the humanity of Christ that Palamas has in mind here. Palamas operates in the realm of metaphors—brother, bridegroom, father, mother—to dramatize the humanity of the divine *Logos.*

It has been pointed out that, whereas the divine Sophia in the great Church of Byzantium is Christ the *Logos,* several Russian Churches dedicated to Holy Sophia, like the cathedrals of Kiev and Novgorod, built in the eleventh century, extol a more feminine image of Sophia, embodied in the icon of the Virgin Mary.[18] Likewise, it is in Russian theology that the question of the female aspect of God has been raised directly.

The material covered so far in this chapter provides a necessary introduction to the speculations of the Russian sophiologists of whom I have to speak now. Undoubtedly, the sources of a sophiology are broader than traditional Orthodox thought. Sophiology constitutes a systematic attempt to discover the feminine element in God and to understand it in terms that are compatible with traditional Trinitarian faith. It was not the first such attempt. Under the influence of the Jewish kabbala and its doctrines on the attributes of God, some Christian humanists of the Renaissance had already tried it.

The kabbala enjoyed considerable fame in the fifteenth and sixteenth centuries, when a number of Christian scholars assumed that it contained a genuine tradition deriving from the Old Testament and supporting the main tenets of Christian theology. The Jewish kabbalists understood God to be a source of emanations rather than the author of a creation. From him as *Ein Sof* (the Infinite) there emanate ten *sephiroth* or attributes: first, Principle or Crown, from which there derive two by two, like gnostic syzygies, Wisdom and Intellect, Mercy and Justice, Victory and Glory. Out of the last two couples, which relate to each other like Father and Mother, two more *sephiroth* proceed, Beauty and Ground. The tenth *sephirah,* Sovereignty, sums up the system of sephiric emanations. Primordial Man (*Adam kadmon*), the heavenly model of man, embodies the *sephiroth* in himself.

The clear outcome of this esoteric doctrine is that the feminine principle has been introduced into the Divinity itself. Some of the Christian kabbalists were to maintain it there, or to interpret it as a medium between God and creation, although this could hardly be achieved without impairing traditional orthodoxy. For Paracelsus (1493-1541), an eminent doctor who lived in Protestant Germanic lands but whose doctrines were questionable by Protestant standards, heaven and earth were born of a primordial matrix, the water which supported the Spirit of God: "Before heaven and earth were created, the Spirit of God brooded over the water and was carried by it. This water was the matrix; for it is in the water that heaven and earth were created, and in no other matrix."[19] This matrix is the primordial motherly substance of all. Then heaven and earth became the matrix of man: "Man emerged from the first matrix, the maternal womb, of the Great World." As the image of the Great World (macrocosm) of heaven and earth, man is the Little World (microcosm). Then man himself became the matrix of woman, who was created out of him. Finally woman "became the maternal womb of all men and will remain so to the end of the world." After the Great and the Little World, she is the "Littlest World": "For the world is and was the first substance, man the second and woman the third. Thus the cosmos is the greatest world, the world of man is the next greatest, and that of woman the smallest and least."[20] As one can see, the discovery of an eternal feminine does not necessarily cause woman to be raised up, but can still place her at the bottom of the scale of being.

The sophiologists were also indebted to the Protestant mystic Jacob Boehme (1575-1624), whose more or less heterodox system integrated evil into God as a necessary motor for starting the movement of emanations. The male and the female principles, which originated in the male and female elements of the divine world—called, respectively, Fire and Light—coexisted originally in Adam. The externalization of woman resulted from Adam's fundamental fault of seeking for companionship outside instead of inside himself, where woman belonged in the primordinal order of humanity.

Another line of thought which had a direct influence on sophiology is more surprising than these classical loci for a doctrine of the eternal feminine. The French sociologist and philosopher Auguste Comte (1798-1857) tried to form what he called the "religion of humanity," in order to give spiritual depth to what he foresaw as the last stage of mankind, the "positive" age destined to succeed the theological and the metaphysical stages. The "Great Being" which he equated both with God and with mankind he described in feminine terms. Comte had a direct influence on the Russian sophiologist, Vladimir Soloviev (1853–1900).[21]

In the thought of Soloviev, the eternal feminine, Sophia, stands at the meeting point of God and the world, belonging to both and at home in both. From the standpoint of creation, she is the "soul of the world," the collective entelechy of the universe which expresses her through "nature"; with the advent of man, she passes from a vegetal and animal life to a spiritual life, becoming now Adam, in whom the created world finds its natural acme and in whom the "soul of the world" reaches its highest embodiment. From the standpoint of the creator, Sophia is the divine purpose and vision in view of which the universe is made, which is already enscribed in it in a hidden manner, and which must be progressively manifested in the history of man until its ultimate fulfillment. These two aspects are one, so that the soul of the world must be equated with the divine purpose: it is a theanthropy, a divine-human reality, what Soloviev calls Godmanhood. With the coming of Christ, immense progress was made in the manifestation of Godmanhood. For Christ is himself the divine Sophia incarnate; the Virgin Mary, as his human mother, embodies the motherly aspect of the divine Sophia; the Church, as his bride, is the body of the divine wisdom. Accordingly, in his *Lectures on Godmanhood,* delivered in Moscow in 1878, Soloviev calls Sophia the world soul, and the body of Christ, the Church, the divine Mother,[22] the ideal mankind, the real form of the Divinity, the manifestation of the Spirit.[23] In the mutual enrichment of the two aspects of Sophia, human and divine, the mystery of redemption takes place: God becomes man and man is deified.

If the overshadowing that descended upon the human Mother with the active power of God produced the incarnation of Divinity; then the fertilization of the divine Mother (the Church) by the active human beginning must produce a free deification of humanity.[24]

In a volume published in Paris, *La Russie et l'Eglise universelle* (1889), Soloviev further develops his concepts. The notion of Sophia becomes less a philosophical theory about the structure of the universe and more a Christocentric view of the process of creation-deification. In this context, it is immediately relevant to a theology of womanhood. For the three incarnations of wisdom are man, woman, and society. In man, the soul of the world, hitherto confined to a subrational state, reaches awareness: "The sensitive and imaginative soul of the physical world becomes the rational soul of humanity."[25] Adam, the male, is mankind, the "image of God," a "universal being," although he is so only potentially and his task is to become so really. Woman and society are born in the course of this transition of man from an ideal to a real universality. Man must first know himself, therefore establishing a dichotomy in himself between the knower and the known: the knowing subject, which Soloviev calls "active," is the principle of manhood, and the known object, which he calls "passive," the principle of womanhood. In thus knowing himself, man activates his embodiment of Sophia as the union of the divine Word and the terrestrial nature: maleness corresponds to the Word and femaleness to nature. Thus Soloviev can write:

> The human individual, being in himself subjectively the union of the divine Word and earthly nature, must begin to realize this union objectively or for himself by an external reduplication of himself. In order really to know himself in his unity, man must distinguish himself as knowing or active subject (man in the proper sense) from himself as known or passive object (woman). Thus the contrast and union of the divine Word and earthly Nature is reproduced for man himself in the distinction and union between the sexes.[26]

For Soloviev, mankind is man; woman is no more than the "complement of man," as society is his "extension."[27] "Man properly so called (the masculine individual) contains already in himself *in potentia* the whole essence of man; it is only in order to realize that essence *actu* that he must, first, reduplicate himself or objectify his material side in the feminine personality, and secondly, multiply himself or objectify the universality of his rational being in a plurality of individual existences organically bound together and forming a corporate whole, human society."[28] In this complex which is the human manifestation of Sophia, woman stands as "object," as "matter," as "passive" correspondent of the activity of the male, as "heart and instinct" contrasting with "reason and consciousness."[29]

In this analysis womanhood is a secondary aspect of mankind, a moment in its development. But this needs to be corrected on two counts.

On the one hand, true mankind is not achieved at the level of individual man. Likewise, womanhood cannot discover its true model in the ideas of passivity, complementarity, materiality, and emotionality, notwithstanding Soloviev's belief that these have a constitutive function in relation to concrete womanhood. The model is to be found in the perfection of these qualities. Man, woman, and society are no more than "a seed," which needs to grow and reach maturity or perfection: "The gradual growth of this seed is accomplished in the process of universal history; and the threefold fruit which it bears is: perfect Woman or deified Nature, perfect Man or the God-Man, and the perfect society of God with men, the ultimate incarnation of eternal Wisdom."[30] These perfect embodiments of the three elements that constitute the visible manifestation of Sophia are no other than Jesus Christ, the Virgin Mary, and the Church:

. . . there is fundamentally only one human being. And its reunion with God, though necessarily threefold, nevertheless constitutes only a single divine-human being—the incarnate Sophia, whose central and perfectly personal manifestation is Jesus-Christ, whose feminine complement is the Virgin Mary, and whose universal extension is the Church.[31]

And again, in a most forceful text:

Mankind reunited to God in the Holy Virgin, in Christ, in the Church, is the realization of the eternal Wisdom or the absolute substance of God, its created form, its incarnation. Truly, it is one and the same substantial form . . . which shows itself in three manifestations that are both successive and permanent, both really distinct and essentially indivisible, calling itself Mary in its feminine personality, Jesus in its masculine personality— and reserving its proper name for its total and universal apparition in the fulfilled Church of the future, the Spouse and the Bride of the divine Word.[32]

On the other hand, if there is a male and a female pole in wisdom as embodied in human life and even as perfectly manifested in the order of the Incarnation, the proper image of Sophia as eternal Godmanhood and soul of the universe remains a feminine image. For, in relation to this world, Sophia is the divine mother of all; in relation to God, she is the eternal bride face to face with the Father, the abysmal fount of Divinity and of nature, of divine and human life.

In September, 1898, Vladimir Soloviev wrote an autobiographical poem describing three personal encounters with the divine Sophia: one in Moscow when he was a child, one in London, and one in the Egyptian wilderness. Each time, the apparition contrasted with some aspect of imperfection in the human situation of Soloviev at the time; and each time it took the form of a vision of beauty filling the sky with blue and gold light, in the midst of which the smiling face of Sophia shone, transforming Soloviev interiorly and changing his relationship to the world. This image of Sophia Soloviev calls "the royal purple of Divinity," "the holy Light"; he addresses her as "flower of God," "eternal Friend," "Model of feminine Beauty."[33]

For Soloviev did not regard Sophia as an imaginary figure or as a philosophical concept, although he used imagination to describe her and philosophy to define her. He had met Sophia in a living encounter. He had seen the eternal feminine, Godmanhood, the first expression of God and the Mother of all things. He even composed this prayer to her, which provides a fitting conclusion to this brief survey of his sophiology:

> In the name of the Father and of the Son and of the Holy Ghost. An-Soph, Yah, Soph-Yah . . .

> O Thou, the most holy divine Sophia, the substantial image of beauty and the delight of the transcendentally extant God, the bright body of Eternity, the soul of the world and the queen-soul of all souls, by the fathomless blessedness of Thy first Son and beloved Jesus-Christ, I implore Thee to descend into the prison of the soul; fill this darkness of ours with thy radiancy; melt away the fetters of our spirit with the fire of love, grant us freedom and light; appear to us in a visible and substantial manner; become thyself incarnate in us and in the world, restoring the fullness of the eons, so that the deep may be covered with a limit and God may become all in all.[34]

As clearly indicated by the beginning of this prayer, with its reference to the kabbalistic formula, *Ein-Sof,* Soloviev consciously drew on non-Christian sources. Largely for this reason, his sophiology could not be accepted as a correct statement of Orthodox theology. More recent attempts to restate a sophiological doctrine have taken care to free it from non-Christian undertones. It is not possible at this point to make a complete survey of these developments, since much of this literature has not been translated from the Russian. Because of the availability of the major works of Sergius Bulgakov (1870-1944) in Western languages, I will say a few words about his version of sophiology.

The relevant works of Bulgakov deal with Trinitarian theology, and easily constitute the most impressive modern investigation of this fundamental Christian mystery. Bulgakov's speculations show a thorough acquaintance with the theological tradition of both East and West. His work purports to be faithful to the central tradition, while carrying it forward to a renewed appreciation of the Trinitarian mystery. It is from this height that it envisions an anthropology, specifically the nature and function of womanhood.

At the heart of the Divinity is the Father, "who is Silence, Mystery, Transcendence, even in the bosom of the Holy Trinity."[35] Seen as God, or, to use traditional language, as the fontal Person or Hypostasis of the Trinity, the Father is the Essence (in Greek, *Ousia*), the ultimate Abyss of Being, unrevealed even to itself, before whom the only possible theology must be negative: we cannot know him unless he reveals himself. The *Ousia* of God can reveal itself, taking on, as it does so, the characteristics of Sophia. The unrevealed Essence reveals itself as ultimate Wisdom, the Source of universal being and of all beings; the apophatic Abyss shows itself to be also and at the same time a cataphatic Ground; the eternal Night is an eternal Light.

In this context, Sophia denotes the revelation of the Father. As self-revelation, or revelation to itself, it is eternal: the Father reveals himself eternally as Wisdom, and this eternal Wisdom is manifested in the two Hypostases of the Son and the Spirit. Together the Son and the Spirit constitute a revelatory Dyad through which the Father reveals himself to himself. They are a divine world expressing the unfathomable richness of the Father. The Father also reveals himself outside the divine world, through the process of creation. Corresponding to the divine Sophia there is a second, creaturely Sophia, the image of the Father manifesting itself in the cosmos and especially in man, the creature in which the cosmos reaches the level of consciousness and becomes able to relate itself freely to God.

The divine Sophia and the creaturely Sophia are not only correlated; the latter is also the image of the former. The Abyss of Divinity reveals itself in a creaturely Image because it has been able first of all to reveal itself in an eternal Image. The divine Sophia of the *Logos* and the Spirit revealing the Father shines through the creaturely Sophia. If the absolute *Ousia* is the Father, the Sophia is the Mother of the created universe, the eternal womb where the creaturely Sophia is conceived. As this implies, the eternal Sophia, the Dyad of the Son and the Spirit, contains already in itself the Image of the world to be made, the Image of man: the divine Sophia is The-anthropy, Godmanhood.

At this point we reach the heart of the problem of man and woman. For Sergius Bulgakov, man is the highest expression and manifestation of the creaturely wisdom at the level of nature. But this sophianic man is not a single individual, any more than the eternal Sophia, the Mother of the world, is a single Hypostasis. As the divine Sophia cannot be adequately revealed in the *Logos* or the Spirit but requires both for its manifestation, likewise the creaturely Sophia in humanity is man *and* woman. The polarity of the sexes constitutes no accident, as the Fathers thought. It belongs intrinsically to the structure of Godmanhood:

Interiorly, in the spirit, man is defined by the polarity of the masculine and feminine principles; and even in his exterior being, he is not only man or woman, but he is precisely man *and* woman, he is this ontological *and* which expresses the fullness of Theanthropy, of the image of God in man.[36]

This insight is formulated differently in *The Wisdom of God*, where the divine Wisdom, as abiding in the Son, defines Adam, and, as abiding in the Spirit, who is himself in the Son, defines woman within the unity of man and woman:

The Son and the Holy Spirit together constitute Godmanhood, as the revelation of the Father in the Holy Trinity. . . . This same relation, since the Incarnation, is reflected in that between Christ and the Church. Human hypostases are reflections of the Logos, the Heavenly Man, the 'New Adam'. But the Holy Spirit, since he abides in the Son, is also a prototype of human hypostases. Thus man, created in the image of God, has been created male and female. Husband and wife, though they differ as two different exemplifications of human nature, manifest in their unity the fulness of humanity and of the image of God enshrined in it. Their union is sealed by the dyad of the Son and of the Holy Spirit, which reveals the Father. They bear within themselves the power of procreation, the image of the unity of the tri-personal God, which is to be traced in the whole of mankind as such.[37]

The relation of man and woman in the oneness of humanity is an icon of the relation between the Son and the Spirit in the oneness of the divine Wisdom: "The masculine principle corresponds to the Logos, the feminine principle to the Spirit."[38] However, Sergius Bulgakov does not confuse the *eros*, or love, which by uniting man and woman contributes to their perfection as the image of God, and sex, the carnal expression of *eros* between male and female which, being vitiated by sin, needs to be reeducated through the asceticism of the monastic life or of sacramental marriage. In the proper order of the universe, the relationship of man and woman is destined to be spiritual, since it is founded on the spiritual differences and complementarities of the masculine and the feminine principles. It can take the form of friendship, when the spiritual complementarities are sustained and united by the psychological complementarities of man and woman. It can also be expressed in sex, when the physical complementarities are introduced in the relationship. But whereas spiritual relationship or friendship, being potentially universal, can be multiplied, the sexual relationship, when it is dominated, as it should be, by spiritual *eros* and by friendship, must be unique. Oriented toward the sacrificial fulfillment of procreation, it needs uniqueness and stability. The ascetic control of sex by the spirit demands also monogamy and the permanence of marriage.[39]

Bulgakov subordinates sex to spirit and, thereby, the sexual differentiations of male and female to the spiritual distinctions of the masculine and the feminine. The general principle is clear: the masculine corresponds to the *Logos* and the feminine to the Spirit. The twofold aspects of creatureliness, masculine and feminine, belong to the very condition of all creatures and therefore obtain even in the world of angels. Insofar as they are images of God, all creatures are made of two principles. In the case of man, where this differentiation is carried into the "psycho-somatic element," this means that "the masculine and feminine principles of the spirit are achieved in the form of man and woman. These are predestined, not only to experience spiritual love (the wife must be the 'helpmeet', that is, the friend, and the husband must be the head, that is also the friend, though showing his friendship in a different way), but also to be 'one flesh'."[40] Eastern theology in general looks at the realities of this world in the light thrown on them by Revelation rather than in what they appear to be in their objectivity apart from the realities of grace. This made it impossible for Bulgakov to describe the feminine and the masculine in empirical terms. Instead of a psychological or sociological description, he provides a strictly theological anthropology: true humanity is divine Theanthropy. It is in that light that we should understand and live the human condition.

> Man is created in the image of God, but this image is precisely the Theanthropy, the image of the Father, The image of the Father is the Son, revealed in the God-Man, and the Holy Spirit, revealed in the Mother of God. Man is created in the image of God as man and as woman, according to the two images of the revelation of fatherhood, the condition of son, and that of mother and daughter. The image of the Son of Man corresponds to that of the Son of God; and they are identical in the God-Man. The image of the Mother of man, and also that of the daughter of God, is revealed in Eve, who, after her Fall, is replaced by the new Eve, Mary. Man is created to be son and daughter of God.[41]

In order to discover the constitutive elements of womanhood as conceived in the divine economy, one should look at what has been revealed of the Holy Spirit, who forms the element of "daughtership" in God and, being on the feminine side of the Theanthropy, presides over all Motherhood on earth. Nowhere has the Spirit been revealed with more fullness than in the Virgin Mary, the Mother of God. Thus the Virgin is the very type of womanhood, the icon of the eternal feminine. "She is, in personal form, the human likeness of the Holy Ghost. "[42] In the works that I have been able to read, Sergius Bulgakov, has not pushed any further his analysis of the feminine as experienced in the human situation.

Other recent Russian Orthodox authors have done so, although they have not started from the sophiological premises of Bulgakov. In spite of what Bulgakov considered to be the traditional antecedents of his Trinitarian theology, sophiology has not been generally accepted. Vladimir Lossky, who—somewhat inaccurately, I believe—summed up Bulgakov's theology in the idea that God is "one person in three hypostases,"[43] called sophiology an "ecclesiology gone astray,"[44] its "fundamental error" being the identification of the Essence (*Ousia*) with one of its attributes or "energies," that of wisdom (*Sophia*). But "God is not determined by any of his attributes; all determinations are inferior to him, logically posterior to his being in itself, in its essence. When we say that God is Wisdom, Life, Truth, Love—we understand the energies, which are subsequent to the essence and its manifestations, but are external to the very being of the Trinity."[45]

Whether this constitutes an adequate criticism of Bulgakov remains a moot question. Yet, whatever one may think of this, the relationship between the Holy Spirit, the Virgin Mary, and womanhood, and the correlative relationship between the *Logos*, the Incarnate Lord, and manhood have survived, without any sophiological connotation, in Paul Evdokimov's volume on *Woman and the Salvation of the World* (1958).

Drawing to a considerable extent on the psychology of Carl Jung, Evdokimov understands the masculine and the feminine in the light of the two psychological principles which Jung calls *animus* and *anima: "Animus* and *anima,* the conscious and the unconscious, introversion and extraversion, the rational functions of thought and feeling and the irrational functions of sensation and intuition, are the infra-complementary parts of the psyche."[46] They belong to the very structure of the soul: *animus,* consciousness, extraversion, the rational functions of thought and feeling are masculine, whereas *anima,* the unconscious, introversion, the irrational functions of sensation and intuition are feminine. For Evdokimov, as for Jung himself, each human being partakes of both, although one series dominates the male while the other dominates the female. However, these distinctions belong to this world and will pass away with its temporality. Eventually, the opposites will coincide and this will be, as hinted at in the Gospel of the Egyptians, one of the characteristics of the Kingdom of God. "A male being and a female being, the many forms of unity in history, are no more than images of the One, of the masculine-feminine in the Kingdom."[47]

In the meantime, both the identity and the differences of the masculine and the feminine are expressed, as Evdokimov interprets it, in the traditional icon of the Deisis: Christ is seated in the center on a throne of glory over the tomb from which he rose, holding the Book of Life in his left hand, his right hand raised in the gesture of blessing; Mary and John the Baptist stand on either side, turned to Christ with their heads slightly bent, their hands opened toward him in a gesture of prayer. This is Christ, the Image of God, the model of mankind, in whom "there is neither male nor female" (Gal. 3: 28), and the two archetypes of the feminine (Mary) and the masculine (John the Baptist). Christ is the universal model, beyond maleness and femaleness:

> This means that there is no exclusiveness, but the total humanity and that each one finds himself in Christ. He is the universal Archetype of mankind, the second Adam containing all in himself, as the first Adam, before the birth of Eve, contained the undifferentiated masculine and feminine. The *ecce homo*—the humanity of Christ—allows no reproduction or imitation, but it is near to all, for all find in it their own truth and their ontological locus as members of the universal, all-encompassing Body. The mystical body of Christ is neither masculine nor feminine, since it is the place where these are integrated.[48]

Mary shows the feminine qualities of receptivity, openness, gestation, hiddenness, fruitfulness, sacrifice. "Living comforter, woman is Eve-Life, who safeguards, vivifies, protects each parcel of the masculine creation . . . As 'Paradise', the Virgin represents grace, the divine philanthropy. . . . Woman, enstatic, is in herself turned toward her own being. The femine acts at the level of ontological structure; she is not the word but the *being*, the womb of the creature."[49]

The masculine qualities appear in John the Baptist: strength, aggressiveness, action, judgment. "Man, the witness, acts through his virility; . . . he is the 'violent one' mentioned in the Gospel, the one who carries away the treasure of the Kingdom. . . . The masculine works at the level of the acts which project it outside of itself. The tool lengthens the arm of *homo faber* and the entire world becomes, as it were, his continued body. . . . Man, ecstatic, is essentially in the extension of himself. . . ."[50] The charisms of man and woman are doled out to them, both in order to fulfill each vocation according to his male or female capacities and also to prepare the eschatological transformation of the Kingdom, where the two will be one. "The divine-human archetype of Christ in his universality is the *what* common to all. . . . The masculine and the feminine are the *how*; and their archetypes show the forms and the means relating to the very personal and concrete destiny of each specific type, in order to actualize the *what* that is common to all."[51] The Christian, whether man or woman, fulfills his calling by orienting his capacities and qualities toward the Image of Christ, by way of the image of Mary or of John the Baptist. He must reach beyond male and female through his male or female characteristics and charisms.

As shown by Evdokimov's reflections on our problem, the speculations of men like Vladimir Soloviev or Sergius Bulgakov cannot be considered typical of Orthodox thinking on the matter of the eternal feminine. The very romantic version proposed by Soloviev was too strongly influenced by heterodox elements to have left profound traces in Orthodox thought. The more theological effort of Bulgakov has itself been strongly criticized as straying away from traditional Trinitarian beliefs. Nothing is left of sophiology in the more recent and more popular outline of an Orthodox position on womanhood written by Mme Tatiana Struve, "The Vocation of Woman."

Biblical in her basic approach and familiar with the great currents of Orthodox tradition, Tatiana Struve starts from the anthropology found in the reading of the Bible by the Greek Fathers of the Church. It is in the image of God in man, itself related to the mystery of the Trinity, that a Christian anthropology resides. The feminine corresponds neither to the dyad of the Son and the Spirit facing the Father (sophiologists), nor to the Spirit facing the two masculine models of the Father and the Son. "We would rather say that, through each of the three hypostases, two manifestations are seen; the one is creative, virile, organizational; the other is specifically sacrificial, uniting gift and love."[52] Thus, the masculine and the feminine would not refer us to the divine Persons in their distinctiveness, but to two aspects of God's action in general, that is, to two aspects of the energies of the divine nature.

Having thus from the start described the feminine as a self-giving, loving element next to a creative and aggressive masculine element, Mme Struve can easily follow this with a survey of the feminine vocation as it appears through the Bible, which is quite obviously filled with accounts of sacrificial behavior on the part of both God and man. She can also relate the polarization of the masculine and the feminine to the Jungian typology of *animus* and *anima*.

> As modern psychology has stressed it, the specificity of the masculine and the feminine derives from the common (human) reality; and, the polarization having taken place in mankind, we meet with the *animus-anima* of Jung, the interpenetration of the masculine and the feminine in each of us. If mankind in its totality is called to the virile vocation of transforming the earth and mastering nature, mankind as a whole is feminine in its eschatological destiny as the bride of Christ.[53]

Woman's vocation is to manifest in herself an aspect of human nature which belongs to all men, but for which she is constitutionally better equipped. Her "primordial function" is to "unify through giving birth and loving," to "be a bond, a revealer of love." Three elements must be joined together in order to bring mankind to its fulfillment, "the divine, the natural, the human."[54] Pulled in different directions by them, man cannot be at peace until they have been reunited. The three calls that man hears constantly are gathered together into a harmony through chastity (in which love is achieved through reintegration, whereas unchaste love divides and destroys). Thus understood, chastity sums up the feminine vocation: it encompasses wholeness, unity, sacrifice, motherhood; and it inspires joy. Woman must teach this to man; for unless man makes himself receptive to God's action in him, he cannot be transformed into a guest worthy of the divine banquet of the Kingdom. As openness to God's action runs counter to the virile drive for domination, man can only learn it from his feminine partner, this "mysterious witness to the role of suffering and oblation."[55]

To the theological models of womanhood presented at the conclusion of the last chapter we can now add a confirmation and a precision. The Virgin Mary has been confirmed as a model, both in terms of servanthood and in terms of ideal. She is both the handmaid of the Lord and the feminine sign in heaven, thus embodying two aspects of womanhood, service and bringing to perfection. More than in the corresponding Catholic reflection, these two aspects are now jointed inseparably.

The precision to be noted derives from the concern of Orthodox authors for the transcendental aspect of the problem of womanhood and for an anthropology that follows a divine model: anthropology rests on theanthropy. The exact whereabouts of the divine archetype of the feminine remains a moot question, one which may well forever escape analysis. Yet it would seem that femininity must somehow be related to the Spirit. This was already the orientation of the third unfinished Catholic model. On this point there is a remarkable convergence of a section of Catholic theology with the quasi-unanimous testimony of Orthodoxy. I do not think that we should follow this with investigations into the Divinity along sophiological lines. Such speculation wanders too far from biblical and patristic sources. What should remain is a concern for depth: to the practical and ethical frame of thought of much Catholic thinking we should join the ontological and eschatological emphases of Orthodox reflection.

8

Protestant Reflections

Turning from Orthodox and Catholic models to the Protestant contribution to a theology of womanhood, we feel a sense of disappointment. Protestantism has contributed little original insight to the problem; indeed, a recent survey of the question by a Protestant author argues that there cannot be a Protestant point of view in such a matter: the "Old Testament places us face to face with the problems that Israel discussed regarding God, and suggests no secret meanings about our nature as women." Likewise,

> the Bible, which provides us with recipes for nothing, will not give us, with a theology of woman, the excuse for a laziness which runs the danger of being satisfied with compelling myths and sacred or magic meanings, instead of a passionate and always approximate investigation. Instead of a metaphysical order to which we should conform, and of consolations that may be found in the sublimation of intolerable or false situations into parables, the Bible frees us from all archetypal forms to throw us forward into the ways of love, where one gropes for an acknowledgement of the contradictions and diversities which love assumes and reconciles. For this reason one cannot expect from a Protestant collaboration a new encyclopedic article on the biblical doctrine of woman. . . . We are therefore reduced, be it with joy, to share the uncertainties and the impatient reflection of our contemporaries on woman's becoming.[1]

Indeed, one may readily admit that while the Bible provides the freedom to use the ordinary means of investigation, it offers no solution to strictly human problems and no answer to purely natural questions. If, however, the Bible is read not only with a contemporary existential focus, but in the context of Protestant history, the answer should be more nuanced. For, whatever modern theology may think of them, there have been Protestant attempts to deal with our questions. In the following pages we will look at the insights of Luther and of Calvin and then examine some contemporary anthropologies.

What strikes me as I seek the Protestant Reformers' insights about woman-hood is that their central concern for problems of nature and grace, law and Gospel, sin and justification did not place them in a situation favorable to elaborate a theological anthropology. In the wake of late medieval theology, the thrust of their thought lay in their understanding of God's acts in the world. But the Ockhamism by which Luther was influenced focused his thought on God's sovereignty, which is, on the side of God, entirely good and noble, yet which often appears, on the side of man, as arbitrary and unmoti-vated. Thus the human condition, which is evil when considered from the point of view of man as a sinner, is nonetheless entirely just and deserved when seen from the standpoint of God's free decision to create this kind of world, or to let sin happen in the kind of world he has made. The order of relationships between men and women are, as instances of the more general relationships within society, arbitrary but nonetheless compulsory and un-avoidable. The human order, as it was to be found at the end of the Middle Ages and during the Renaissance, was accepted as carrying divine sanction.

Luther's contribution to a Christian reflection on woman is, like so many of his endeavors, full of paradoxes. His general understanding of the Gospel is meant to bring spiritual freedom to all the faithful. As images of God, men and women are equal; in the order of redemption they are equally called to justification and to life with Christ. Yet the natural order does not assign woman any other function than what corresponds to her sexual and procre-ative organs. Luther's commentary on Genesis identifies mankind with Adam the male, seeing woman as adjunct to him for the sake of procreation:

> Man is a more excellent creature than heaven and earth and everything that is in them. But Moses wanted to point out in a special way that the other part of humanity, the woman, was created by a unique counsel of God in order to show that this sex too is suited for the kind of life which Adam was expecting and that this sex was to be useful for procreation.[2]

Had there been no sin, woman would have been the equal of man. As things are, she is not. It is Adam who, "in his own person," is "the most beau-tiful creature." In Paradise Adam would have needed woman's sex only to procreate. In the present life, "after our nature has become corrupted by sin, woman is needed not only to secure increase but also for companionship and for protection." Woman "manages the household," a good and valuable thing which frees her husband for his own pursuits. "The final cause [of the wife] is to be a mundane dwelling place to her husband." More fundamentally, however, she must also be treated as "the medicine which she is," namely the medicine which, through matrimony, provides a legal outlet to sexual desire, thus providing man with a remedy against sexual sins by making lawful what otherwise would be illegitimate. "We are compelled to make use of this sex in order to avoid sin." Human beings "are compelled to make use of intercourse with their wives in order to avoid sin. As a result we are begotten and also born in sin, since our parents did not copulate because of duty but also as an antidote or to avoid sin."[3]

Dwelling on this theme, Luther pushes to an extreme the old idea that one of the purposes of marriage is to act as a remedy for concupiscence. Yet this is not all. Marriage is not only remedial; it is also shameful now, whatever it would have been in Paradise. "Parents are compelled to hide in darkness to do this."[4] While there is great joy in marriage, even in our corrupt nature, this joy "is contaminated by that leprous lust of the flesh which was not present in righteous Adam." In a sense, married love is the highest love: "It burns as fire and seeks nothing more than a mate. . . . All other loves seek something else than that which is love, but this love alone desires the beloved completely."[5] Such a love, however, is no longer pure: "It is so hideous and frightful a pleasure that physicians compare it with epilepsy or falling sickness. Thus an actual disease is linked with the very activity of procreation."[6] What happens to woman herself in this conundrum of the fallen state? Since her function is shameful, she also participates in the shame of sex. "In paradise, woman would have been a help for a duty only" (namely the duty of procreation). "But now she is also, and for the greater part at that, an antidote and a medicine; we can hardly speak of her without a feeling of shame, and surely we can not make use of her without shame."[7] It is not surprising that Luther's approach to our topic has been called a "genitalism."[8] Not is it astonishing that Luther took a lenient view of polygamy, not least in the disgraceful episode of the bigamy of Philip of Hesse.[9] In polygamy, also, women are a medicine for their husbands. Their own feelings need not be taken into consideration and are never prominent in Luther's mind, since the will of God is that women obey men. By the same token, Luther permits adultery when one of the partners cannot perform the sexual act.[10]

Given these principles, woman cannot count for much. The procreative purpose affects her entire being, which is strong for that purpose and weak in all other faculties. Furthermore, her place in the present world has been vitiated by the fall. "To me," Luther exclaims, "it is often a source of great pleasure and wonderment to see that the entire female body was created for the purpose of nurturing children. . . . In procreation and in feeding and nurturing their offspring, they are masters."[11] In everything else they are inferior and incompetent: "They cannot perform the functions of men, teach, rule, etc." Add to this the curse brought about by the fall, and the proper functions of women are now beset with miseries:

From the beginning of that time [of conception] a woman suffers very painful headaches, dizziness, nausea, an amazing loathing of food and drink, frequent and difficult vomiting, toothache, and a stomach disorder which produces a craving, called pica, for such foods from which nature normally shrinks. Moreover, when the fetus has matured and birth is imminent, there follows the most awful distress, because only with utmost peril and almost at the cost of her life does she give birth to her offspring.[12]

All in all, woman bears the brunt of the curse, man's share of it being reduced to the burdens of leadership: "The female sex has been greatly humbled and afflicted, and it bears a far severer and harsher punishment than the men."[13] It seems little consolation for woman to think, as Luther advises her to do, that her punishment might well have been worse: Moreover, "Eve has been placed under the power of her husband."

The rule remains with the husband, and the wife is compelled to obey him by God's command. He rules the home and the state, wages war, defends his possessions, tills the soil, builds, plants, etc. The woman on the other hand is like a nail driven into the wall. She sits at home. . . . Just as the snail carries its house with it, so the wife should stay at home and look after the affairs of the household, as one who has been deprived of the ability of administering those affairs that are outside and that concern the state. She does not go beyond her most personal duties.[14]

This is the will of God. Yet women try to revolt against it, and "if they are unable to do more, they at least indicate their impatience by grumbling."[15]

Luther, here, has used several medieval themes: the natural inferiority of woman (inherited from Aristotle), the notion of concupiscence and of marriage as an alleviation of concupiscence (one of three "goods of matrimony" of Augustine), the arbitrariness of God's action (a theme of the Nominalist school). Set in the context of his pessimistic concept of the nature of man in his fallen state, these points build a dreadful picture of man and woman and of their mutual relationship. Redemption and justification transform the spiritual dimension of man, but without changing anything in the structure of his fallen estate. We then are faced with a paradox: sex and, accordingly, woman as defined by sex are both evil and holy. This was pithily expressed in Archbishop Cranmer's opinion, embodied in *The Bishop's Book* of 1537, that "the act of procreation between men and women" which is "of itself and of its own nature damnable," has been, for Christians, "sanctified by the Word of God."[16] Or, in Luther's own words, "Therefore for the sake of Christ marriage must be holy and pure, and sexual intercourse, which in itself is most indecent, must be chaste and honorable."[17] In the context of Luther's concept of sin and justification, this is only one instance of the universal situation of man as sinner and yet justified. However one judges this wider context, it was not conducive, in the sixteenth century, to a well-balanced assessment of womanhood.

Calvin's contribution to our problem is more refined than that of the spontaneous and boisterous Luther; and some evaluations of it have been extremely laudatory. In his book on "man and woman in Calvinist ethics," André Biéler regards Calvin as a reformer of the relations between man and woman, after the darkness of the Middle Ages had brought about a complete moral decadence and at the very time that woman was starting on her progressive emancipation in modern society.[18] Yet Biéler's elaboration on this theme shows nothing more than what could be found in a medieval conception of man and woman. Calvin's stress lies heavily on the moral aspects of feminine behavior. This was well in line with the prevailing emphasis of Western thought, though Calvin more underscored it than was usual before him. This was partly due to the moral decadence of Renaissance mores, much more corrupt than those of the Middle Ages, and to the high ascetic ideals which Calvin proposed to, and to a great extent imposed on, the citizens of Geneva. It was also due to the fact that Protestant thought from the beginning refrained from listing marriage among the sacraments of the Gospel. The basic reasons for this are to be found in Luther's understanding of the Gospel, which was related essentially to the promise of justification. The sacraments of the Gospel are, for him, those which directly express the promise of justification, while other ceremonies and rites of the Church which do not directly express this promise are not sacraments of the Gospel even when prevailing usage does call them sacraments.

Whatever the validity of this reasoning, it effectively removed marriage from the realm of the sacred and placed it among secular realities. Indeed, had practice followed theory, this could have entailed a sacralization or a sanctification of the secular: once all human conditions were given the status and the dignity of vocations according to the spirit of the Gospel, human activity as such could have become holy in itself. The Puritans went far in this direction. In practice, however, the ethical overstress of Calvinism and of its sequel, Puritanism, made such a sacralization of institutions hardly possible. Likewise, Pietism, which was an outgrowth of Lutheranism, stressed the ethical and subjective dimensions of man's life. In both cases, marriage tended to become a private matter which was not the concern of the Church as such and could be abandoned to the care of secular authorities. As a natural rather than a sacramental institution, marriage came to be regulated mainly by the prevailing culture of society. The anthropology which is unavoidably implied in matrimony ceased to have a theological dimension.

There is even some irony in presenting Calvin as an emancipator of woman.

We read in his *Commentary on Genesis* that the punishment on woman for "having trespassed over her limits" consists in "being put back in them more narrowly." The difference between Paradise and the fallen state of man does not, as far as woman is concerned, lie between freedom and subservience, but between subservience and slavery. "She had indeed been subject to her husband, though this was an honest and by no means harsh subjection, but now she is placed as it were in slavery."[19] Admittedly, Calvin speaks of woman with a delicacy which is alien to Luther, and he parts with the Scholastic tradition, which Luther had not done, on the important matter of the purpose of womanhood: Eve was not given to Adam only to bear his children, but to be his companion. "As if," he objects, "she had been given to him only to sleep with him, and not to be the inseparable companion of his life."[20] Her purpose, which she is to learn from the account of her creation, is to "help him live more comfortably."[21] Eve is created from Adam in order to teach Adam to recognize himself in her "as in a mirror," and to teach Eve "to be willingly subject to her husband."[22] Indeed, "mankind, which was like a partly built edifice, has been perfected and finished in the person of the woman." Until then, "the male was only half the man"; once Eve had been created, Adam "saw himself complete in his wife, where he was only one half formerly."[23] For "man was created by God to be a creature of society. Then mankind could not subsist without woman." Through their legitimate union, "man and woman are united in one body and one soul."[24]

Yet if Calvin teaches the companionship of man and woman, he maintains the subservience of woman to man. Woman has in truth no name, since her name "means nothing else than 'woman of man.' "[25] So many of the women of the Old Testament never appear because they are, as befits them, "without a name of their own, being hidden in the shadow of their husbands."[26] For Calvin, woman enjoys more dignity than for Luther: polygamy is "a corruption of the true and legitimate marriage," and those who defend it today are "fanatics."[27] Yet man, who must "show himself to be her head and leader," may not, as Jacob did with Rachel, give her too much freedom.[28] She should be treated like a minor; and "holy heads of households should do all they can and omit nothing, in order that no spot of vice remains in their wives or their children."[29] In the proper order of society, woman stays at home, whether she is a virgin, a wife, or a widow. This is Calvin's commentary on the rape of Jacob's daughter Dina:

> Dina is kidnapped and raped because, having let her father's house, she went away and wandered in greater freedom than belonged to her. She should have stayed quietly at home, as the Apostle advises it (Titus 2:5) and as nature itself teaches it, for this virtue, which a common proverb attributes to women, that they must be keepers of the house, applies to

girls. For this reason the fathers are taught to keep their daughters under narrow watch if they want to protect them from all indignity. . . . One cannot doubt that Moses blames a part of the fault on Dina, when he says that she had gone out to see the girls of the area, whereas she should have stayed in the tent, within her mother's sight.[30]

The difference between man and woman in Calvin's eyes is also clearly brought out by his appreciation of the killing of adulteresses in Old Testament times. This was entirely proper, whether death was by stoning, as enjoined in the Law (Lev. 20:10), or by burning, as was done, he asserts, "by the common consent of all," before the Law was formulated: "It is most certain that this was done by divine inspiration, so that the holiness of matrimony would be protected by the guidance and mastery of nature as by a very solid fence." Calvin acknowledges that husband and wife have the same obligation of loyalty to each other. Yet he justifies the execution of the wife who has committed adultery, "whereas husbands who have fornicated with unmarried women are not subject to capital punishment." The purpose, he asserts, "was not only to punish impudicity, but also the dishonor of the husband by his wife, and next the furtive mingling of his posterity." The Law was actually more elaborate than this would seem to show, since, in Deuteronomy 22:22 and Exodus 16:40, capital punishment is inflicted on both the guilty wife and her male partner in sin. The sinning husband, however, went unpunished if his adultery was committed with an unmarried woman. Clearly, Calvin's standards of judgment in this case, like those of the Law itself, betrayed an assumption of the male superiority in marriage and a corresponding assertion of male pride.

After she has heard this, it is little comfort for woman to be told that her beauty is like that of Sara, God-given, or that it is entirely proper to marry a woman for her beauty, as long as "reason is always the mistress that will contain and bring into obedience the excess and the superabundance of love."[31] For male arrogance has provided the basic standard of discrimination between man and woman. Calvin's understanding of the Gospel inspires him with touching exhortations to men and women alike to live in faith and holiness. Yet, for all their genuine concern for the tasks of woman as mother, these texts add nothing to what was said on the same topic before the Reformation.

The purpose of this chapter is not to sketch the history of Protestant approaches to the problem of woman. Were we to do this, we would have to speak of the unorthodox speculations of Paracelsus,[32] of the aberrant views of Emanuel Swedenborg (1688-1772) on "heavenly marriage,"[33] of the interesting and important elements that can be drawn from the works of Schleiermacher (1768-1834)[34] and from the reflections of Søren Kierkegaard on woman, especially in *Either/Or* (1843) and in *Stages on Life's Way* (1845). We would also refer to less well-known authors, like Theodor Culmann (1824-

1863), for whom the fall begins with the creation of the female sex and the division of man into a duality away from his original solipsism (*Christliche Ethik,* 1867). Such an investigation would result in several, and to some extent contradictory, visions of woman, in which a great deal of philosophy, anthropology, and psychology would enter.

In the twentieth century, especially since the publication in 1951 of Karl Barth's long essay on man and woman in his *Church Dogmatics,* Protestant reflection on woman has aimed chiefly at recovering a strictly biblical view. Such an approach owes practically nothing to the Reformers, who turn out to be singularly unhelpful, and it differs both from "the mysticism of the Catholic woman and the modernism of her existentialist rival."[35] Such is the avowed purpose of Charlotte von Kirschbaum's slim volume, *Die wirkliche Frau* (1949):

> As one will see, I have tried, in the last chapter, to keep away from the Catholic doctrine of woman (Gertrude Von Le Fort) as well as from the existentialist theories (Simone de Beauvoir). These are two ways that we cannot follow. Our problem is to seek for the bases of an evangelical doctrine of woman.[36]

Accordingly, Charlotte von Kirschbaum's method is to comment on biblical passages, especially on the texts of Paul in Ephesians 5:21-32 and in 1 Corinthians 11 and 14. The picture which emerges shows man and woman as coresponsible before God and therefore as radically related to each other, whether it be in the common vocation of marriage or in the special charism of celibacy. Yet, within this unity of man and woman, woman remains "subordinate" to man. Far from being arbitrary, this expresses the basic order of redemption: the subordination of the Church to Christ.

> On the one hand, the obedience of woman and her subordinate position must witness that Christ is the prototype of all subordination; on the other, Christ glorified, the head of all domination and authority, is at the source of the authority assigned to man. The assertion that man is the head of woman is acceptable, as long as it is not separated from its Christological context.[37]

If this is so, the subordination of woman to man makes sense because it images and announces other ordered subordinations: that of the Church to Christ and that of Christ to the Father. In spite of Charlotte von Kirschbaum's statements to the contrary, this perspective remains close to that of Gertrude Von Le Fort: the being of woman is symbolic; its value derives from its transcendant pattern; and it calls for interpretation. It makes ultimately little difference whether the interpretation leans, like that of Gertrude Von Le Fort, toward postbiblical myths, or, like that of Charlotte von Kirschbaum, it wishes to remain strictly within biblical categories. The symbols that are invoked by the one and by the other differ in degrees, not in kind.

Charlotte von Kirschbaum was undoubtedly influenced by the theology of Karl Barth, even though Barth's consideration of "man and woman," in his *Church Dogmatics,* III/4, followed the publication of her short volume on the question. Barth made a systematic attempt to eliminate all possible myths about sex and specifically the myths that have been current in recent or contemporary thought. The myth of romanticism exalts woman to a quasi-divine level. In its Christian forms, it dominates, the thought of Schleiermacher. It is widespread in the Catholic and Orthodox searches for an "eternal feminine." And it pervades some of the "mystical" and more or less heterodox movements within Protestantism, as in the thought of Jacob Boehme (1575-1624), or outside of it, as with Nicholas Berdyaev (1874-1948). "We definitely reject," Barth proclaims, "every phenomenology or typology of the sexes."[38] Here as elsewhere, the dominant motif of Barth's theology is to follow the Word of God in its purity as it reaches us today.

It is not unimportant that the treatment of "man and woman" in the *Church Dogmatics* is set in the context of a long chapter on "the command of God the Creator." This provides the background of the question as an ethical problem: man and woman are called to follow God's command, and to fulfill what God intends by the creation of the sexes, participation in which is inescapable for all human creatures. Each human being is man or woman; each is also called to participate in the other sex and thus to reach the fullness of his own by relationship with the counterpart which unavoidably faces him or her in the unity of what Barth calls "fellow-humanity." Within the meaning of the Christian commitment, following God's command is a free act which itself becomes the source of further freedom. Thus, the question answered in terms of the man-woman relationship has been asked in terms of "freedom in fellowship." Man is called to be free. This freedom is achieved in fellowship. The typical fellowship to which man is universally called, whether he is married or not, is that which ties man and woman together.

When seen in the light of God's call, this relationship must be, in Barth's terms, "demythologized," "dedemonized," and "decentralized." Demythologizing drives away the fundamentally pagan idea, that the practice of sex opens a door into the divine, leads to a mystical realm of heavenly delights, raises man above his temporal condition. Sex must be limited to what it is, a basic human experience which implies an ethical demand. By dedemonization sex escapes the bounds of the sex organs in the strict sense. It belongs to a human being, or rather, since it is an instrument of relationships, to human beings, who must always be considered in their total personalities. "The point is that here particularly it is a question of the whole man and not merely of the use which he makes or does not make of his physical sexual organs." Sex is "a point of transition, having its own weight and honor in the whole, but not breaking loose from the whole."[39] There is no such thing as pan-sexuality. The whole in question (the *pan* of the Greek language) is man face to face with God, whether he is male or female. Decentralization means that, whereas the problem of man and woman finds its focus in marriage, it is itself broader, enveloping as it does everything that a human being does, for a human being is always a man facing woman, or a woman facing man, and he remains this even face-to-face with God. "It belongs to every human being to be male *or* female. It also belongs to every human being to be male *and* female: male in this or that distant relationship to the female, and female in a similar relationship to the male. Man is human, and therefore fellow-human, as he is male *or* female, male *and* female" (italics mine).[40]

When he asks, "What is the man in his sex, and the woman in hers?"[41] Barth rejects all typology: there is no way of knowing beforehand what maleness or femaleness may imply in the circumstances to which the Word will call and in which the divine command will be heard. Speculative attempts at defining man or woman in symbolic or metaphysical terms can do no more than canonize human preconceptions, to which the command of God is by no means bound. Admittedly, "such schemes can sometimes render us heuristic, exegetic and illustrative purposes." They can help us to read the text, but "it is not for us to write the text at all."[42] In other words, they can assist us in understanding ourselves and God's design; but they are neither the design nor a blueprint of ourselves. Only one basis can provide man with security for his self-understanding and for his relationships with others and with the other sex: "That man and woman—in the relationship conditioned by this irreversible order—are the human creature of God and as such the image of God and likeness of the covenant of grace: this is the secure theological knowledge with which we ourselves work and with which we must be content."[43] Man and woman together form God's image. Yet they enjoy no foreknowledge of what masculinity or femininity, as called by God's command in a concrete set of circumstances, may demand of them. "Life is richer, and above all the command of God is more manifold, than might appear from preconceived opinions."[44]

Barth draws from this a series of consequences: each sex has always its right place, and the relationship of both sexes is always irreversible, even if what this place will be cannot appear beforehand; human beings should be content with the sex that God has given them; they should not attempt to reverse their sexual roles; they should not try to transcend the polarity of the sexes, a temptation which is particularly attractive in the ascetic traditions and which always ends up by recreating the myths of a sexless, bisexual or transsexual humanity. These attitudes are flights from the command of God. Human beings have the duty of establishing relationships with the other sex, for "in obedience to the divine command there is no such thing as a self-contained and self-sufficient male life or female life."[45] This does not imply for all the duty to marry, but the duty to face the other sex in an attitude which Barth sums up under three heads: "They are to consider one another, to hear the question which each puts to the other, and to make responsible answer to the other."[46]

Out of this dialogue emerges an "order." As man remains man and woman remains woman, as they become partners without becoming identical, an order appears in which man and woman are fully equal before God, free in the Gospel, yet each with a proper place in relation to the other, "in such a way that A is not B, and B is not another A but B. . . . Order means succession. It means preceding and following. It means super-ordination and sub-ordination."[47] Thus Barth maintains a subordination of woman to man, which he considers to be implied in God's command to them. In all humility and obedience, for he stands before God, man must be "ordered, related and directed to woman in preceding her, taking the lead as inspirer, leader and initiator in their common being and action." Conversely, as man takes this position as a "primacy of service," woman, knowing that she loses nothing and does not thereby become inferior, for she also stands before the Lord, must "recognize that in order she is woman, and therefore B, and therefore behind and subordinate to man."[48]

At this point, it seems to me that Karl Barth has unwittingly reintroduced a myth: the myth of over and above, of before and after, of man the leader and woman the follower. This, of course, is justified for him by what he understands to be God's command, as found in the Old Testament (in the myth of Genesis) and in Paul, particularly in the Epistles to the Ephesians and to the Corinthians. But this is precisely the question: must the biblical witness be understood in this sense only? Can we not conceive that Christian freedom, the freedom of man with woman and of woman with man before God as coming to them in the Redeemer, has not itself been redeemed from the obligation of superiority and inferiority? In final analysis, Karl Barth has accepted an elementary form of what he has denounced in its developed forms, namely "a metaphysical order to which we should conform."

Emil Brunner's approach to the question of womanhood is disconcerting, beset with paradoxes or contradictions. In *The Divine Imperative,* originally published in German in 1932, Brunner insists on a point that he will maintain in his later writings: "Woman is not only physically different from man, she is also different in soul and spirit. . . . It is certain that the Creator who has created body and soul as a unity, has also created the mental and spiritual nature of woman different from that of man."[49] This was Thomas Aquinas's contention, based on Aristotelian hylomorphism. Brunner does not base it on technical philosophy, however, but on what he takes to be the fundamental purpose and rule of woman's being, as perceived by common sense, namely procreation: "So long as it is only women and not men who bear children and nurse them, so long also also the domain of woman will be essentially different from that of man."[50] In other words, it is from the physiology of woman that one may judge her mind and her soul. This is maintained in *Man in Revolt* (1937): Sex affects not only the body and the physiological functions but also the "psychical and spiritual being" of man and woman.[51] Accordingly, the difference between them is a "difference in kind,"[52] affecting the whole person, soul and body.

In spite of this, Brunner insists, against Karl Barth, that each human being is, in himself, the *imago Dei,* regardless of sex. "It is going too far to assert that the male and female existence of humanity is identified with the *imago Dei.*" What must be asserted is that "sex belongs, not only to the nature which has been created by God, but also to the *imago Dei,*"[53] a very peculiar doctrine, since it would imply that the human nature as created by God is not itself the image of God, and that the *imago* is an additional perfection. This obscurity affects Brunner's anthropology deeply, which wavers between a biblical, an Aristotelian, and a Platonic concept of the soul. The body is an instrument for the soul. In an Aristotelian psychology the soul is essentially linked to her body, whereas a Platonic psychology sees the soul as an entity in and by itself, which happens to operate, in this life, through a body. The *Dogmatics* describes the body as "the means of expression and the instrument of the spirit and the will. . . . [it] is full of the symbolism of [man's] divine-human destiny, and is admirably suited for its realization."[54] By contrast, "the spirit . . . is that aspect of human nature by means of which man can perceive his divine destiny and, knowing and recognizing this, can receive it, and transmit it to the body, as the instrument through which it is accomplished."[55] Here Brunner speaks in terms of a twofold anthropology. At other times he refers to a threefold anthropology, spirit (or *imago Dei),* soul (or psyche), and body. Thus, we read in *Man in Revolt:* "The differentiation of the biological sexual function in the man and the woman has its exact counterpart in the mental and spiritual nature of both sexes, although . . . it recedes in exact proportion to the measure in which the spirit, and the personal spirit in particular, becomes strong."[56] Accordingly, man and woman are body (biology, where sex reigns), mind and spirit (psychology, where sex reigns, as this is the counterpart of the first element), spirit (where the influence of sex recedes as the spirit waxes stronger). This hesitancy between several anthropologies illustrates the difficulty of accounting for antithetic notions at the same time: the belief that the image of God applies equally to man and woman in themselves rather than in their mutual relationship does not tally with the idea that man and woman differ "in kind," in "nature," and therefore in the totality of their body and soul.

This basic inconsistency leads to others. Emil Brunner makes woman a special kind of human being, whom he describes in relation to the body, even when the adverb "spiritually" is used:

> . . . it may be said that also spiritually the man expresses the productive principle and the woman expresses the principle of bearing, tending and nourishing. The man turns more to the outside world, the woman turns more to the inner realm; the man inclines to be objective, the woman to be subjective; the man seeks the new, the woman preserves the old; the man roams about, the woman makes a home.[57]

Pointing out the excesses to which woman is prone, Brunner continues:

> For her the relation between husband and wife is far more central than it is for her husband; in this she loses her universal destiny, her spiritual task, she allows herself to be persuaded by her husband that she belongs to the home and has no other responsibilities outside. She lays far more emphasis upon the fact of sex, she is far more sexual than the man, although the instinct within her, from the purely organic point of view, is not so acute and passionate. If the husband is falsely free, she is falsely bound; and if the husband is impersonal and intellectual, she tends to be personal and natural in a wrong way.[58]

This sort of psychological description has been taken for granted by men for centuries. Karl Barth rightly protests that there is no warrant for it in Christian Revelation. Brunner himself admits that "such a theory of sex is of course, like all such theories, to be accepted with all due reserve." Yet he makes it the cornerstone of his own understanding of woman, for he takes it as normative of what, in keeping with the divine imperative, woman should be: the "sexual disposition . . . helps to determine the whole psychical and even the spiritual nature of the man and the woman. Just as the whole physical nature of man is connected with and indeed penetrated by the organic sex function, so also is his psychical and spiritual being."[59]

In this case, one fails to understand why sex should disappear in the next world. Yet this is Brunner's belief. "The sex element belongs to the sphere of earth, not to that of heaven, to the temporal, not to the eternal."[60] "The sexual quality and function of man is full of the symbolism of true community.

The love between the sexes, the love of man and woman, is the earthenware vessel in which true love, *agape,* is to be contained; it can therefore be thrown away when the course in the preparatory school has achieved its end."[61] One may well ask what happens then to the spirit of man and woman, penetrated as they are, in Brunner's view, with sexuality. Anthropology and eschatology are at odds at this point.

Another inconsistency affects Brunner's description of the relationship of sex and spirit. This relationship is inescapable, since spirit is affected by the basic function of sex. Woman is motherly in all her being because she is destined to be a mother physically. Likewise, male aggressiveness dominates man's social and spiritual endeavors, because the male functions as the initiator in sexual relationships. Brunner's doctrine of original sin, however, introduces a dichotomy between these interpenetrating elements of human nature:

> Sin has entered into the sex relation in such a way that the sex nature and the personal life, sexuality and spiritual destiny, the sex creature and the spiritual creature have become separated. Shame is the expression of this separation, surprise at the fact that man is both the one and the other. Man now feels, and rightly, that the personal-spiritual element and the sexuality which he now has are incompatible, and thus he feels that from the point of view of personal existence sex does not belong to him; it is low, and base, humiliating, animal nature.[62]

This is, of course, dependent on a very profound notion of sin as a radical self-alienation of fallen man: sin penetrates as far as the connection in man between the physical and the spiritual. But there seems to be no corresponding description of overcoming this estrangement through grace, of the incomparable newness that the Christian reality has introduced into human self-understanding and into human relationships, of the freedom to which the faithful are called in Christ Jesus. Thus, in some passages, Brunner expresses some sympathy with the theories, which however he does not fully endorse, which identify man with the luminous, heavenly aspect of reality, and woman with the chtonic, infernal, demonic, dark aspect. Man is Apollonian and woman Dionysiac. Admittedly, Brunner clearly condemns this typology as incompatible with the biblical statement, "Male and female he created them." He objects that such a mythology deals with abstractions, and not with persons.[63] The struggle between "Apollo and the chtonic deities" does oppose man and woman; but it takes place within each of them in the form of a combat "between the brightness of the spirit and the darkness of passion," between "spirit and nature," between "spirit and sex."[64] In Brunner's anthropology, however, this struggle results in the profound feeling of shame which takes hold of man and woman at the very thought of nakedness and sexuality. At this point, it seems to me that Brunner does not describe a universal experience. The shame in question may well be a product of "civilization" rather than a requirement of the human condition. Were he to be logical in holding such shame as normative, he ought to add that men and women should be ashamed of each other no less than of themselves; and that the male should be particularly ashamed of the female who attracts him away from the spirit toward the divinities of the earth to which she is germane.

It seems ironical that Karl Barth, who explicitly rejects the sort of typology of womanhood that Brunner accepts without trusting it completely, should be quite assertive about the "order" in which men and women stand in relation to one another. Brunner seems more hesitant. At least in *The Divine Imperative* he concludes, though somewhat against his own arguments, that "a true marriage is only possible where the wife is in every way equal to the husband in independence and responsibility."[65] *Man in Revolt* paints a different picture. Physiological typology is taken as normative, as shown by the transition from "is" to "must" in the following text:

> The man is the one who produces, he is the leader; the woman is receptive, and she preserves life; it is the man's duty to shape the new; it is the woman's duty to unite it and adapt it to that which already exists. The man has to go forth and make the earth subject to him, the woman looks within and guards the hidden unity. The man must be objective and generalize, the woman must be subjective and individualize; the man must build, the woman adorns; the man must conquer, the woman must tend; the man must comprehend with all his mind, the woman must impregnate all with the life of her soul. It is the duty of the man to plan and to master, of the woman to understand and to unite.[66]

Brunner logically adds, "In these distinctive qualities there lies a certain super- and sub-ordination."[67] Thus we are back in the myth of man the leader and woman the obedient follower.

In these instances, the Protestant tradition has not proposed a theological model for womanhood. At its worst, it has repeated clichés that have no special theological relevance, at times giving them theological sanction. At its best, it has tried to discover a strictly biblical anthropology. It has preserved ideas coming from the older Catholic tradition, especially in its medieval form, and it has borrowed notions from contemporary secular research, chiefly psychological and phenomenological. Given the Reformation emphasis on the pure Gospel, one may wonder if a strictly Protestant theological anthropology is possible and therefore if a Protestant doctrine of womanhood may be formulated. This need not be a disparaging remark. Indeed, it coincides with the contention of Françoise Florentin-Smyth in her essay quoted at the beginning of this chapter. Karl Barth has made the most thorough attempt to detail a theology of womanhood. The result is a very biblically inspired reflection which contains valuable insights on the interrelationship of man and woman and on their being interrelatedly the image of God. Emil Brunner has proposed what is to me a very pessimistic view of sex and of mankind in general, one most unlikely to inspire anyone with much devotion to the task of being a man or a woman...

One will have noticed that all the authors mentioned have steered clear from any consideration of models properly so called: neither Mary, nor the Holy Spirit, nor the divine Sophia have been called upon to tell us what woman is. This is in keeping with the common Protestant stance on Mariology, although there is no reason why Protestantism should avoid a reflection on the Spirit, if such a reflection can bring some light to bear on our topic. The basic concern to remain close to Scripture and to avoid theological elaborations that tend in a myth creating direction may still explain the absence of Pneumatological considerations at this point.

It would seem that with the outmoded anthropology of the Reformers, with the passing of the predominant influence of Karl Barth, with the unpopularity of the neo-Calvinism of Emil Brunner, and with the corresponding rise of phenomenologically oriented theologies, the Protestant woman is left to the perspective opened before her by Françoise Florentin-Smyth: to share with joy "the uncertainties and the impatient reflection of our contemporaries."[68]

9

Toward an Anthropology

A Christian anthropology should keep a double focus, on man as he is and on what the Christian tradition so far has said about him. By "man as he is," I understand man as he experiences himself in our time. For we cannot directly experience mankind in any other way. Whether or not we assume that man has physically and spiritually evolved as he has developed culturally, we can experience only the present point of such an evolution. Therefore, an anthropology cannot deal in the first place with man as he was created. This has been the basic tendency of theologians who have considered the question of man in the light of the first chapters of Genesis: from this they are likely to pass, through speculative reflection, to certain assumptions about the nature of man, distinguishing the four aspects of pure nature, actual nature before the fall, fallen nature, redeemed nature. Nor can anthropology speak of man as reflection may determine his chief essential and existential features, though this has been the basic tendency of philosophers. Anthropology concerns man as he lives today. Only from this vantage point can one reach conclusions that will be valid for the men of all times and civilizations, although one cannot be certain a priori that such will effectively be the case. Accordingly, a theological reflection on woman should not take as its chief focus the feminine image of the Virgin Mary, even though this image has long been close to centrality in the faith of large numbers of Christians. The Virgin Mary ought to come within the scope of our study only insofar as she is a woman and thus participates in the general structure of womanhood, if such a structure is to be discovered. For this reason, the ancient or modern models of womanhood which present Mary as the theological pattern for all believing women suffer from a radical fallacy.

One cannot build a theology in historical isolation anymore than in the abstract. Consideration of woman today will avoid abstraction. Insertion of our thought in the continuity of Christian tradition will avoid isolation. What we see and think of woman today is necessarily tied to what was seen and thought formerly. The difficulty comes when we try to assess what in this tra-

187

dition remains normative and what was too influenced by local or temporary conditions, by contingent cultural patterns, by human prejudice, and by philosophical bias to be valid for today. Our historical survey has shown that the theological stance concerning woman, her function in mankind and her place in the Church, was dominated originally by Jewish, Greek, and Roman patterns of thought and behavior. Into these forms that were borrowed, even the Jewish ones, from the societies of the day, the Christian Revelation, in the wake of the Abrahamic, Mosaic, and Prophetic revelation, wedged an element of newness, of fermentation, perhaps we may even say of revolution. Yet this element could only take shape in the context of prevailing cultural forms, which to a great extent contradicted it. And so forms of thought or behavior essentially alien to the Christian message have carried through the centuries the seeds of transformation which this message entailed. As I see it, the task of a theological reflection on womanhood lies here: we should disentangle the inner message and its containers. For these, whether they were biblical or came to the fore in the course of the Christian tradition, have, like old skins bursting with new wine, shown themselves to be in disharmony with their content.

A central affirmation is undoubtedly to be kept: man (as *anthropos* or *homo,* that is, both man and woman) is created in God's image. This holds true for today as well as for any other period. It is sufficiently asserted in all the biblical and traditional data to be beyond discussion. But what cannot escape discussion is the precise meaning of this "image." Some options have been proposed that cannot be avoided, although we need not investigate the question of the effects of sin upon this image, for the determination of these effects should naturally depend on the previous identification of the image. In the main, I would distinguish two possibilities.

1) The image of God lies in the spiritual nature of man (I take the word "nature" in this context to cover the data with which man starts life, that which is given to him and which he has to develop, "cultivate," through what must be called culture). In his spiritual nature, man is endowed with faculties which allow him to act in ways radically different from animals. He thinks and he wills. By his intellectual and voluntary powers, he is the natural image of God, which will be transformed and elevated by grace to a higher level through new strengths corresponding to these faculties, namely faith (transforming the intellect) and love or charity (transforming the will). By and large, this was the Scholastic approach. It was deeply indebted to Augustine's analysis of the mind in connection with Trinitarian reflection. Both Augustine and his medieval followers could thus relate the image of God to the inner relationships of the Holy Trinity as known through Christian Revelation: the in-

tellect corresponds to the Word, and the will to the Spirit. Hence man is an image of the Holy Trinity, of the Persons in God, of God's inner life, rather than an image of the divine nature in its undividedness. To the question of what in man corresponds to the Father, the Augustinian-Scholastic answer would have pointed to the very essence or being of man, which is the source of all his potentialities, as the Father is the fountainhead of the divine life. A later author of considerable importance, Saint John of the Cross (1542-1591) identified the most basic element of the Trinitarian image in man with the power of memory, memory here implying not only the retention of knowledge and experience, but also the continuity of man with his own self.

If this analysis is applied to the problem of womanhood, it allows an interesting conclusion. According to the Aristotelian contention, the intellect predominates in man (as *anêr* or *vir*), whereas the third faculty prevails in woman (the will being affectivity and love rather than the modern will-to-power). If this is correct, it follows that man and woman are differentiated at the most fundamental level of their spiritual existence. For in this case man images the Trinity with the chief focus on the Son, whereas woman images the Trinity with the chief focus on the Spirit. In this case, the anthropologies that make the female soul distinct from the male soul, and those which assign to woman a pneumatic function analogous to that of the Spirit, become plausible.

2) With a concern that is more biblical than speculative and that looks to the earlier rather than the later Christian tradition, the image of God in man may be identified with the duality of human existence. It is not as Adam or as Eve that human beings are images of God, but in their interrelatedness as Adam and Eve, or rather as Adam-with-Eve and Eve-with-Adam. A totally different perspective opens. There may be differences in it concerning the extent to which the duality of mankind, and therefore the image, includes sex in the strict sense. Is the duality inscribed in the structure of mankind a psychological and functional dichotomy to which the complement of physiological sex is superadded (though not necessarily in a later time sequence)? Or does the duality of man and woman imply maleness and femaleness necessarily and from the beginning? Under the influence of Origen and of Gregory of Nyssa, the separation between sex and the duality of the image as man-and-woman tended to prevail among the Greek Fathers. This in turn tallied with the efforts of the monastic and ascetic movement to bring man to the level of an angelic, sexless life. The ambiguity and, at the same time, the rich possibilities of this approach are patent. Should the image reside in a man-woman relationship beyond sex, then the abolition of sex would be theoretically possible in this life. Man and woman must relate to each other, though not necessarily through sex. New spiritual relationships may be envisaged, as in the case of *mulieres subintroductae*. The fact that such ill-fated experiences were soon discontinued simply shows that what was theoretically possible was not prac-

tically feasible; yet this need throw no doubt on the basic principle that the image of God lies in the interrelationship of man and woman.

It would seem to follow from this that neither man nor woman alone is the image of God. In the concrete life of Christians, the image would not be a datum so much as an ideal. The faithful should develop and deepen the image of God in themselves or, better said, their participation in the image of God. How this may be done will depend on the option that has been made concerning sex. If sex itself belongs to the basic structure of the image, then there would seem to be no way to fulfill oneself as the image of God but through the companion of the other sex who will allow us to become, together with her or him, a fully developed image. The image is androgynous and must be actualized through marriage. From this point of view, the ascetic and monastic movements would appear to have been fundamental misorientations. The sacrament of the image would be matrimony. Needless to say, although this path was a distinct possibility, it has never been followed in orthodox Christianity.

If, on the other hand, the image lies in the self-differentiation of mankind as man-woman, yet has been set from the beginning beyond physiological sex, then we face a very different horizon. Manhood and womanhood are two ways of being human, each of which needs the other as its spiritual and psychological complement, even though physiological complementation need not be sought. Neither man nor woman is the image of God; but man and woman participate in the image only to the extent that they share in the functions and characteristics of the other.

In both cases, man will be associated with the Word and woman with the Spirit. No justification for this is needed other than the historical fact of the Incarnation of the Word as the man Jesus of Nazareth and the typification of the Church as the realm of the Spirit's activity, under feminine images, as has been the case throughout Christian tradition, in continuity with the symbolism of the Old Testament where Israel is the bride of Yahweh.

In both cases, too, the image results from creation: man is created in the image of God. The Incarnation and the redemption and sanctification of mankind add nothing new to this; no added level of grace is needed. Yet the Incarnation transforms the context of human life and assigns to it a goal that could not even be discerned before, the goal of deification through the sacramental and mystical life, that is, through the transformation of human existence by the advent of God into it.

In view of these different trends of the tradition, one conclusion seems to be justified. The image of God cannot be a solipsist endowment of each human being by himself, On this point Scholastic theology must be overcome. Yet I cannot see the image as residing specifically in a man-woman relationship, whether this takes place at the level of sex through the sacrament of marriage, or at a spiritual level through the cooperation and complementation of man and woman in Church and society. This would seem much too narrow, as it would in fact exclude from the image the entire monastic movement, although this was effectively for centuries the heart of the Church in both East and West. If the image lies neither in the soul of man as an entity by itself, nor in the togetherness of man and woman, then only one possibility remains. It resides in the interrelatedness of man with others, regardless of whether these are men or women. The seat of the image is the *person*, as distinguished from the solipsist individual. A person is interrelated with others; to be a person is to be a center of interpersonal relationships. This expression does not mean that relationships bring together totally constituted persons, but that an individual becomes a person through such relationships. I would therefore say that, insofar as man is born an individual, he is not in the image of God; yet as soon as he interrelates with others (which means, in practice, as soon as a midwife or a doctor or his mother picks him up) he then begins to become a person. Thus man is in the image of the Trinity, in which the Persons are essentially interrelated.

Biblical tradition has focused on man and woman this interrelatedness of the image of God, for the simple reason that the most basic type of human relationship is the one that unites men and women. More than any other one, this relationship calls each of them out of self-centeredness into a new and rather different way of being human, teaching each of them forms of thought or intuition with which they would not otherwise be so familiar and ways of sharing and loving to which they would otherwise remain strangers. This, I would maintain, happens whenever two persons relate to each other, regardless of whether they are men or women. The man-woman relationship is, nonetheless, the very type of this happening. I would therefore conclude that the image of God in man lies in man's interrelationship with others as exemplified in the man-woman relationship, or, equivalently, in the man-woman relationship as the type of all human relationships.

Such a conception of the image allows us to preserve the valuable insights of the Augustinian-medieval conception. For man relates himself to other human beings through the aspect of his personality which seeks association with others. Human association is radically different from the types of associations that prevail among animals, in that it is free: man can enter into a group or withdraw from it at will, according to his likes and dislikes, his decisions, and his conceptions of himself. In other words, human relationships are not restricted to the tribal networks of associations into which man is born. Men are normally, in the course of their development, called on to transcend the limitations of their clan, caste, class, city, province, nation. Such movements beyond set relations are consummated in the intellect and the will. Accordingly, it is not entirely erroneous to see the seat of God's image in the two faculties of the soul which classical psychology calls the intellect and the will. Yet these provide only the tools with which one may become the image of God. They themselves are not the image; they are preconditions of it.

We have described the image of God in man in nonstatic terms. Man must grow into the image which the grace of God destines him to be. What this entails cannot fully appear unless we also consider the final purpose. Toward what climax is the spiritual development of man headed? Image of God, in the context of Christian Revelation, means image of the Trinity. The Trinity is neither an abstract concept nor merely a way of speaking about God. Some modern authors give the impression of understanding Trinitarianism as a form of thought which primarily affects man and only secondarily tells us something of God. As such, it only points to man's ultimate inability to think about the absolute in other than dialectical fashion: the absolute is reached by human thought only at the crosspoint of three lines of reflection, each of which corresponds to one aspect of the Divinity. But the Christian tradition sees much more in the doctrine of the Trinity. The Three Persons are real; and there is no God or Divinity outside of them. It is not correct even to say that Godhead is a reality equally shared by three transcendent Persons or centers of awareness and attribution. Godhead is not a fourth reality in which the Three meet. It is the very reality of each divine Person, and it is what each Person is in itself, in relationship to the other Two. These are not aspects of the Divinity (the "modalist" or Sabellian error) but genuine centers of being: three centers of the same transcendental being.

These remarks point the direction in which we must seek for the ultimate scope of the image of God in man. Man is invited by creation and by grace to fulfill himself through participation in the life of the Three Persons. He is the image of God to the extent that he himself experiences the Three-ness of the divine life. This of course cannot be achieved by any merely human means, or reached at the end of an ascetic process of self-purification along neo-Platonic or yogic lines; it is itself a gift from God, who, little by little, measuring man's progress with man's capability to progress, brings each man into oneness with himself.

There are several traditional names for this process. The Orthodox tradition, faithful to the emphasis of the Greek Fathers, calls it a "deification," a term which obviously remains highly symbolic yet which adequately expresses what then takes place: man's own life becomes itself Trinitarian. It is the very life of God in the recesses of the human being. The Latin tradition has also used the term "deification," though its Scholastic representatives have preferred to use other terms, like elevation to God, or beatitude, or transformation into God. For example, Thomas Aquinas writes: "It belongs to the rank and dignity of man to be raised to the divine realities inasmuch as man has been made in the image of God."[1] Or: "As to its object, beatitude is simply the Supreme Good; as to its act, it is the Supreme Good in the beatified creature, not absolutely but insofar as the creature is able to share in it."[2] The *Summa against the Pagans* develops the point that the human intellect can be raised to the vision of the divine Essence by "participation" in a "divine light."[3]

As used by the Western mystics, the language of participation becomes less guarded than with the systematic theologians. Thus John of the Cross, who blends a rich mystical experience with a Thomistic theology, defines man, in some remarkable texts, as "God by participation." In the "spiritual marriage," he writes in *The Spiritual Canticle*, "the soul becomes divine, becomes God through participation, insofar as is possible in this life."[4] Then the soul "enjoys in security and quietude the participation of God."[5] Such a union is of course a union to the Three Persons of God:

> Granted that God favors her [the soul] by union with the most Blessed Trinity, in which she becomes deiform and God through participation, how could it be incredible that she also understand, know and love—or better that this is done in her—in the Trinity, together with it, as does the Trinity itself! Yet God accomplished this in the soul through communication and participation. This is transformation in the Three Persons in power and wisdom and love, and thus the soul is like God through this transformation. He created her in His image and likeness that she might attain such resemblance.[6]

These expressions—union with, transformation into, participation in, deformity—are not the language of a few schools only. They indeed express a theological consensus which is echoed by the more guarded style of the Councils. Thus the Constitution *Verbum Dei* of Vatican II, quoting a formula already contained in Vatican I's Constitution *Dei Filius,* says:

> In Divine Revelation God has wanted to show and to share himself and the eternal decisions of his will concerning man's salvation, "that they may participate in the divine wealth, which utterly exceeds the human mind's comprehension."[7]

If such is the Catholic tradition concerning man as image of God, no distinction may be made between men and women at this level. The image of God follows upon the presence of God in man, the Three Persons in each human being. Men and women are alike in this respect. No specific Trinitarian relationship is proper to women or to men. Woman therefore cannot enjoy a special relationship to the Spirit which would not also be open to man, just as man cannot have a special relationship to the Son which would not also be open to woman. The various attempts that have been made to define man or woman by analogy with the Son or the Spirit cannot be followed; they would lead to a differentiation within God which simply does not correspond to the reality. The sophiological efforts in that direction can only lead to erroneous Trinitarian views.

A similar conclusion may be reached by reflection on the mystery of Christ, the "only mediator between God and man" (1 Tim. 2:5) and therefore the savior of men and women equally.

If man is defined, as "God by participation," if the purpose of the Christian life is a deification by the elevation of man into the realm of the divine, it follows that there is only one perfect man, only one man who entirely fulfills the definition of humanity, in whom participation in God and deification are totally and absolutely achieved: this is Jesus Christ. Being the assumed nature of the Word of God, his human nature fully participates in the divine life. The classical concept of the "communication of properties"[8] between the divine and the human in Jesus is the ineluctable consequence of the extent to which the humanity of Jesus shares the divine life. "Out of his fulness we all have received grace upon grace" (John 1:16). That is, in the mystery of God's design for mankind, the assumption of the humanity of Jesus into the realm of the divine through its personal link with the Word becomes the means by which every man can be raised to deification. Jesus is the only model and the only mediator. His grace is, in the Scholastic phrase, *gratia capitis*,[9] a grace which, as head of the human race, he shares with all who believe. Men and women stand on the same footing in relation to the grace of Christ. Here there can be no distinction. It is impossible to hold that men would find the divine-human model of their perfection in Jesus Christ, whereas women would find theirs in the Virgin Mary.

The focus of Trinitarian and Christological reflection invites us to take very seriously the conclusion of our biblical study. Christianity implies the total emancipation of woman, the complete removal of the inferiority in which society has kept her and which the authors of the Old Testament attributed to a curse pronounced at the beginning of mankind as a result of an original sin. Facing their call to the Trinitarian life, men and women cannot be differentiated. Likewise, they are alike in relation to Christ. This is further supported by the sacramental order, in which, in contradistinction to that of the Old Testament, men and women receive the same sacraments. Unlike the rite of circumcision, there is no baptism for men that would not also be a baptism for women.

Through the mystery of baptism, the primal order of the universe is restored. This entails a reversal of values for society, where men have dominated women, reduced to a form of slavery. Does it also imply, as our biblical study also seemed to show, that women should be, as in the Eden described in Genesis, the spiritual model of human perfection? On this point, the final answer cannot be provided by the Old Testament. The authors and redactors of Genesis could conceive of a restored order of the universe only as a return to the beginning. Lacking other terms of comparison they could image this Edenic ideal only by contrast with the daily experience of their times. Thus they presented Eden as the reverse of history, and the lot of Eve before the fall as the reverse of her lot after the fall. Instead of physical, mental, and moral inferiority, they crowned her with spiritual superiority over Adam. In effect, however, the Incarnation did not restore a previous order but instored a new one. The realm of redemption, even as it will be fully achieved in the Kingdom, is not Paradise. It is an entirely new domain. In it, the model of human perfection can be neither manhood nor womanhood; it cannot be a concrete human person, whether male or female. The model is the God-man, the Word made flesh. There is no other to be sought. Thus, the Christian reality is different from that which the Old Testament described as the Edenic order of the universe. The perfection of mankind does not reside in Eve or even in Mary, but only in the Lord Jesus. And what faith perceives in him is neither maleness nor even manhood alone, but manhood as transformed by the pervading presence of the divine *Logos,* that is, Emmanuel, God-with-us, God become one of us. Accordingly, a Christian anthropology must transcend the differentiation of the sexes which still dominates the prelapsarian anthropology of the Bible. The model of woman, as the model of man, is the Word of God Incarnate.

Several of the trends examined in the last few chapters have connected woman in a special way with the Spirit. We should now face the Pneumatological question as it relates to a Christian anthropology. The differentiation of mankind into male and female has been seen as somehow patterned on the differentiation between the *Logos* and the Spirit in God. This has been facilitated by the linguistic phenomenon that the word for "spirit" in the Semitic languages (*rouach* in Hebrew; *rōūchā* in Syriac) is of the feminine gender. While neither Latin nor Greek or standard Russian theology was directly affected by this linguistic pressure, Russian sophiology has been influenced by it. This could be grounded theologically in the prophetic application to Israel of the concept of the bride of Yahweh, which was followed by the patristic analogy between the *Ecclesia tou Theou* (the Church of God) and the bride of the Lord. Accordingly, the relationship between Christ and the Church his bride is seen as an image of the eternal relationship between the Word and the

Spirit in the dyad of the divine processions. It is significant that the controversies over the *Filioque* did not hurt this analogy in either East or West, for Greek theology, which tends to deny the eternal procession *ab utroque,* nevertheless teaches that, in his mission in this world, the Spirit is also sent by the Incarnate Lord: thus the analogy between the Church and the Spirit may still be deemed acceptable at the level of the order of the Incarnation. Russian theology, which has been less averse to the doctrine of the procession *ab utroque,* could more easily entertain the notion of an eternal prototype for the marriage between Christ and the Church in the union of the *Logos* and the *Pneuma.*

The meaning of this analogy depends in the first place on the theological conception of the Holy Spirit in God and, secondarily, on the understanding of the specific elements of womanhood which would relate to the Spirit. This line of thought I find particularly attractive, although I entertain some reservations about it. On account of this, I will attempt to present it systematically.

Whatever its exact description may be, the image of God in man is not a static quality. It does not simply imply a likeness, a proportionality, a resemblance between God and man. Furthermore, it entails that the reality which is God's image has become a channel of divine power and presence. This is inseparable from the statement that the image "shares" in what it represents. But what does sharing imply? One can envision it in at least two different ways. God himself, may be thought of in his oneness or in his threeness. Does the image of God in man refer to the oneness of God, to what classical theology calls his "nature"? Or to the differentiated life of the three Persons? In his oneness, God appears, in relation to creation, as the divine ground of all things, as the abyss in and out of which the Three Persons are seen and by which they are sustained, since the content of each Person is no other than the totality of the divine nature. In his threeness this eternal abyss of being manifests itself in three types of life, which we call Father, Son, and Spirit. It can then be looked at from the standpoint of each of the Persons. The Father is ultimately identified with the very notion of divine abyss: he is the abysmal depth of the divine, never to be contacted directly, never to be seen in himself, for he manifests himself only through the two Persons who proceed from him, the Son and the Spirit. The one who tries to see the Father can only reach the Spirit and the Son, the Father standing behind them as the ground from which they come, to which they point, but which they never show face to face. No one has seen the Father. Yet the one who sees the Son sees the Father also, for the Son is all that the Father is, except fatherhood, except origin and abyss. And the one who sees the Spirit sees the Father also, for the Spirit is the Spirit of the Father, sent to do the Father's work in the wake of the incarnation of the Son. The Son, or Word, expresses the Father: this is his life, and his being consists precisely in this manifestation—manifestation to himself in all eternity and to man by creation and redemption. He reflects, in the sense of receiving and sending back all that the Father is. He keeps nothing for himself and he has nothing of his own, for all that he has is the Father's. All that he is is the divine nature as present in, and given to him by, the Father. The only element that defines him as a distinct Person is precisely this distinctiveness of being the one who receives in order to give back.

As for the Spirit, his personality, though clearly affirmed in the tradition, is more difficult to visualize. For if the Father has given all he is to the Son, except the precise fact of being the Father and the origin of all, nothing would seem to be left to specify the Spirit. Christian theology has attempted to see the Spirit as the one who returns, who gives back to the Father what came from him: thus he is called the bond of the Trinity, the link of love between the Father and the Son. This is obviously a neo-Platonic diagram: the emanation from the One through the Son returns to the One through the Spirit. Following Gregory Nazianzen and Augustine, most classical thought has understood the Spirit on the pattern of the spiritual faculties of the soul: the Son would correspond to the intellect, and the Spirit to the will. In the Latin Middle Ages, Richard of Saint Victor saw the Three Persons as three phrases of the self-substantive divine love: the Lover (identified with the Father), the Beloved (identified with the Son), and the love which unites them (being the Spirit). Sergius Bulgakov explained the Spirit as necessary to the fullness of fatherhood in the First Person: in human experience, the fullness of fatherhood requires not only a son, but a son and a daughter, otherwise the generative powers of the father have not been fully tested and he has exercised fatherhood with only one-half of mankind. Likewise, the divine Fatherhood would require two Persons, whom we call Son and Spirit, these corresponding to sons and daughters in mankind.

In any case, the Spirit is the more mysterious of the divine processions. In relation to man, he does not reveal, for the only revealer is the Son; but he manifests what has been revealed. He does not redeem, for the redeemer is the Son; but he sanctifies those who have been redeemed, guiding them into all the truth. In relation to the Father, we cannot know for certain what he is, except that he is neither the Father nor the Son, and that all that he is and does is related to the Father as the ultimate fount of divine life, and to the Son as the one to whom all that the Father is and has already been given. His very existence as God emphasizes the gratuitousness of the divine life: he is supernumerary, logically unaccountable, unnecessary, yet He is. His being is the supreme challenge to man's intellect. How can we conceive in God himself, what strikes us as superfluous? He is also the supreme challenge to man's love. How can man love the One who is without self-consistence, being totally gift, of whom one cannot even say that the Father gives himself to him (as He does to the Son), the One who never manifests himself, but always points to another; enlightens, but has no light of his own that he can show; guides but never guides toward himself?

Thus, the Christian life is lived in the Spirit, but never directed toward him. The Spirit is the one "in whom we live and move and have our being" (Acts 17:28). If, in relation to man, there is a divine Person who functions as "the air we breathe"[10] as the womb that bears and nourishes, it is the Spirit. If the Father is the eternal abyss, in whom the Second and the Third Persons subsist, if the Son, being constituted by the Father's total self-gift, contains in himself the eternal types of all created beings, it is yet the Spirit who bears this world in himself, guiding it, from the first moment of creation, toward the Father, watching over it as over the waters of chaos and bringing order into it, preparing it for the Incarnation and guiding the Church of the Lord Incarnate to fulfill its function in fidelity and holiness. The Spirit is the last and final agent, in whom all things find their eschatological dimension. He is the one who overcomes the divisiveness of the created world, bringing all things to reconciliation and unity.

These remarks throw light on the theologies that find a special correspondence between womanhood and the Spirit. The Father's eternal partner (what the sophiologists would call the divine Sophia) is the dyad of the *Logos* and the Spirit. As I understand it, this is the true meaning of the doctrine of *Filioque:* in his own procession, the Spirit remains in the Son, thus maintaining the Oneness of the two Persons who proceed from the Father. This unity of the Father's eternal coequal is a di-unity, a di-archy, differentiated into two distinct Persons. On this pattern the created image of God will be bipolar, reflecting back the Son and the Spirit, in a unity of oneness and differentiation. Within mankind as image of God, one pole corresponds to the Son and the other to the Spirit. The Spirit is the divine model of woman, because he is the Third, the last, the one in whom divinity reaches the fullness of its manifestation, just as woman, in the story of Genesis, is the perfection, the bond, the acme of mankind. Thus maleness would correspond to the Son, femaleness to the Spirit; and both together constitute the image of God, just as the diarchy of the Son and the Spirit full manifest the Father.

It so happens that in human experience woman does fulfill some of the functions of the Spirit and somehow acts in a manner more reminiscent of the Spirit than of the Word of God. Woman in history has been hidden, mysterious, incomprehensible, active yet gearing her activity toward another, a husband or a child. In most countries of Western civilization, she has no real name, since she loses her name at marriage and acquires a name which is not hers. She works at home, and even when she works outside, she holds less glamorous jobs than men, being more often than not the adjunct of a man, for instance, as a secretary or a typist. The task where she excels relate to education, so that she may be seen there as a mother more than as a wage earner or as the author of a creative activity she may call her own. The qualities commonly attributed to her are humility, receptivity, fidelity, patience, care for others, concern for continuity, tradition, and unity. The comparison is plain between these aspects and what Christian theology says of the Spirit; and the conclusion that woman is meant by divine design to be the image of the Spirit is very tempting indeed.

However, this line of thought runs into a difficulty. The characteristics thus assigned to womanhood cannot be seen in the simple context of "nature," in which they would represent and correspond to the will of the creator of nature. As far as man is concerned, nature, that is, the datum with which man starts, does not exhaust his environment. For man has built and is continually building a culture, which he adds to and with which he transforms nature. This raises a major question regarding the origin of these characteristics of woman: Do they derive from nature or from culture? If from nature, then woman's destiny is fixed once and for all; and one may define her task in relation to the Spirit, whom she somehow resembles. But if from culture, then woman cannot be simply related to the Spirit: culture—that is, society and education—has given her what seem to be her major qualities. And one may conceive of another type of society in which a different culture would assign her other tasks. The old myth of a land of Amazons is highly relevant here. Woman can be conceived of as other than she is. In other words, what she seems to be neither derives from nature nor represents an unalterable law of her being. It ensues from culture and has been produced by certain types of civilization. Another type of civilization can emancipate her from the yoke of her traditional functions and attitudes.

Precisely, the Christian message, as we have determined it so far, has been one of liberation. The advent of Christ means the possibility of woman's escape from the curse, for the curse is now lifted from all who believe. Woman is no longer secondary and subservient; she is second insofar as the first waits for her coming; and she typifies mankind in its perfection, bringing to its climax the process of creation begun with Adam. What therefore the Spirit represents cannot be a final predetermined model for woman, any more than the Word (in his divinity, or in his incarnate life as Jesus Christ) is a final, predetermined model for man. Christ is a model for all, men and women alike. In these conditions, the Spirit is indeed relevant to woman, insofar as he presents her, not with a destiny, but with a vocation; and he is equally relevant to man, to whom also he offers a possible option.

What this amounts to is that both man and woman, realizing themselves as images of God, imitate the eternal image, the unity of the Word with the Spirit as the revelation and manifestation of the Father. But they may be spiritually attracted to, and they may imitate more specifically either of the two Persons who constitute the eternal image. The Son and the Spirit confront us with distinct, though related, callings, to which certain qualities correspond and which are to be manifested through certain behavioral patterns. That most women who care enough to think about it would find it congenial to carry out the tasks of the Spirit does correspond to the data that have accumulated so far regarding woman in history. Nonetheless, as woman in history is an inextricable mixture of nature (God-made, necessary) and of culture (man-made, contingent), one cannot assert with any degree of certainty that this will be true of all women at all times, or that it is more natural or better for woman to imitate the Spirit and to conceive of herself as an approximation of the Spirit, destined to reach spiritual and psychological fulfillment through the tasks of the Spirit as exemplified in the so-called feminine virtues and qualities. It would even seem that the more a woman has progressed in Christian holiness—that is, the freer she has become from the curse and its consequences in society—the freer she is to follow paths that society does not usually recognize as legitimate feminine pursuits. Thus Joan of Arc, leading a victorious army against the English and Burgundian factions, does not make much sense and is to be considered a freak of history, unless one thinks of her in the words of Charles Peguy, as *la sainte la plus grande après sainte Marie.*[11] Likewise with Saint Catherine of Sienna, who brought Pope Gregory XI, much against his own judgment, back from Avignon to Rome in 1377.

The more a woman becomes God-like, the freer she is to take positions of leadership, because on the one hand she can imitate equally well the Son and the Spirit in keeping with her charism of the moment, and, on the other, she has risen above the demands and prejudices of society. At the same time, if women may be called to male virtues and situations usually associated with the Son, men also, raised by grace above the conditions imposed on them by society and culture, may become notable examples of classical feminine virtues and be characterized by humility, hiddenness, and devotion to others, thus achieving in their work a sort of motherhood over the Church and the world. And this has characterized many saints.

The previous considerations have been made from the standpoint of God as Three Persons. We have seen how the doctrine of the image relates man and woman to the Son and the Spirit; and we have found that such a relationship can only be a matter of call, grace, and choice. There is no set pattern for either man or woman. Each may grow into a living image of the Word or of the Spirit, or of both, since each is structurally related to both. The response to one's vocation, the types of piety and of activity, the attractions and achievements that predominate in a given person result from grace and its charisms, not from predetermined orientations of men toward the Word or of women toward the Spirit.

This is consistent with the basic theological principle that the works of God *ad extra,* that is, creation and all that is comprised by it, are effected by God in his unity, in what has traditionally been called the divine "nature." Although creation is usually connected with the Father as the ultimate source of all things, the act of creating cannot be attributed to any of the Three Persons exclusively. It is a common action, an activity of the divine nature which belongs equally to the Three. Accordingly, all that is made by God proceeds equally (though not in the same way) from the Three Persons. Differentiation belongs to the order of the imagination, pedagogy, and manner of speaking, not to the ontological order. There can therefore be only one fundamental attitude of the creature toward God: receptivity. For the creature is essentially constituted by the reception of God's action, a reception which is so total that it makes this creature to be. Man, just as woman, is purely receptive of God's will and action. Mankind has agreed to call receptivity a feminine attitude, since in most societies woman has been attributed chiefly receptive functions. If this is so, then womanhood is the very type of creatureliness. All mankind, and all creation seen from the standpoint of the reception of the creative act, is feminine. Therefore, if we remain within the context of the feminine type as determined by our culture, it is not the female, but the male, who is the anomaly. All creation being receptive and feminine in relation to God, a male type of activity, like aggressiveness, drive to power or domination, can only be an attempt to escape the realm of creatureliness, an attempt, needless to say, which in the long run cannot but fail. Original sin is the pride by which the feminineness of mankind, symbolized by Ishah, tries to become God.

We are thus led to a paradoxical conclusion: even within the myth of the male and the female as it predominates in Western culture, the female is, for man and woman alike, the normal type of attitude and behavior. This would seem to confirm our previous conclusions that the male-female myth is basically incorrect and that in the proper order of creation, which the advent of the redeemer has begun to restore, the relationship of man and woman is not what society has made it. This relationship demands the possibility of a choice, not indeed of physiological functions, which belong to the order of nature, but of spiritual attitudes, personal purposes and ambitions, even all the psychological qualities belonging to the order of culture.

A further conclusion is warranted. If the coming of Christ was intended to restore the order of creation and nature over against that of sin and culture, and if the order of nature, insofar as woman is concerned, has been reversed by the order of culture, as culture developed within Judaism and in the context of the Greco-Roman empire, then the Christian faith should have entailed, as its ineluctable consequence, the liberation of woman from the societal yokes that burdened her. It is my view that Saint Paul at least saw this clearly, but shied away from the revolutionary consequences that this implied for society. The Fathers of the Church successfully created and preserved, within the framework of their society, a realm of freedom for the women who would select it as their way of life. Thus the ascetic life and the order of virgins, guaranteed at least spiritual freedom to women. Other attempts that were made here and there to give women equality with men within the structure of the Church eventually floundered before the pressures of societies dominated by the male principle.

In general, the Church was offered to woman as the realm of her liberation. With the exception of the priesthood and episcopacy (and, later, the diaconate, too) women have been equal to men before the sacraments. Insofar as the organizational structure of the Church was patterned on that of Roman society (and this pattern was consciously adopted for diocesan organization), woman was deprived of her legitimate Christian freedom.

The question should now be asked: has not the time come for the Church to reverse its compromise with the society of the Roman Empire and return to what it was originally meant to be, the realm of redemption, of liberation, specifically the liberation of woman from her cultural subservience to the dominant male principle in society? That the Church is the realm of freedom must not remain an empty statement; it ought to be experienced as a fact by all those who are not yet free. It would be easy to show that the universal sacraments of the traditional Catholic way of life provide the dimension of freedom and therefore of liberation: they bring about freedom from sin and weakness (baptism, confirmation, penance), freedom from dispersion and disunity (eucharist), freedom from sickness (unction), freedom from solitude and loneliness (matrimony). Positively expressed, this means the freedom to live and to act, to unite with all men in the Lord, the freedom to be healthy, to love, and to have a family. As to the sacrament of orders, its special function, connected with the presidency of eucharistic worship, does not need to confer similar types of freedom, because it assumes the freedom of the other sacraments in the one who is ordained. Clearly, this is just as relevant to a woman as it is to a man.

Thus, in the experience of the early Christians, the Ecclesia was the mother of freedom, the realm of liberation. The records of the mystics through the ages show that this feeling of freedom never left the Church, even though it has not been realized by all the faithful. Why prolong now an ambiguity that resulted in the first place from a necessary compromise with the society of the Roman empire? Why not take the steps to make the Ecclesia of today the effective instrument and symbol of liberation? It is only a matter of manifesting what the Church already is and always has been in her very essence.

Before spelling out the implications of the principle we have established, several more general consequences in the area of anthropology ought to be examined. For evidently a theology of womanhood can only follow on a theology of mankind.

1. Man as human being cannot be properly defined as a union of soul and body, whether these terms are understood in their Platonic or their Aristotelian sense. Whenever the terms soul and body are used, they act only as symbols representing the two levels of man's existence here on earth. He is on earth and yet, insofar as he lives in the Ecclesia, he is already in heaven. Man can properly be defined only in relation to his call to participation in the life of God the Father by union to Christ in the power of the Holy Spirit, *Homo erectus, homo faber, homo sapiens,* and all the other expressions describing some phase of human evolution or some function or aspect of man, must ultimately be subsumed under the concept of *homo eschatologicus or homo parousiaticus or homo transfiguratus,* or simply *homo mysticus:* man as transparent to the divine, as the image of God, is the type and pattern that all men are called to exemplify. Man must be defined teleologically, by the spiritual entelechy which guides him toward the Father, the source and goal of all beings.

2. The human community is mankind. One can designate by this term the collection of all individual men and women, or, in a sense which is more familiar today, the organic, the not yet completed but certainly growing unity of all men and women at the level of both nature and culture. But in fidelity to Christian Revelation and the Catholic tradition, one point must be added: the human community can be only the Ecclesia, since it must be the unity of those who are called to deification. The contemporary question "Is the world for the Church or the Church for the world?" has no recognizable meaning once we have identified the unity of man with God with both the entelechy of man's collective evolution and the teleology to which this evolution tends. The only recognizable unity of mankind is not the world, or the United Nations, or the technological interdependence of nations, or the *Pax Americana,* or the *Pax Sovietica,* or whatever world Empire may still come into being. It is the Church. Just as the true man, and the model for all human beings is Jesus Christ, so the true mankind, and the model for all attempts at achieving the oneness of man, is the Church of Christ. Accordingly, the suggestion that the future of Christianity may lie in a diaspora situation is acceptable only for a more or less near future. As far as the absolute future is concerned, however, it is a fallacy: the Church can encompass no less than the universe. The dimension of catholicity guarantees her adequacy to mankind and her ultimate iden-

tity with it, although the implications of catholicity still need to be worked out and implemented. Likewise, the modern distinction between the "real" Church and the "institutional" Church derives from the delusion that man and mankind can be abstracted from bodily existence without losing their reality. This fallacy is just as patent as regards the Ecclesia as it is regarding mankind, since the Ecclesia and mankind are two aspects of the same reality.

3. Within the community that I may now call ecclesial man, the concept of race has neither content nor validity. It is based on appearances, on empirical evidence of differentiations within mankind which have not stood the test of scientific investigation. Differences of pigmentation, of facial features, of height, of hair color and fluidity, whatever their distant origins, have no consequences on the data with which man starts in life, except insofar as they coincide with diverse cultural value systems. In other words, culture rather than nature gives the illusion that the concept of race corresponds to reality. The corporate unit which mediates between the individual and mankind cannot be the clan or the tribe, formations that are closely related to the family insofar as they rest on bonds of parental ancestry and of blood. The laws of exogamy and endogamy prevailing in tribal societies show sufficiently that the tribe is part of a broader corporate body made of other clans and tribes with which matrimonial interchanges are thought to be proper. This broader corporate body, in its fully developed form, constitutes the nation. The nation is essentially patterned on mankind, being itself a smaller version of the pluralism of origins, colors, and linguistic differentiations within mankind. It cannot be defined by unity of race or of language, but by community of history. It is precisely the nation which has shaped and is shaping the culture of man all the world over, whether the nation is old, as in Asia, more recent, as in Europe, very recent, as in America, or emerging, as in Africa. The nation has also shaped the Church and its history. This principle has been recognized in diverse ways by the Orthodox Church with its practice of national autocephaly; by the Catholic Church with its lukewarm attempts to nurture "Eastern rites" next to the Latin rite, which expresses the former national unity of the Roman empire of the West, and with its recent initiatives toward the formation of national conferences of bishops; by the Churches of the Reformation, with their separate developments along national lines. Admittedly, there are legitimate and meaningful differentiations within national boundaries (provinces); and several nations may be included within one state (Wales, Scotland, and England within Great Britain). By the same token, historical events have at times merged several nations into one or, on the contrary, split one nation into several (Belgium has recently become two nations, whereas the various cantons of Switzerland form only one nation today). These facts do not detract from the statement that the typical corporate unit within mankind is the nation, shaped by shared history, tradition, and culture, and that

the typical unit within the universal Church with which a Christian can meaningfully identify is neither the local parish or congregation nor the diocese, but the national church with its specific religious ethos. Man defines himself by his participation in mankind and, next, by his participation in a nation.

4. Within this corporate context, man is a self. That is, he is a center of awareness. Awareness both relates him to those other selves with whom he is in contact and distinguishes him from them. Thus, selfhood must not be conceived only as a principle of individuality by which one man would detach and separate himself from other men; it is also a principle of relatedness. A self is a person, structurally related to other persons; and this structural relationship is experienced existentially by all men, at a minimum within the confines of the family, from which center it tends to expand and embrace more and more relationships. A self is potentially related to all men, even though the limitations of existence are such that although he relates and identifies more concretely with only a selected number of persons and really understands only a limited number of civilizations and cultures. The balance of self-awareness demands both the universal potentiality of relationships with all men and the actuality of limited relationships with some men. The generality is necessary to the breadth of the concrete relationship; and the closeness of the concrete relationship is required for the depth of the universal.

It is in this context that the relationship of man and woman ought to be seen. For among all human relationships, the one that joins two persons of different sexes has a capacity for concreteness that can never be reached by relationships within one sex. There alone can a unity and union of soul, mind, understanding, sympathy, and concerns be expressed bodily in a union and unity of sexes. Nowhere else can the universal unity of man with man become so concrete and particular.

In the Christian context, the self is not turned on himself and self-enclosed. What constitutes it, Christianly speaking, as a self is its calling to become the image of God. In the self, the collective and the individual aspects of mankind converge to the point of coinciding; it is destined to participate in the divine life. The self of the secular man is called to become ecclesial man; and the self of ecclesial man lives on earth while already sharing in heaven, encompassing in himself all that the Three Persons of the Divinity are, because they dwell in him, thus making him the image of God. All that was said above concerning the image refers to the self.

The meaning of sex, and thereby the differentiation of mankind into two sexes, appears clearly in this context. Sex is a means of relationship. It is, properly speaking, the means to make most concrete and particular the oneness of the children of God and their sharing in his life, by bringing the whole body into play as the expression of this oneness. Sex experienced and satisfied demands a one-to-one relationship, that is, the stability of marriage rather than general promiscuity, polygamy, or divorce, for only in such a relationship can two persons be fully committed to expressing their participation in the image of God through their union. As to sex denied, which has often been the standard for the more spiritually sensitive sections of the Church, it also has a purpose when, in the traditional vocabulary, such a denial is motivated by aspiration after "the Kingdom of God." Its purpose is to make visible the belief that relationships among human beings can also be fully developed at another level. Men and women do not become the image of God through sexual unity, but through the relationship of friendship or love, which may, but need not, be expressed through sex. On the contrary, because it particularizes a virtually universal potential for relationships, sex restricts the universality of a man's ties and contacts. Human beings, therefore, are given the choice between universality and particularity, between spiritual friendships that may be multiplied and a sexual relationship which cannot be. In both cases, however, in a Christian universe, it is still the same image of God which is then experienced and actualized, though in different ways and to various degrees.

That mankind is divided into two sexes, then, means that it is called to unity, not by necessity or destiny, but through choice and love. It means that men are to actualize the image of God in themselves by seeking the sort of relationship with others that, for them, may best develop and express the image.

5.   In this case, womanhood and manhood have a meaning—that of showing the possibility of, and the vocation to, relatedness with others in the progressive manifestation of the image of God. We run into difficulties as soon as we look for a specific meaning of each that would not also be that of the other. The establishment of relationships requires at least two terms. Hence man and woman, the male and the female sex. Yet at all levels but the strictly sexual one, the roles of both may be interchanged. There is no dominant and no subservient half, no leader and no led, no superior and no inferior, no intellectual and active and no sensitive and passive, no reasoning and no intuitive section of mankind. Each person can be both, the variations depending not on sex but on the congeries of heredity and circumstances which make up the individuals of either sex. On this point, the findings of contemporary psychology, at least in the Jungian school, and those of physiology corroborate the conclusion that we have arrived at theologically.

In these conditions, the question of the specificity of man and woman is irrelevant, except in the obvious area of sexual intercourse and of the following tasks of pregnancy, birth, and feeding which determine woman's physiology. For everything else, including education, men and women are alike by nature, whatever differences have been bred into their customs and habits by differing cultures. One may still ask how Christian women and Christian men understand themselves and each other as they go through the stages of their lives. On this point, however, very little can truly be said, as this self-understanding again is a matter of culture. It varies according to the type of society one lives in, to the roles and functions expected of, and available to, men and women in that society, to the sort of education provided for them. Without entering into details of a nontheological nature one can put forward some norms which ought to shape society in a Christian order of things and should at any rate help form the Christian's attitude and response to the culture of his times.

The Christian tradition was not wrong in specifying diverse roles and functions for woman as virgin and for woman as mother, although it tended to neglect her as wife, which was obviously a major oversight. It often provided the additional category of widow, a category which is bound to exist—although one may doubt its specificity, except in cultures where widows do not as a rule remarry. Seen from the standpoint of the image of God, of participation in the divine nature, of progressive "deification," the virgin, the wife, and the mother have in common that their life is focused on relationships. This is particularly evident in a sexually oriented civilization like that of the second half of the twentieth century. Before marriage, the girl is frequently involved in the relationship called dating, but whether she dates or not, she relates to all sorts of friends of both sexes at school, at home, and in society at large. In marriage she is closely related to her husband in love and companionship. As mother she relates to her children in love and responsibility. So is all this true of the man, since to be a human being implies relatedness to God and to other human beings. The theological self-understanding of each depends on what these relationships mean to each person. What they do in fact mean is a matter of sociological investigation. How they are experienced and translated in language and behavior is a topic for psychological studies. How they ought to be experienced may be considered proper matter for moral philosophy and theology. At this moment we can only look into some doctrinal or dogmatic elements of this self-understanding.

Woman as virgin is placed before a choice that will largely determine what life she will live. She has to decide freely in what way she is to respond to the call to participate in the divine life. Will she do it, as most in fact do, through the relationships of marriage? Supposing her answer is affirmative, how will she find a suitable companion who will make this possible? What will her reaction be to sexual intercourse, to pregnancy, and to motherhood? These questions build up the girl's self-understanding. They show her becoming the image of God through the preparation and the anticipation of the human relationships to come that are to shape her life. In all this, however, the main question has not yet been formulated, although it underlies all others: how spiritually free will she remain through the bonds into which she will enter freely? This may often be asked at the level of a superficial freedom, relating to freedom to work or to have her own friends. The true level where the question is apposite is that of spiritual life: will she be able to share her life constantly with others and still preserve the core of interior silence in which alone she can experience God's presence? That is, theologically speaking, the ultimate question that needs to be faced at this stage of life.

Woman as virgin has the choice. Indeed, she is specified by the fact that she has not yet chosen. As soon as she chooses, she orients herself toward a way of life which already participates of that which is to follow, though their choices are not final until they are sealed by marriage. The other option is that of celibacy as a stable way of life, which the Christian tradition has called "virginity for the sake of the Kingdom." Here the questions that ought to be answered for a satisfactory self-understanding are reversed. Granted that the center of such a life will be relationship to God and the awareness of God's image in oneself, will it still be possible to grow in the human relationships that are necessary to the full flowering of the image of God? Will it be possible to lead a life of friendship, including friendship with persons of the other sex, without which the possibilities of human relationships are not exhausted? What sort of career can make this feasible? What sort of community, of companionship, of sharing with others? The answer need not be a religious community, although it will be in many cases. Yet it must be a choice of a way of living *sui generis,* for which no abstract pattern can be given beforehand, except the very pattern endorsed by a given religious community, or the one corresponding to the career selected.

Woman as wife can be defined in only the most general of terms: she has linked herself permanently to a certain man. The specificity of this relationship, however, depends on the personalities involved. Theology can indeed provide doctrinal and ethical norms for such a relationship. A wife, like a husband, ought to deepen her awareness of the depths of traditional theology concerning what Pius XII called "the redemptive value of marital union."[12] Scripture and the theological tradition from the time of the Fathers to our own have reflected on the analogy between the unity of Christ with the Church and the unity of man and woman in marriage. How this sort of insight can be incorporated into the specific experience of a man and a woman in marriage is theirs to discover. Such a discovery implies a degree of spiritual sensitivity and commitment that may be rare and that is not promoted by the main trends of secular society. Whoever has this insight, however, will easily solve any conflict arising between the concrete, particular relationship of marriage and the broader and always needed relationships of friendship and social life. For marriage is only one type of unity, and man needs many types. The woman who is so enclosed in the universe of her marriage that the outside world counts only as a commercial adjunct to the amenities of life together can hardly be ecclesial man as described above. The dimension of universality must never be lost if God's image is to develop in the framework of marriage. For this reason it is absurd to hold that the Christian ideal of marriage requires the wife to stay at home, busy with the care of her husband and children and with the chores of the household. The Christian ideal demands a proper balance of the particular and the universal. And this can best be achieved by most women through involvement in some tasks of society outside the home. This is a matter for each woman's choice of the way most appropriate to her own spiritual development.

Woman as mother has occupied the main seat in the preoccupation of Catholic churchmen, as witness our survey of contemporary theological models for womanhood. This tallies with the place and function of motherhood in the very idea of the Church. But when seen in the wider context of womanhood, this insistence on motherhood has been exaggerated. Woman is not only mother. She is also wife. And before being wife, she is unmarried girl. In the early Church, woman as virgin held the center of attention. This simple fact shows sufficiently that the recent stress on woman as mother is not normative for the Catholic tradition. The time has come to redress the balance and to give equal importance to the three basic stages of womanhood. Be that as it may, motherhood remains a major category, one that is more questionable in modern civilization than in the past. One cannot avoid the problems raised by the rising ghost of overpopulation, by the practical necessity of some forms of birth control, by the availability, with the manufacturing of progesterone and other pills, of new methods of birth control, by the spread of the social acceptability of premarital intercourse, by the resulting multiplication of unwed mothers, and by the growing leniency of society and law on such matters as abortion. I will not deal with these questions at this point, since I intend to speak of ethics in the next chapter. From the doctrinal point of view, motherhood is open to woman as one of the ways to fulfill her calling as a human being. In the context of Christian freedom, the notion of free motherhood becomes a proper theological category. That is, the Christian woman who enters marriage chooses a way of life which does not entirely take away her own further choice of motherhood. By choosing marriage, she accepts motherhood, but it still remains for her to choose it within the context of her marriage in relation to the children to be born to her. Thus, planned parenthood, birth control, or what Pius XII preferred to call "regulation of offspring,"[13] is a live option for every married woman. The only moral problems that need to be raised in this area by Catholic ethics concern the morality of the contraceptive intention and of the means taken to avoid procreation. It is enough for the moment to note that the principle of the regulation of offspring is entirely consistent with the theological concept of womanhood as outlined in this chapter.

Enough has been found in the preceding pages that extols motherhood and its spiritual marvels. I would add that, in the long run, it is up to each woman to discover motherhood, just as she had to discover both virginity and the marital relationship. The principle of Christian liberation frees woman from society's concept of marriage and motherhood. Rather, the Christian woman is tied to a doctrine of motherhood which sees the mother as the very embodiment of the Ecclesia helping ecclesial man in his birth and growth. How she will implement and experience this in her relationship to her own children is left to her initiative, her sensitivity, and her spiritual insight.

In the context of the theology outlined here, a Christian anthropology is normative only as regards the divine model—the Holy Trinity revealed through Christ and made active in our life by the Holy Spirit—and the eschatological goal of divine participation by man and woman. Within the context of the Ecclesia, the sacramental life and the elements of asceticism necessary to human personal development are also normative. But how these are lived, experienced, and practically understood by each man or woman is a mystery that each must enter under the Spirit's guidance. Accordingly, one cannot define woman. One can only present her with the divine model, with the means of participation in the divine life, and with the records of experience and self-understanding that have been left by great women. What this may mean in the concrete case of each woman cannot be described in advance. In this sense, there is no specific theological model for womanhood any more than there is one for manhood. The models are for mankind, to be diversified and specified according to the charisms of each person. Ecclesial man (which includes woman) is always in the making. What must be offered woman as her Christian ideal is an open future, a perspective of successive self-understandings as virgin, wife, and mother (and we may add, although this need not be elaborated upon, as grandmother and as widow). The vertical dimension of self-understanding can be pointed out normatively: it corresponds to the traditional doctrine on the image of God in man and on its development through the spiritual life. The horizontal dimension cannot be normatively described: it has to be invented anew by each Christian.

10

Controverted Questions

The baptized woman enters a realm of freedom in which she is in principle, freer than any other woman. The hitch, however, has always come from the practical impossibility, until our own day, of implementing this freedom in a world which does not yet recognize it. If the Church has already escaped the dominion of sin and death, the societies in which Christians live are still steeped in sin and death. It makes little difference at this point whether society is Christian or not. The institutions of Christian society are still dominated by the fall. The ideal society cannot exist in this world. No Christian can in practice enjoy the full freedom to which he or she is heir. No one can expect to enjoy it except in the never-never land of utopia.

Two problems are raised by this dichotomy between the principle and its corresponding ideal, on the one hand, and the reality of societal life, on the other.

First, there is no theological reason, although there may be an abundance of empirical or political reasons, why the very structures of the Church should not try to embody the spiritual freedom of the children of God, which neither the secular nor the sacred *polis* can possibly implement. Yet, the Church progressively abandoned the principle of Christian freedom in its application to the life of women within its own ranks and concerns, and in areas that could conceivably have escaped secular prejudice and social pressure. Instead, it adopted the principle of harmony with secular society. The early Fathers indeed endeavored to guarantee to woman the possibility of spiritual freedom within the confines of the Church: to that effect they instituted and organized the ascetic way of life which later evolved into the religious orders of women as these survive today. At the very same time, the reversed process was taking place. Whereas the earlier Church admitted women to the important functions of prophecy and the diaconate, a number of reasons—among which we may note a reaction against licentiousness and heresy and the sheer weight of the secular, with its prejudices, customs, and legalities —induced the later Church to close to women all activities directly connected

211

with the three functions of Christ as teacher, prophet, and king. Thus women have been completely eliminated from preaching, liturgy, and government. Though uneven, this process became totally effective with the disappearance of the medieval vestiges of feminine authority in the Church, the monastic foundations presided over by an abbess who counted monks and priests within her jurisdiction. Whatever motivations and justifications may explain the peculiar phenomenon by which the Church eventually closed doors which the Gospel and the early tradition had left open to women, the theological question is unavoidably mooted; can the adoption of secular standards ever be justified when it results in restricting the freedom of the Gospel? Both Protestant and Catholic thought have expressed the fundamental dignity of the Christian by reference to the tasks of Christ as teacher, prophet, and king. This is even basic to Vatican Council II's treatment of the theme of the people of God and of the laity. Yet women have not been admitted, nor did Vatican II plan to admit them, to any function in which teaching, preaching, or government are actively exercized. Not only has woman been ineligible for any priestly or hierarchial task, she has not even been allowed to do in the Church all that a layman can do, as witness the fact, whereas we have had "altar boys" for centuries, we have had no "altar girls" until quite recently, and this in only a few areas.

Second, the present moment in the evolution of secular society creates possibilities, opens up opportunities, and raises questions that could not be faced before. Modern society has gone a long way toward emancipating woman from male tutelage, although great distance still has to be travelled before men and women become truly equal and responsible in purely secular matters. The political evolution and the social emancipation of our times could have been foretold. The progressive adoption of permissive laws concerning divorce, remarriage, contraception, and abortion is not entirely surprising. Once the principle of the total equality of human beings has been accepted as a political basis, there is no justification for further practical restrictions on what a man or a woman may do. Biological research has changed the very nature of contraceptive interventions, thereby placing the problem of birth control in a light where one can arrive at philosophical or theological judgments other than were formerly justified. Patently, this evolution places before the Church certain inescapable questions, relating to the task and function of woman in the organism of salvation and to her legitimate Christian freedom in areas where total secular freedom will soon be available to her. In other words: should the Church continue to deny woman access to positions of authority, and specifically to the sacrament of orders? Can the Christian woman lawfully avail herself, as a Christian, of the sexual freedom that is now hers as a modern woman?

I will take these questions successively, beginning with the theological problem of ordination.

The problem of women's ordination may be looked at canonically. We then run into Canon 968§1: "A baptized male alone can validly receive sacred ordination." The canon by itself is not as impressive as the long history behind it. It does sum up twenty centuries of Church history, including the period of the New Testament. Exceptions regarding orders have been factual only in the two areas of the diaconate and of the quasi-episcopal jurisdiction of some medieval abbesses. Neither the priesthood nor episcopacy have ever been opened to women, except in early heterodox circles connected with gnosticism or Montanism. The argument of canonical precedent against the ordination of women to the priesthood is unimpeachable.

However, a purely canonical argument can never be ultimate in the theological field. What has never been done can still be done if good reasons militate in its favor. The Church has never ordained women. But she has not committed herself to never ordaining women.

The theological arguments against the access of women to the priesthood are striking by their very poverty. The patristic Church never raised the question. There were, of course, good reasons for this. The status of woman in the society of the times did not permit her to take up positions of authority. The Jewish background of the Church made it unthinkable. The Roman and the Greek world made it impractical. In such conditions, the possibility of a woman leading the congregation in prayer never became an option for the Church in general. What was possible for some Montanist circles might have been acceptable also to the great Church in limited sections of the Empire. The general access of women to positions of authority would have been a very different proposition. For this reason, women deacons never had a chance of heralding the advent of women priests.

The question was raised to an academic level of discussion in the intellectually free world of medieval schools and universities. The Scholastics faced it, showing in this less inhibition than most contemporary theologians. Nevertheless, their answer was negative: maleness belongs to the essence of the sacrament of orders. Thomas Aquinas understands this to derive from the nature of the sacrament, rather than merely from positive law. "Even should all the acts of ordination be performed, a woman does not receive the sacrament. For, as the sacrament is a sign, what is done in a sacrament requires not only a reality, but the sign of it. . . . Superiority cannot be indicated by the female sex since woman is in a state of subjection. Therefore, she cannot receive the sacrament of orders."[1] This follows from Thomas's opinion that woman is subject to man, both in the work of procreation, and, for her own guidance, in all other matters. In keeping with this, Thomas opines that women who held the title of deaconesses never actually received the diaconate. They simply performed works otherwise done by deacons, "like reading the homily at church."[2]

The same conclusion is reached in the early Franciscan school. For Bonaventure "it is the doctor's healthier and more prudent opinion that women not only must not or cannot be ordained *de jure*, but moreover cannot *de facto*."[3] This does not come "from the Church's institutions," but "from the fact that it would not fit the sacrament of orders." However, the reason given for such a sacramental impossibility is not woman's inferiority and subservience, but the mediating function of Christ, which can only be signified by the male sex: Man "alone can naturally represent this sign and can actually bear it through reception of the [sacramental] character."

The treatment of this question by John Duns Scot is particularly relevant. Duns Scot does not argue directly from feminine inferiority, like Thomas, or from the nature of the priestly function, with Bonaventure. The basis for his conclusion that a woman cannot be validly ordained is simply the ecclesiastical practice. This must derive from the will of Christ; for the Church would be guilty of a serious injustice if she took it on herself to forbid women access to such a great sacrament:

> This is not to be considered as specifically determined by the Church, but it comes from Christ. The Church would not presume to deprive the entire female sex, without any guilt on its part, of an act which might licitly pertain to it, being directed toward the salvation of woman and of others in the Church through her. For this would be an extreme injustice, not only toward the whole sex, but also toward specific persons: if by divine law the priestly Order could licitly pertain to a woman, this would be for the salvation of [some] women and of others through them.

That Christ did not want woman to be ordained seems patent: otherwise his mother would have been raised to one of the degrees of the sacrament of orders. This restriction was in keeping with natural reason, since "at least after the fall, nature does not permit woman to hold a place of predominance in mankind." Yet the very scope of the injustice of antifeminine legislation in this matter makes Duns Scot recoil: the Church cannot possibly be responsible for it. Duns Scot of course does not ascribe an injustice to Christ: Christ has his own reasons, of which man is not judge.

The position of this great Franciscan shows that the contemporary question about woman in the Church was indeed raised in the later Middle Ages. On this point, Duns Scot was the first modern man, for he was the first to perceive the inherent injustice of a law that bans women from one of the sacraments of the New Covenant. Thus, the anthropology of Thomas Aquinas and the majority among the Schoolmen was not necessary to the Catholic synthesis. If indeed, woman is less fully human than man, only a fully human being can have access to the priesthood, where, standing before the community in *persona Christi*, he is destined to represent the one who is the perfect model of humanity. This sort of argumentation loses all validity in an anthropology which recognizes the full humanity of woman. Duns Scot's concept of the Church made it unthinkable for him that the Church could be responsible for such an injustice to womanhood. In this, Duns Scot indeed stood in the great Catholic ecclesiological tradition, which cannot attribute sin to the Church. The puzzling point for the contemporary mind is that his concept of God's omnipotent will made him accept the idea that God himself had decided the matter. The distinction between good and evil was commonly attributed to God's arbitrary decision in later medieval theology and reached final fruition in Calvin's extreme view of predestination.

Thus we reach a dilemma. Because we hold Saint Thomas's idea of God rather than Duns Scot's, we cannot attribute to God the decision to restrict priesthood to males. Yet, because we do not share Thomas's anthropology, we recognize the injustice that Duns Scot sees in the current discipline of the sacrament of orders. It remains to put the blame where Duns Scot could not put it: on the Church, or more correctly, on the men of the Church who have so far been unable or unwilling to rise above their social and psychological conditioning.

In keeping with the position arrived at in the last chapter, I cannot accept the objection drawn from the supposed relationship of woman to the Holy Spirit. The priesthood is immediately connected with Christ as high priest of his Church. On account of man's relatedness to Christ, only a man could be a priest, the tasks of woman coming under the aegis of the Third Person. Among contemporary authors, this remains the position of Jean Galot, who also sees in it the explicit will of Christ:

> The women who followed Jesus to Jerusalem and who the day after will be so closely associated to his Passion are not invited to the first Eucharistic meal. The Master wants to entrust the eucharistic celebration only to the Apostles, and to them alone he addresses the words: Do this in memory of me. This is his deliberate will.[5]

Such a line of thought is based on a myth, the myth that the account of the Last Supper in the Gospels and in Saint Paul's first epistle to the Corinthians is a strict historical account of what actually took place in the upper room, rather than a projection of what the Christian communities were actually doing at the time of the writing. The safest thing that may be said here is that we really do not know what Jesus did at the Last Supper. Moreover, why should the practice of the primitive Church remain normative for all times unless it is supported by doctrinal reasons that have perennial value? Galot does find such a reason in the incarnation: "Now it is in a man that God willed to show himself in the incarnation; it is consequently in men that he wills to continue to show himself in the Church, according to his divine power."[6] But this is a patent *non sequitur*: the fact of the incarnation of the Word in the man Jesus proves nothing whatsoever about a male priesthood within the Church.

Thierry Maertens, who authored a valuable study of woman in the Bible, prefers an agnostic conclusion: the question of the ordination of woman cannot receive an answer now.

> The Christian ministry, particularly in the liturgical gathering, constitutes the most important step of the unique mediation of Christ. Can we conceive that a woman may someday fulfill this mediating function? It is not possible to answer this question. One could not even envisage it as long as society was built on the only mediation of the male. Today, the sociological and cultural conditions allow us at least to posit the question, but the answer rests with the Holy Spirit: he alone calls to the priesthood.[7]

This is not altogether satisfactory. For what shall we tell a woman who believes herself called to the priesthood by the Spirit? Obviously, the Church will not change her way of acknowledging the divine call to the priesthood unless theology feels able not only to ask the question which is already implicit in the social conditions of the times, but also to answer it affirmatively.

Luc-Henri Gihoul, whose book on the subject tries to find an acceptable version of the "eternal feminine," concludes that the arguments against women priests are not persuasive: "We have sufficiently said that, in the present state of our knowledge, no scriptural, theological, psychological, social or other argument is apodictic or convincing."[8] His personal attitude, however, remains close to the agnosticism of Maertens:

> As to the question of the admission of women to the priesthood, the problem is up in the air: partly because the arguments are false, partly because they are hardly relevant in view of the changed social and religious conditions, partly because they do not carry conviction. At any rate, a growing number of theologians are concerned about the weakness or the obscurity of the arguments hitherto proposed, and they foresee the day when it will be possible and necessary to reexamine the whole question completely. This will not come about by recrimination and pressure; it will only arise from the breath of the Spirit in the intelligence and the heart.[9]

In any case, Gihoul cannot be counted among the advocates of women's ordination: he prefers to wait for the Spirit to manifest his intentions more clearly.

During the last session of the Second Vatican Council, Jean Daniélou, now Cardinal, summed up the only position that would seem compatible with the nonvalidity of the arguments against the accession of women to the priesthood:

It is my opinion that, immediately, and therefore before the end of the Council, the Church ought to authorize the ordination of deaconesses. As to the possibility of women priests, there is no fundamental theological objection to it.[10]

This position on deaconesses followed from the conclusion of Daniélou's historical essay of 1961 on the "ministry of women in the early Church": "We have three possible ways of ordering the ministry of women: lay, clerical, religious. It may be said that all three are equally traditional."[11] In other words, the introduction of women into the clergy is just as traditional as the status of religious women or as the identification of women with the order of the laity. The accession of women to the second and third degrees of the sacrament of orders, the priesthood and the episcopate, would indeed go beyond historical precedent. But the diaconate, in the Catholic tradition, already belongs to the sacrament of orders. The deaconesses of the distant past effected enough of a breach in the wall of opposition to make it possible now to go further.

The access of women to all the degrees of the sacrament of orders logically tallies with the anthropology outlined in the preceding chapter. I also think that it follows from the study of the process by which the early Church began to liberate woman, applying to her the basic principles of Christian freedom, and then disenfranchised her in reaction against schismatic movements, against ambiguous situations, and against licentiousness. Let me briefly recall the outlines of the story.

Greek and Roman traditions rendered the age of the Fathers unfavorable to a systematic promotion of women. Yet from the early days women shared the burden of spreading the Gospel and were, for instance, "co-workers" with Saint Paul. The care of the closed gardens of virginity, to which the Fathers without exception devoted themselves, eventually had effects far and wide. The Middle Ages saw a remarkable, though limited, growth of feminine influence in the Church. Abbesses not infrequently wielded authority over monks. Women were counted among the great mystics. Neither the Church nor the society of France balked at the idea of an eighteen-year-old-girl, Jeanne d'Arc (1412-1431), heading the French army against the English during the most famous episode of the Hundred Years' War. Condemned as a witch by an illegal tribunal in 1431, Jeanne d'Arc was rehabilitated by the Church in 1456, beatified in 1909, and canonized in 1920. Indeed, women featured prominently at many turning points of medieval history. Even in the so-called "Dark Ages" we may mention Radegunda (d. 587), retired queen of the Franks, wife of Chlothar I, who studied the Fathers' works at her monastery of the Holy Cross at Poitiers. Gertrude of Nivelles (abbess, 626-653) and Bertilla of Chelles (d. 705) were great abbesses. Gonzague Truc, who names these women in his *Illustrated History of Woman,* adds that Rabban Maurus (776-856) dedicated his commentaries on the books of Judith and Esther to the wife of Louis le Débonnaire (778-840) and that philosopher and theologian Gerbert d'Aurillac, who became Pope Sylvester II (pope, 999-1003), corresponded with Empress Adelaide (c. 931-999), wife of Emperor Otto I;[12] a number of other prominent women appear in this correspondence. At the end of the Middle Ages, Renaissance ladies like Vittoria Colonna or Marguerite de Navarre exercised a great influence, the first in the Oratories of Divine Love which flourished in Italy, the second among Reformist circles in France. Women remained influential in the Church in the seventeenth century, but Bossuet's crushing of Madame Guyon in the controversy over Quietism marked the end of their influence. Yet a new concern for the education of women was developing at the very time of Bossuet's triumph. In 1687 Fénelon published his pioneering *Treatise on the Education of Girls,* and the Jansenists strongly upheld the right of women to read and study the Bible. All in all, however, neither Fénelon nor the Jansenists could achieve the necessary breakthrough. Ecclesiastical antifeminism remained well-established.

If none of the theological arguments brought forward to justify this state of the matter has persuasive value, then we must squarely face the question: should not the tide be finally reversed? It is the conclusion of this book that all ecclesiastical disabilities of women should now be raised, that women should be admitted to all sacraments and to all positions of authority, ministry, and service. The freedom of the Christian, imparted to all in baptism, should remove all man-made barriers between human beings.

Such a position neither threatens the traditional theology of the sacrament of orders nor denies the fact that the higher forms of it were never bestowed on women. Moreover, the problem today is no longer sacramental; it is Pneumatological. It does not relate to who is or is not a fit subject for the reception of a sacrament. It rather concerns the theology of the Spirit. The ages which admitted women to prominence in the Church were strongly charismatic periods. As witness the reaction against Montanism, women were discarded from places of influence, discouraged from prophesying, and banned from the reception of the diaconate by fear of charisms. Yet if charisms come from the Spirit, no one may limit the Spirit's freedom to grant his gifts to whom he wants. The remedy of chaos is not obstruction; it is the all too neglected art of discerning the spirits.

On the one hand, the canonical and theological tradition, still embodied in Canon 968, §1, that the male sex is necessary to the valid reception of the sacraments of orders, is a *post factum* justification of a common practice. It is by no means a normative conclusion flowing from undoubted premises. On the other hand, the compelling argument for the ordination of women cannot be drawn from the secular conquests of the older feminist movement or the newer women's liberation movement. That women are achieving equality with men in the professional functions of modern society is irrelevant. Those who build their case for women priests or women ministers on the basis of feminine emancipation in society can never reach a persuasive conclusion. For we are not at this point dealing with society, but with the Church; and we should not base our views on political and social convenience and opportunity, but on the Gospel and on the dynamics of the coming Kingdom. Neither here nor anywhere else should the Church take the world as its norm. The norm should always derive from the Gospel. When she restricted women in the past, the Church followed society rather than the Gospel. I am afraid we would not be better off with the opposing decision today, were it still grounded in the same premise.

The true ground for change is that the Spirit may call whom he wants to lead his people. Indeed, those who associate woman with the symbolism of the sacred ought to go a little further and not stop at the symbol. Paul VI's assertion that woman "is, for us, mankind as adopting the best attitude facing the attraction of the sacred" cannot logically remain the last word concerning this matter. When woman is seen as "the sign of a goodness which appears to us as having no bounds, the mirror of the ideal human being as conceived by God in his own image and likeness,"[13] this recognition ought to extend to the women of flesh and blood who embody the symbol. The symbol can have meaning only if it is reflected in the actual life and place of women in the Church. This strengthens the conclusion already reached: the symbols given by the Spirit must not remain empty, any more than the Word spoken by the mouth of God must return to him void. There is a symbol only where there is a symbolic reality. The symbol is womanhood, and the symbolic reality is woman. The role of woman in the Ecclesia is that to which the Spirit calls her. And once the Spirit has been acknowledged, no one may reserve his assent.

In the perspective of the last chapters, woman has appeared to us as a human being endowed with a certain biological function and with psychological and existential opportunities implied in that function. At the level of symbolism, she has been seen as symbolic of human relationships by the very fact that the relationship between man and woman is the primary relationship of mankind. At the cultural level, it belongs to each woman to develop herself as she wishes within the spectrum of the possibilities open to her by the cultural environment; in modern society, it belongs also to her to enlarge this spectrum of the possibilities open to her by the cultural environment; in modern society, it belongs also to her to enlarge this spectrum indefinitely by joint action. In the context of the Christian faith, woman has the vocation of deepening and understanding her relationship to God and more precisely to the Persons of the Word and the Spirit, with the possibility both of finding in the divine archetype of all relationships the justification of her tasks and of questioning and challenging the cultural patterns in which she lives.

Such a perspective entails a doctrine about marriage and about love. This is not the place to develop it at length, as I have purposely restricted my topic to woman as such, not to all the problems that may be connected with womanhood. Marriage I cannot see in any way other than has been consecrated by the Catholic tradition, as a sacrament of the Christian life, permanent, indissoluble, monogamous as well as monandrous. It is a sacrament because in it the incarnational dimension of the Gospel appears at its most eloquent: the very personality of human being, body and soul, channels the grace and the love of God. Whatever inferiority between man and wife society has devised, there can be only equality in the Gospel. Contemporary movements which demand total equality for husband and wife do reflect a Christian ideal in spite of their secular inspiration. The community of man and wife in marriage cannot be defined alone or even primarily in terms of sex. It must be seen and experienced in terms of love and community so profound that they are expressed and built up through sexual union. Although Catholic theology has, until recently, stressed procreation as the primary purpose of marriage, in keeping with the Augustinian doctrine on the "goods" of matrimony, this purpose should be set in the broader context of a relationship of love which must be its own end to the very extent that love here below participates in God's very life. One cannot but welcome the contemporary concern for authenticity in sexual relations, for this corresponds to the intrinsic structure of Christian marriage.

It follows from the "high" conception of sacramental marriage which I am outlining that sex can have no meaning, sense, or direction outside of a permanent relationship and, for a Christian, outside of the participation in God which is signified by the sacramentality of marriage. Premarital and extramarital sex are tragic and self-condemning mistakes. The ideal of the virginal life does keep its traditional value as witnessing to a form of the love of God which transcends sexual relations. One need not speak of superiority or inferiority between virginity and marriage, a concern which is more quantitative and visual than spiritual. One should rather defend the equal value of both marriage and celibacy and their sanctifying power for those who are called to either of them.

Contemporary developments in society raise a number of problems that are unavoidable for those engaged in Christian marriage: problems of sexual behavior, birth control, divorce, the right to abortion. These pertain to the realm of moral theology, not to a theology of womanhood. To examine them from the happenstance of the Christian woman may indeed add a helpful dimension to moral judgment; yet such a horizon can change neither the basic principles nor the general conclusion to be drawn from them. The theology in question is embedded in a sacramental reflection on marriage no less, and perhaps much more, than on a natural law. This reflection again stands in need of a feminine accent. And if the conclusion of this book is correct—namely, that man and woman cannot be Christianly specified otherwise than as human beings—then the feminine accent in moral theology cannot alter any basic proposition concerning ethical behavior.

On the matter of birth control I have explained my stance elsewhere in reference to the encyclical *Humanae vitae*.[14] More recent literature has offered no convincing reason to shift the position which I formulated then. Briefly, the ethics of birth control cannot prescind from critically studying the morality of contraceptive methods, unless one makes exceptions to the principle that the end never justifies the means. I cannot see how such an exception can be made even in favor of some higher good,[15] for it would then become impossible to determine with any degree of probability what context would legitimate similar exceptions. In other words, acceptance of the exception nulifies the whole principle. And once the principle has been abandoned, the ultimate moral barrier to the manipulation of human beings has also vanished. There would be no qualitative difference between such a manipulation for the sake of birth control and that with which Adolf Hitler boldly experimented in his "ultimate solution" to the Jewish question. The classical objections of Catholic ethics, which *Humanae vitae* reasserted, remain valid. One may question, however, the extension of these objections to new means of birth control, working in a biological way, in which the distinction between nature and culture, necessity and biology is blurred to the point of extinction.

Secular woman's aspiration to freedom from unwanted pregnancy arises today from economic, demographic, financial, cultural, social, and psychological conditions no less, and perhaps more, than from selfish or erotic motives. On the one hand, I cannot see by what stretch of imagination those could be considered equivalent to basic Christian categories and commitments. On the other, concern for the Kingdom of God, which ought to be basic to all the faithful and which is central to Christian ethics, does not dispense the Christian woman from her responsibility and coresponsibility in, to, and with society. Accordingly, birth control ideas and ideals may be shared and, to an extent, endorsed by the Christian concern for a more spiritual and less selfish life. In view of the impending population explosion, of the dire straits of larger families in crowded areas, and of the growing sense of the integrity of the bodily relationship in the context of interpersonal love, birth control acquires the consistency and goodness which make it possible to view it as a Christian concern. The growing medical reservations about the side effects of birth control pills may well end up in wider recourse to mechanical means of contraception which, with classical Catholic ethics, I consider to be morally unacceptable. But ethical norms may never be derived from social facts. The freedom of the Christian woman, like that of the Christian man, can come to fruition only in the context of the order of justice, which is an objective order. It will be assisted in this area by further medical and biological research, not by the disregard of ethical objections.

This is obviously not the place for a full discussion of ethics. But it is clear from the preceeding pages that I regard situational ethics as morally wrong, intellectually absurd, and practically confusing. The **morality of an action** does not derive only from the situation; it depends on a total context which involves, besides the situation, the objective morality of the act that is to be performed and the personal intentions of the doer. It would be **equally** mistaken to make Christian ethics depend exclusively on any of these three elements, situation, object, and intention. The contemporary secular trend focuses on situation and circumstances; Protestant ethics have usually been focused on intention; classical Catholic ethics, while taking account of all three elements, has given pride of place to objective morality. Because ethics cannot be only a matter of a good intention, the question of an objective morality of the means of birth control must be taken seriously.

The systematic moral theology developed since the seventeenth and eighteenth centuries has therefore been focused on the three aspects of an action (the object of the act, the intention of the doer, the circumstances). A good act requires the goodness of these three aspects; an act is more or less evil (or less good), as one or more of these aspects is not good. This approach to the morality of an action, which is indispensable to teachers, counsellors, and confessors, does not exhaust the morality of the Gospel. The Christian who examines his behavior should first see himself in the light of the Gospel. The Christian call to perfection, "Be perfect as your heavenly Father is perfect" (Matt. 5:48), implies an invitation to daily heroism. The love to which the disciples are called is, like God's own *agape* manifested in the Lord Jesus, lived in self-giving. In other words, the life of the faithful should aim much further than the negative morality implied in the analyses of action by moral theology. From the point of view of the Gospel, Christian ethics is an ethics of the Kingdom, manifesting here below, in witness and anticipation, the perfection of the saints in God. In the light of this, one should assess one's own life and set goals of self-discipline and asceticism which are necessary to the self-purification needed of those who have heard "Blessed are the pure of heart, for they shall see God" (Matt. 5:8).

Sexual ethics, and all the practical problems that modern life raises in relation to sex, must be placed in this eschatological perspective. Then, the problem no longer lies in determining the minimal morality of an act; it is to seek the Kingdom of God and its justice, and everything else, including the spiritual instinct to select the correct course of action, will be given from above. Indeed, the modern mentality, which gets most impatient with what it interprets as the hairsplitting of moral theologians, remains sensitive to a call to perfection even when it feels unable to answer it. The greatness of Pope Paul's encyclical *Humanae vitae* was its reiteration of this call to perfection implied in the Gospel; its weakness was a language that was hardly comprehensible to most contemporaries.[16]

After this remark on the ethics of the Gospel, need we examine the burning problem of abortion? The freedom to obtain legal abortions is certainly among the goals of the movement for feminine liberation today. For this reason it cannot be shunned. Yet we must approach it again from the lower point of view of a minimal morality rather than from the higher standpoint of the ethics of the Gospel. For it cannot be raised in the perspective of the perfection of the Kingdom to which we are called. It can only be faced in the twilight morality of the world in which we still live.

For moral theology, the current question is not whether abortion may be legalized, but whether Christian believers may have recourse to legalized abortion. The legalization of abortion is a social problem. On this point the groups which lobby against legalization of abortion often labor under a great deal of confusion as to the proper issue.

Be that as it may, the moral problem is relatively easy to solve in theory, whatever difficulties must undoubtedly assail those who have to make practical decisions in this area. The equivalence of abortion with murder, which may be read in the average textbook of moral theology, results from an oversimplification. Thomas Aquinas himself did not equate the human fetus with a human being before the infusion of a spiritual soul, a phenomenon which he believed to follow conception by several months. Voluntary interruption of the process of life cannot be identified with murder. It is exactly what the words say and no more: the ending of a process that would otherwise produce a new human life, a new human being. Thus the exact question is not: when is there a human soul? It becomes: when is there new life? When does the biological process of pregnancy produce a life which is no longer that of the mother only?

If the human fetus may be considered an organ of the mother, an abortion may be morally permitted according to the principle of subsidiarity, like any other major surgical intervention in bodily processes. As soon as the fetus can no longer be regarded as an organ of the mother, but must be seen as another being, then direct abortion by killing the fetus enters the category of the slaughter of the innocent. Admittedly, it may be remarked that the surgical intervention in question may directly affect the placenta rather than the fetus. In this case again, it would not qualify as killing, because the organ that has been directly interfered with can only be a maternal organ. The principle of subsidiarity may be applied to the excision of an organ for the good of the person of which it is a part.

Thus it would seem that relatively simple clarifications based on classical categories of moral theology may help to face the contemporary problem. It should go without saying that the use of freedom must be responsible, that weighty reasons alone may justify such a drastic action as an abortion, and that the burden of education and of self-discipline increases as technology and social permissiveness make more concrete freedoms available.

But one must still ask the fundamental question of the Kingdom of God and its call to perfection: are abortions compatible with the ethics of the Gospel? Can they have any meaning in relation to the eschatological fulfillment to which Christians tend? Can an earnest seeker of the Kingdom stop along his way in order to obtain an abortion, and what would she gain thereby in relation to what alone is necessary, her progressive discovery of God in Christ? Such questions should be answered only in light of the coming Kingdom.

The spread of social and political freedom to the realm of marriage and family life shows clearly that mankind is at last on the verge of overcoming the two previous states in which men have lived, the matriarchal and the patriarchal organizations of society. The advent of woman to total social equality with man spells the doom of all previous types of civilization. Insofar as this permits the Christian woman to manifest in her way of life the internal and sacramental freedom she enjoys under the Gospel, this revolution of human mores is to be welcomed. Yet it goes without saying that one may remain critical of some forms already taken by the feminine liberation. This criticism need not entail a fight against the new mores, since these do correspond to some cherished principles and objectives; but it does mean a free refusal to share in some of the liberties gained by woman in the secular world. Thus, the principle of divorce and remarriage cannot be accepted in a Christian concept of the relationship between man and wife. The Christian should, on this point, struggle in favor of the possibility of divorce and remarriage in the eyes of the state, but reject the very thought of himself or herself adopting the successive polygamy or polyandry which divorce and remarriage amount to. The Church can never abandon her traditional belief in the permanent relationship of marriage.

This is not to say, however, that certain accommodations cannot be sought within the freedom of the Gospel. For instance, it is morally inconceivable— although this is the standard practice for both Catholic and Portestant missionaries—to break up the polygamous relationships of converts to whom prescription has in fact given natural and societal rights and duties that ought to be honored. At the other end of the spectrum, whereas the Church cannot admit divorce, she may consider new causes for annulments of marriage which would correspond to and derive from the psychological problems of contemporary men and women. Thus I can see no theological objection to interpreting the early breakdown of a marriage relationship as implying that there had never truly been a voluntary commitment to permanent marriage. Or: the long existence of an impediment of physical impotence suggests the possibility of a parallel impediment of psychological incompatibility, even though this may not always be discerned before the progressive collapse of mutual relationships. These questions cannot be solved here: they raise points of Canon Law, of moral theology, and of sacramental theology that need further study. It is sufficient for the purpose of this book to show in what direction the freedom of the Gospel as applied specifically to the status of woman in the Church, seems to be pointing.

The controverted questions briefly examined in this final chapter may well constitute the frontier of the next major turmoil in the life of the Catholic Church, following the attempt at self-reform initiated by John XXIII. Although these reforms may be far-reaching, there is no reason to envisage them otherwise than with serenity. Indeed, the anxiety and the panic that seized many in the wake of Vatican II have been immeasurably wasteful and have certainly not shown much depth of Christian conviction and of confidence in the God-given structures of the Church. I would suggest now that the liturgical reforms, the canonical adjustments, the institutional updating that have taken place in the last few years, and that are not yet completely effective, will be looked upon as elementary in comparison with the infinitely more thorough self-reform implied in the accession of women to the full freedom which they should enjoy in the Church. Even such a step as the introduction of a married clergy of the Latin rite would mean very little in terms of a reform of the Church as a whole: married men tend to be no less one-sided in their views and projects than single men. Sharing initiative, responsibility, and spiritual power with women would bring about much more altered ways of acting and thinking in both clergy and laity. It would undoubtedly have a cathartic effect that the halfhearted reforms of the last few years cannot possibly equal.

Should we balk at the idea of introducing into the already hard pressed Church such a leven of self-transformation? Yes, indeed—unless we believe that the Catholic Church today is still the Ecclesia to which the words of eternal life were entrusted, against which the gates of hell shall not prevail, and in which the Spirit dwells, leading it unto all the truth.

Conclusion

In the course of this volume, I have abstained from venturing outside a strictly theological point of view. I would not claim, however, to have reached the anthropology of the last two chapters without the help of philosophical reflection, and so by way of conclusion I will indicate briefly which contemporary nontheological trends I find particularly congenial to my way of thinking.

Let us begin with the person who is undoubtedly the universal father of contemporary thought, Karl Marx.

In the writings of the younger Marx one major point about woman deserves to be remembered. This is the idea that the primary test of man's relationship to nature (understanding by this term the material elements of his surroundings and the other human beings who together with him constitute the human species), and therefore of man's relationship to himself as part of nature, is no other than his relationship to woman:

> In the relationship to woman as the prey and the handmaid of communal lust, is expressed the infinite degradation in which man exists for himself; for the secret of this relationship finds its unequivocal, incontestable, open and revealed expression in the relation of man to woman and in the way in which the direct and natural species relationship is conceived. The immediate, natural and necessary relation of human being to human being is also the relation of man to woman. . . .[1]

Marx's starting point itself remains excessively masculine. For although he refers to man's relation to woman, he omits the correlative importance of woman's relationship to man in order to test her own place in relation to nature, to mankind, and to herself. Once this has been corrected, however, the fact remains that a human being's relationship to persons of the other sex provides a criterion of his relationship to himself, to his own sex, and to mankind

226

as a whole. Thus, one's concept of femininity holds the key both to personal behavior and to theoretical anthropology, whether this is conceived as descriptive of existing behavior or as normative of moral attitudes and orientations.[2]

More recent philosophical writings about woman have highlighted an element of major importance. Mme Yvonne Pellé-Douel, starting her study from phenomenological considerations, insists on the difference between "nature" and "culture."[3] Nature is the datum with which man starts and is confronted. Culture is the human superstructure built upon the basis of nature. Once this distinction has been understood, it is obvious that nature in the form of a natural law cannot be considered a normative limit to human activity and behavior, however much it may constitute a *de facto* limit in the actual situation of a given man. Like the wider problem of anthropology, the problem of womanhood must be raised at the two levels of nature and of culture. Womanhood is a datum of nature; and its natural function is sufficiently described anatomically and observed physiologically. As a cultural development, however, womanhood can only be what mankind makes it to be. This in turn can be looked at from a descriptive standpoint, as is commonly done by ethnologists and sociologists, who observe the data of the diverse human civilizations, or from a normative angle which attempts to determine what womanhood ought to become in the ongoing process of culture. On account of its possibilities as normative reflection, a theology of womanhood, or a theological anthropology, would be of interest even to unbelieving philosophers, insofar as these desire to record the achievements that culture has added and is able to add to nature.

Modern psychology offers us an element of major importance, namely Carl Jung's typology of *animus* and *anima*. As analyzed in *Two Essays in Analytical Psychology*,[4] *anima* is the unconscious aspect of man's soul, in which he compensates for his one-sided masculine image and behavior with hidden, but real, feminine features. Reversely, *animus* is woman's unconscious male counterweight to her own femininity. *Animus* typifies the masculine and roughly corresponds to the conventional male figure of a given society, whereas *anima* typifies the feminine and roughly fits the conventional image of woman in society. It is of paramount importance that, whereas *animus* and *anima* characterize respectively male and female personality, each nurses its reverse and counterpart in its unconscious depths. Thus a man's concept of woman unknowingly corresponds to his own unconscious, while a woman's concept of man corresponds likewise to her own unconscious. This is to say a concrete human being is exclusively neither male nor female. He is constituted by a more or less unstable mixture of the two principles. Virile elements are active in ths psyche of woman, as feminine elements reside in man. To an extent that can hardly be exaggerated, human balance rests in the conscious integration of *animus* by woman and of *anima* by man, an incorporation which is often facilitated by marriage, when the person selected fits the interior image of the other sex present and active in one's soul.

In the light of this, one may well hold, with Edith Stein, J. J. Buytendijk, Michael Müller, and many others, that masculinity and femininity are not aspects of humanity, but rather ways of being human.[5] Each is a complete way and, perfect in itself, conveys an adequate experience of being human. Yet each is never by itself. For it implies a relationship to, and a contrasted share in, the other way. The way of being human of which, according to the predominance of the characteristics of one sex, one is not usually aware is confined to the unconscious, where it is nonetheless active. Accordingly, the two ways are not exclusive. The ideal human being does not choose one way over against the other. He rather lives one way at the primary level; and he shares the other, thus living it at a secondary level.

This psychological approach shows a certain convergence with both the existentialist reflection of Simone de Beauvoir and the anthropology of other authors working in the perspective of structuralism.[6] In all these shcools of thought, no typology of womanhood determines woman's being. Whatever typology of the yin and the yang may be discovered in human experience illustrates aspects of all human beings, who are all male and female in a certain sense and to a certain degree. The existentialist doctrine that man and woman are what they make themselves to become is correct enough as an analysis of fact, though singularly unhelpful as a norm of conduct. For it is not enough to be free; one should also know what to do with freedom. Simone de Beauvoir's identification of the man-woman relation with the master-slave relation results from an unacceptable oversimplification of the facts.

On the contrary, I find a great deal in common between the conclusions to which the present theological investigation leads me and the reflection of Abel Jeannière. Here, all determinism as to what woman is or ought to be has been abandoned. Yet we are not left in existential darkness. It is in her relationship to man that woman discovers herself as woman; and she does not exist as woman except in that relationship. Likewise, man does not exist as man except as related to woman. Womanhood and manhood jointly point up the relational structure of mankind. Each person is fully a human being in this relationship. Whereas the fundamental relationship of master and slave (with its concrete forms: rich and poor, capitalist and worker, governor and governed) is disjunctive; that of man and woman is unitive. This analysis does not lead directly to a description of womanhood; yet it places the problem of womanhood in the context of a sexual anthropology.

Finally, although theology should not attempt to be sociology, it cannot ignore the situation in which woman lives in the contemporary world. For this reason many assumptions made by past theologians should not be discarded.

The Fathers of the Church could not foresee what far-reaching changes the evolution of society would entail in the situation of man and woman and what requirements would ensue for the proper location of a theological anthropology. Likewise, the tenets of ancient and medieval science and psychology should no longer dominate a theology of womanhood, even when these conclusions or some of them were shared by Thomas Aquinas, have been embodied in canon law and in sacramental theology, and still largely dictate or inspire the general attitude of the Church's magisterium toward woman and her function in the Christian community. The conquests of the feminist movement cannot be questioned. Woman is politically and socially equal to man; she enjoys the same civic and legal rights; all careers are, in principle, opened to her. It is up to woman herself—and by this I mean, not to woman as an abstract idea, but to each woman—to make her choice among the opportunities that are available and to orient her life and career in her own way. Discriminations that continue to divide men and women in politics, business, and social life must eventually go; and the sooner the better. The theological question does not lie at that level.

The theological problem consists in reevaluating for today and tomorrow the models of womanhood that have been proposed in the Church. Although we cannot be satisfied with the solutions of yesterday, we will still find in Christ himself, in whom "all the jewels of wisdom and knowledge are hidden" (Colossians, 2:3), the principles of Christian anthropology. The proclamation of Christian freedom is as old as the Gospel.

Notes

NOTES TO CHAPTER 1

1. Besides the standard commentaries and dictionaries, see Joseph-Marie Lagrange, *Le Judaïsme avant Jésus-Christ* (Paris, 1931); Roland de Vaux, *Les Institutions de l'Ancien Testament*, 2 vols. (Paris, 1965); Louis Bouyer, *Man and Woman with God* (London, 1960); Pierre Grelot, *Le Couple humain dans l'Ecriture* (Paris, 1961); Lucien Legrand, *La Virginité dans la Bible* (Paris, 1964); Thierry Maertens, *La Promotion de la femme dans la Bible* (Tournai, 1967); Marie Welles Clapp, *The Old Testament as It Concerns Women* (New York, 1934); Elsie Thomas Culver, *Woman in the World of Religion* (New York, 1967); Clarence Vos, *Woman in Old Testament Worship* (Delft, 1968). For a totally absurd interpretation of Genesis, see Theodor Reik, *The Creation of Woman: A Psychoanalytic Inquiry into the Myth of Eve* (New York, 1960).

2. The Old Testament translations are taken from the Jerusalem Bible.

3. The New English Bible translates, in keeping with Hebrew and RSV: "closed the flesh over the place."

4. Johannes Leipoldt, *Die Frau in der antiken Welt und im Urchristentum*, 2nd ed. (Leipzig, 1955), pp. 72-116.

5. On the Therapeutes, see Philo, *The Contemplative Life* (Loeb Classical Library, *Philo*, IX [Cambridge, Mass., 1941], 113-169). The following quotations are from chap. 9, p. 155 and chap. 11, p. 165.

6. Pierre Bonnard, *La Sagesse en personne annoncée et venue* (Paris, 1966).

7. Daniel Lys, *Le Plus Beau Chant de la création* (Paris, 1968).

NOTES TO CHAPTER 2

1. Johannes Leipoldt, *Jesus und die Frau* (Leipzig, 1921); *Die soziale Gedanke in der altchristichen Kirche* (Leipzig, 1951), and *Die Frau in der antiken Welt und im Urchristentum*, 2nd ed. (Leipzig, 1955); Madeline Southard, *The Attitude of Jesus toward Woman* (New York, 1927); G. F. Moore, *Judaism in the First Centuries of the Christian Era*, 3 vols. (Cambridge, 1925-1930); Joseph Bonsirven, *Le Judaïsme Palestinien au temps de Jésus-Christ*, 2 vols. (Paris, 1935); P. Ketter, *Christus und die Frauen*, 2 vols. (Stuttgart, 1944-1949); Fritz Blanke and Franz Leenhardt, *Die Stellung der Frau im Neuen Testament und in alten Kirche* (Zurich, 1949); Krister Stendahl, *The Bible and the Role of Women* (Philadelphia, 1927). Unless otherwise indicated, translations from the New Testament will follow the Jerusalem Bible.

2. Gerhard Delling, *Paulus' Stellung zu Frau und Ehe* (Stuttgart, 1931); Else Kähler, *Die Frau in den Paulinischen Briefen* (Zurich, 1960).

3. For another interpretation, see Jean Daniélou, *The Ministry of Women in the Early Church* (London, 1961), p. 10.

4. Leopold Zscharnack, *Der Dienst der Frau in dern ersten Jahrhunderten der christlichen Kirche* (Göttingen, 1902); Henry Wheeler, *Deaconesses Ancient and Modern* (New York, 1889); Henri Chirat, *L'Assemblée Chrétienne a l'âge apostolique* (Paris, 1949).

5. For another interpretation, see Joseph Bonsirven, *Le Divorce dans le Nouveau Testament* (Paris, 1948).

6. See R. H. Charles, *The Revelation of St. John* (Edinburgh, 1920) I, xxix-lxi; Raymond Brown, *The Gospel according to John* (New York, 1966) I, lxxxvi and ciii-civ.

7. Irenaeus, *Adversus haereses*, IV; Eusebius, *Historia ecclesiastica*, III, 23.

8. André Feuillet, *L'Apocalypse* (Paris, 1963).

9. Yves Congar, *Le Mystère du Temple* (Paris, 1958).

10. Frederick H. Borsch, *The Son of Man in Myth and History* (Philadelphia, 1967).

11. Anscar Vonier, *The Spirit and the Bride* (London, 1935); Héribert Muehlen, *L'Esprit dans l'Eglise*, 2 vols. (Paris, 1969).

NOTES TO CHAPTER 3

1. Jean Daniélou, *Théologie du Judéo-Christianisme* (Paris, 1958).

2. *Stromata*, III, 45. See *Ante-Nicene Fathers*, II (New York, 1926). My translations of Greek and Latin texts being largely my own, I will refer to standard English translations for purposes of information only.

3. *Stromata*, III, 66.

4. *Stromata*, III, 91 ff.

5. *Gospel of Thomas*, no. 112. See Robert M. Grant, *The Secret Sayings of Jesus* (New York, 1960), p. 197.

6. *Second Epistle of Clement*, chap. 12 (*Ante-Nicene Fathers*, VII, 517-523).

7. *Second Epistle of Clement*, chap. 14.

8. *Questions and Answers in Genesis*, bk. I, no. 27 (Loeb Classical Library, Philo, Supplement I [Cambridge, Mass., 1953]).

9. Daniélou, pp. 23-25.

10. R. H. Charles, *The Apocrypha and Pseudepigrapha of the Old Testament*, II (Oxford, 1965), 298-299.

11. *4 Esdras* 10:27. See Philo, *Questions and Answers in Genesis*, bk. I, no. 26.

12. Discussions on the authorship of *The Shepherd* need not affect the bearing of the book on our theme. See Stanislas Giet, *Hermas et les Pasteurs. Le Trois Auteurs du Pasteur d'Hermas* (Paris, 1963).

13. Daniélou, pp. 46-49.

14. *The Shepherd*, Vision I, chap. 1 (*Ante-Nicene Fathers*, II, 9-55).

15. Vision II, chap. 4, no. 1.

16. Vision III, chap. 3, no. 3.

17. Vision III, chap. 10, no. 3-6.

18. Two remarks may be added here: 1) Rodè appears in Acts 12:13 as the name of the maid who opened the gate to Peter after his miraculous escape from jail. Thus, Rodè may be given a symbolic meaning as to the shelter which is the Church. 2) Both in Greek (the language of *The Shepherd*) and in Hebrew (which is relevant here since *The Shepherd* is a Judeo-Christian work) the letters D and M are geometrically equivalent: D = 4 and M = 40. The vowel difference (è = 8, o = 70, ô = 800) may be disregarded, as the consonants suffice for the permutation of letters.

19. Vision I, chap. 1, no. 1.

20. Georges Blond, "Les Encratiques et la vie mystique" in *Mystique et Continence* (Paris, 1952), pp. 117-130.

21. Epiphanius, *De haeresibus*, XLI (P.G., 41, 1039), refers to the Apotactites. The codex of Theodosius (XVI, tit. V, lex 7 and 11) associates these to the Encratites, Hydroparastates, Saccophores, See D. T. C., vol. 1, col. 1646.

22. As for instance by Athenagoras and Tertullian; this is the topic of Tertullian's *De monogamia.*

23. *Stromata*, II, chap. 23 (S.Chr., 38, pp. 138-144).

24. Jean Daniélou, *The Ministry of Women in the Early Church* (London, 1961), originally an article in *La Maison-Dieu,* no. 61, 1960.

25. Eusebius, *Ecclesiastical History*, III, 31.

26. On Montanism, see ibid., V, 14-19 and Pierre de Labriolle, *La Crise Montaniste* (Paris, 1913).

27. Irenaeus, *Adversus haereses*, bk. III, chap. 11, no. 9 (S.Chr., 34, pp. 202-205).

28. Hippolytus, *Philosophoumena*, bk. VIII, chap. 12 (*Ante-Nicene Fathers*, V, 9-153).

29. Epiphanius, *De haeresibus*, XLVIII, 2 (P.G., 41, 857).

30. Ibid., XLIX, 2 (881).

31. Eusebius, *Ecclesiastical History*, V, 3.

32. Ibid., V, 1.

33. Pierre de Labriolle, *Histoire de la litérature latine chrétienne* (Paris, 1920), p. 143.

34. *Passio Perpetuae et Felicitatis*, I, 3 (P.L., 3, 24-25).

35. Ibid., III, 2 (41).

36. Ibid., VI, 3 (55).

37. Ibid.

38. Tertullian, *De pudicitia*, I (*Fathers of the Church*, XL [New York, 1959]).

39. *De virginibus velandis*, 16.

40. On allegorical exegesis, see Henri de Lubac, *L'Exégèse médiévale*, 4 vols. (Paris, 1959-1964); *L'Ecriture dans la tradition* (Paris, 1967).

41. On Tertullian's theological method, see Joseph Moingt, *Théologie trinitaire de Tertullien*, vol. I (Paris, 1966), chap. 3.

42. *De exhortatione castitatis*, 9.

43. "Nihil novi Paraclitus inducit; quod proemonuit, definit; quod sustinuit, exposcit" (*De monogamia*, 3).

44. *De monogamia*, 5.

45. *De cultu feminarum*, I, 1.

46. Ibid., I, 8.

47. *Ad uxorem*, I, 1.

48. *De cultu feminarum*, II, 1.

49. Ibid., II, 2.

50. Ibid., II, 4.

51. *De monogamia*, 9.

52. *Ad uxorem*, II, 9.

53. *De virginibus velandis*, 16.

54. Ibid., 17.

55. *Ad uxorem*, I, 5.

56. *De monogamia*, 16.

57. *Ad uxorem*, I, 5.

58. On Philo, see Jean Daniélou, *Philon d'Alexandrie* (Paris, 1968); *Colloque national sur Philon d'Alexandrie*, Lyon, 11-15 Sept. 1966 (Paris, 1967).

59. *Legum allegoria*, II, 23-25 (Loeb Classical Library, *Philo*, I [Cambridge, Mass., 1962], 241).

60. *Questions and Answers on Genesis*, bk. I, no. 25.

61. See the theory of sex in Aristophanes' speech in Plato's *Banquet*.

62. *Questions and Answers on Genesis*, bk. I, no. 25.

63. On gnosticism, see Eugène de Faye, *Gnostiques et gnosticisme* (Paris, 1913); François Sagnard, *La Gnose valentinienne et le témoignage de saint Irénée* (Paris, 1947); "Introduction" to *Adversus haereses*, bk. III (S.Chr., 34); G. Quispel, "Introduction" to the *Letter of Ptolemaeus to Flora* (S.Chr., 24); Hans Jonas, *The Gnostic Religion* (Boston, 1958); Robert M. Grant, *Gnosticism and Early Christianity* (New York, 1959); *Gnosticism: A Source Book of Heretical Writings from the Early Christian Period* (New York, 1961).

64. Hippolytus, *Philosophoumena*; Clement of Alexandria, *Stromata*; Irenaeus, *Adversus haereses*. A systematic study of the gnostic library discovered in 1946 at Dag-Hammadi (Egypt) is still to be made.

65. Hippolytus, *Philosophoumena*, VI, 35. See F. Legge, *Philosophoumena*, II (London, 1921), 34.

66. Origen, *Commentary on St. John* (P.G., 14, 21-830); Irenaeus, *Adversus haereses*, bks I and II.

67. *Adversus haereses*, bk. I, 1, 1.

68. Clement of Alexandria, *Excerpta ex Theodoto*, 21 (S.Chr., 23, p. 99). See Olivier Prunet, *La Morale de Clément d'Alexandrie et le Nouveau Testament* (Paris, 1966).

69. *Excerpta ex Theodoto*, 22 (S.Chr., 23, p. 101).

70. Ibid., 68 (S.Chr., p. 193).

71. *Gospel of Thomas*, 112 (Grant, *The Secret Sayings of Jesus*, p. 197).

72. Clement, *Stromata,* III, 13, where it is attributed to Julius Cassianus, a Valentinian; *Gospel of Thomas,* 23 (see Grant, *The Secret Sayings of Jesus,* pp. 140-141, with the explanations on pp. 76-77); *Martyrium Petri,* no. 9 (see M. R. James, ed., *The Apocryphal New Testament* [Oxford, 1924], p. 335).

73. See above, n. 4.

74. *Adversus haereses,* bk. I, 13, 2-3 (P.G., 7, 584-585).

75. See above, n. 64.

76. *Recognitiones,* III, 59-61 (P.G., 1, 1307-1309; see *Ante-Nicene Fathers,* VIII, 129-130); *Homiliae,* II, 33 (P.G., 2, 100; see *Ante-Nicene Fathers,* VIII, 235).

77. Oscar Cullmann, *Le Problème littéraire et historique du Roman Pseudo-Clémentin* (Paris, 1930).

78. Jean Daniélou, *Théologie du Judéo-Christianisme,* pp. 71-76.

79. See *Didachè,* I, 1-6 (*Early Christian Fathers* [Philadelphia, 1953], pp. 171-172).

80. *Pedagogue,* I, IV, 1 (*Ante-Nicene Fathers,* II, 209-296).

81. Michael Spanneut, *Le Stoïcisme des Pères de l'Eglise, de Clément de Rome à Clément d'Alexandrie* (Paris, 1957).

82. This is the theme of bk. II, chaps. 10-12.

83. *Stromata,* II, 23.

84. Ibid., IV, 20.

85. Ibid., II, 23.

86. Ibid.

87. *Pedagogue,* II, 8.

88. *Stromata,* III, 12.

89. Ibid.

90. *Commentary in Matthew,* XVII, 33. My treatment of Origen is indebted to Henri Crouzel, *Virginité et mariage selon Origène* (Paris-Bruges, 1962). See also Crouzel, *L'Eglise primitive face au divorce* (Paris, 1971). For the quotation, Crouzel, *Virginité et mariage selon Origène,* p. 22.

91. *Fragment in 1 Cor.,* XXXIX (Crouzel, p. 33).

92. *Homilies in Luke,* XIV (Crouzel, p. 63).

93. Crouzel, p. 86.

94. Crouzel, p. 105.

95. Crouzel, p. 161.

96. *Homilies in Josuah,* IX, 9 (Crouzel, p. 138).

97. *Selecta in Exodus,* XXIII, 17 (Crouzel, p. 137).

98. Quoted in Crouzel, p. 142, n. 1.

99. Eusebius, *Ecclesiastical History,* VI, 21 and 36.

100. Justin, *Dialogue with Trypho,* no. 100 (P.G., 6, 710-711). See *Writings of Saint Justin Martyr,* in *Fathers of the Church,* VI.

101. *Adversus haereses,* III, 22, 4 (S.Chr., 34, p. 380).

102. Ibid., II, 22, 4 (p. 382).

103. Ibid., III, 21, 9 (p. 370).

104. *Epistula apostolorum,* no. 43 (M. R. James, p. 501).

105. Ibid.

106. Ibid., no. 45 (p. 502).

107. *The Gospel according to the Hebrews* (M. R. James, p. 33).

108. Ibid. (p. 5).

NOTES TO CHAPTER 4

1. Louis Bouyer, *La Vie de saint Antoine. Essai sur la spiritualité du monachisme primitif* (Paris, 1950); *Le Sens de la vie monastique* (Turnhout, 1950); *La Spiritualité du Nouveau Testament et des Pères* (Paris, 1960).

2. Gonzague Truc, *Histoire illustrée de la femme*, 2 vols. (Paris, 1940-1941), I, 81-84; James Donaldson, *Woman: Her Position and Influence in Ancient Greece and Rome, and among the Early Christians* (London, 1907), pp. 1-75.

3. Truc, I, 85-115.

4. The term "neo-sophistic" is applied in general to the philosophical style of the third century, characterized by rhetoric, eloquence, and exaggeration.

5. *Recognitiones*, VII, 32 (P.G., 1, 1387).

6. Basilius of Ancyra should not be confused with St. Basil of Caesarea (329-379), to whom the *De virginitate* has sometimes erroneously been attributed.

7. A. Vaillant, ed. and trans., *De Virginitate de St. Basile. Texte vieux-slave; traduction française* (Paris, 1943), p. 5.

8. Ibid., p. 7.

9. Ibid.

10. Ibid., p. 31.

11. Ibid., p. 33.

12. Ibid., p. 7.

13. Ibid., p. 9.

14. Ibid., p. 59.

15. The concept and the ideal of "apatheia, ataraxia" are also basic to Stoic philosophy.

16. Basilius, in Vaillant, p. 59.

17. Ibid., p. 61.

18. My references will be to the edition of *The Banquet* in S.Chr., 95 (Paris, 1963); an English translation will be found in *Ancient Christian Writers*, 27 (Westminster, Md., 1958), 38-162.

19. S.Chr., 95, p. 213.

20. Ibid., p. 69.

21. Ibid., p. 71.

22. Although the Church is fully manifested only with the advent of Christ, its history goes, in the words of Vatican II, "from Abel the just to the last of the elect" (*Constitution De Ecclesia*, no. 2). This expression is itself borrowed from the Fathers.

23. S.Chr., 95, p. 59.

24. Ibid., p. 111.

25. Ibid., p. 49.

26. Ibid., p. 39.

27. Gregory of Nyssa, *On Virginity*, chap. 7 (S.Chr., 119, pp. 349-359). Also, John Chrysostom, *On Virginity*, chaps. 2-3, 8-10 (S.Chr., 125).

28. John Chrysostom, *Letter to Theodora* (S.Chr., 117, pp. 71ff).

29. *On Virginity*, chaps. 15-17 (S.Chr., 125).

30. *Homily in Genesis IV*, no. 18 (P.G., 53, 154).

31. *On Virginity*, chap. 19 (S.Chr., 125, p. 159).

32. Ibid., chap. 25 (p. 175).

33. *Letter to Theodora*, chap. 14 (S.Chr., 117, p. 167).

34. *Letter to a Young Widow* (S.Chr., 138, p. 159).

35. *Carmen ad Olympiaden* (P.G., 21, 897-918).

36. *On Virginity*, chaps. 40 and 50-58 (S.Chr., 125).

37. Ibid., chap. 37; *On the One Marriage* (S.Chr., 138, pp. 161-201).

38. *On the One Marriage* (p. 191).

39. *On Virginity* (S.Chr., 119, p. 351).

40. *Homily Quales ducendae sint uxores* (in *Opera omnia*, ed. Montfaucon [Paris, 1832] III, 259).

41. Ibid.

42. *The Banquet* (S.Chr., 95, p. 185).

43. Ibid. (pp. 305-307).

44. *On Virginity* (S.Chr., 119, p. 269).

45. Ibid. (p. 397).

46. Plotinus, *Ennead* I, bk. VI, nos. 6-9. See Stephen MacKenna, *The Enneads of Plotinus*, I (Boston, 1916), 84-89.

47. *On Virginity* (S.Chr., 119, p. 503).

48. Chrysostom, *On Virginity* (S.Chr., 125, p. 351).

49. Ibid., chap. 7.

50. Gregory of Nyssa, *On Virginity*, chap. 7 (S.Chr., 119).

51. Ibid., chap. 14.

52. Ibid., chap. 2.

53. Ibid., chap. 14 (p. 433).

54. Chrysostom, *On Virginity* (S.Chr., 125, p. 377).

55. Ibid., chaps. 1-2.

56. Chrysostom, *On the One Marriage* (S.Chr., 138, p. 199).

57. Chrysostom, *On the Epistle to the Hebrews, XII*, Homilia XXVIII, no. 7 (P.G., 63, 202).

58. *On Virginity* (S.Chr., 125, p. 367).

59. *Letter VIII to Olympia* (date: 404) (S.Chr., 13, pp. 121-122).

60. P.G., 33, 1564 d.

61. P.G., 33, 1565 a.

62. Chrysostom, *Homily VIII on Genesis I*, no. 4 (P.G., 53, 73).

63. Ibid.

64. Ibid., no. 3 (P.G., 53, 72).

65. *On Virginity*, chap. 12, no. 2 (S.Chr., 119, pp. 399-411). See *On the Creation of Man*, chap. 16 (S.Chr., 6).

66. *On Virginity* (p. 411).
67. Ibid. (pp. 401-403).
68. Ibid. (p. 421).
69. Dietrich Ritschl, *Memory and Hope* (New York, 1967), p. 95.
70. *On the One Marriage* (S.Chr., 138, p. 183).
71. Ibid.
72. *Homily Quales ducendae sint uxores*, in *Opera*, III, 260.
73. Ibid., pp. 260-261.
74. *On Virginity* (S.Chr., 119, pp. 259-263).
75. Ibid., pp. 263-271.
76. Ibid., pp. 271-274.
77. *Homilia XV in Genesis II*, no. 3 (P.G., 53, 122).
78. *Homilia XVII in Genesis III*, no. 9 (p. 145).
79. Gregory Nazianzen, *Oratio VIII*, no. 8 (P.G., 20, 502). On Macrina the younger (c. 327-379), elder sister of Basil and Gregory of Nyssa, see Gregory of Nyssa, *Life of Macrina the younger* (P.G., 46, 959-1000).
80. *On His Own Life*, verse 60 (P.G., 21, 590).
81. *On the Priesthood*, bk. I, chap. 5 (*Opera*, I, 443-444).
82. *On Saint Thecla* (*Opera*, II, 897-899).
83. Ferdinand Cavallera, *Saint Jérome*, I (Paris, 1922), 123-129.
84. *Laudiac History*, 41, 1 (*Ancient Christian Writers*, 34 [Westminster, Md., 1965], p. 117).
85. See above, n. 35.
86. *Letter VIII to Olympia*, no. 12 (S.Chr., 13, p. 138).
87. *Therapy of Hellenic Diseases*, chap. 5 (S.Chr., 57, p. 244).
88. P.G., 36, 289-292. See J. Bernardi, *La Prédication des Pères cappadociens* (Paris, 1968).
89. *Life of Saint Melany* (S.Chr., 90, p. 151).
90. *The Pilgrimage of Etheria* (S.Chr., 21).
91. *Second Letter of Clement*, no. 12 (*Early Christian Fathers* [Philadelphia, 1953], pp. 197-198). See H. Achelis, *Virgines Subintroductae. Ein Beitrag zu 1 Cor., VII* (Leipzig, 1902).
92. Charles Williams, *The Descent of the Dove* (New York, 1956), p. 11.
93. *Contra eos qui subintroductas habent virgines*, no. 12 (*Opera*, I, 303).
94. Eusebius, *Ecclesiastical History*, bk. VII, chap. 30. See Penguin Classics ed., (London, 1965), p. 318.
95. Jean Daniélou, *The Ministry of Women in the Early Church* (London, 1961), p. 22 ff.
96. Henri Leclercq, "La législation conciliaire relative au célibat ecclesiastique" in Hefele-Leclercq, *Histoire des Conciles*, vol. II/2 (Paris, 1908), appendix VI.
97. C.O.D., p. 6.
98. Socrates (c. 380-c. 450), *Ecclesiastical History*, bk. I, chap. 11 (P.G., 66, 1485). The same information is given by Sozomen (c. 400-c. 450), *Ecclesiastical History*, bk. I, chap. 23 (P.G., 67, 925).
99. Socrates, ibid. Synesius (c. 370-c. 414), a neo-Platonist philosopher

who studied under Hypatia in Alexandria, was elected bishop o *239*
410, when, apparently, he was not yet baptized; his remaining \
P.G., 64, 1021-1756.

    100. Hefele-Leclercq, vol. I/2 (Paris, 1907), pp. 1029-1045.

    101. Hefele-Leclercq, vol. I/1, pp. 620-624.

    102. Ibid., pp. 312-313.

    103. *Apostolic Constitutions,* bk. I, chap. 8 (P.G., 1, 579). S
chap. 29 (986-987).

    104. *Apostolic Constitutions,* bk. I, chap. 9 (586-588).

    105. Ibid., bk. III, chap. 9 (782-787).

    106. Ibid., bk. VIII, chaps. 24-25 (1122).

    107. Ibid., chaps. 19-20 (1115-1118).

    108. Dionysios of Alexandria, *Canonical Epistle* (P.G., 10, 1282).

NOTES TO CHAPTER 5

    1. *Epistola CXXVII,* no. 5 (P.L., 22, 1088).

    2. Roman girls were commonly called by the feminine form of their fa-ther's name (Flavius, Flavia); often they were simply designated by numbers (Quinta, Sexta).

    3. A. C. Johnson, P. L. Coleman-Norton, F. C. Bourne, *Ancient Roman Statutes* (University of Texas, 1961), p. 10. On Roman women, see Gonzague Truc, *Histoire illustrée de la femme,* 2 vols. (Paris, 1940-1941), I, 117-151; Theodor Birt, *Frauen der Antike* (Leipzig, 1932); Johannes Leipoldt, *Die Frau in der antiken Welt und im Urchristentum,* 2nd ed. (Leipzig, 1955), pp. 16-24; Gulielmo Ferrero, *Le Donne dei Cesari* (Milan, 1925); Jerome Carco-pino, *Daily Life in Ancient Rome* (New Haven, 1940); J. Assa, *Les Grandes Dames Romaines* (Paris, 1958); James Donaldson, *Woman: Her Position and Influence in Ancient Greece and Rome, and among the Early Christians* (Lon-don, 1907), pp. 77-147.

    4. Johnson, Coleman-Norton, Bourne, p. 3.

    5. Ibid., p. 10.

    6. "On the Vestal Virgins he [Numa Pompilius] conferred high honors, among which was the right of making a will while their father lived, and of doing all other juristic acts without a guardian" (ibid., p. 4).

    7. On the vestals see R. Schilling, "Vestales et vierges chrétiennes dans la Rome antique," *Revue des Sciences Religieuses,* XXXV (1961), 113-129. Gonzague Truc mentions some of the mishaps in vestal history: in 114 B.C., three of the vestals were accused of fornication and buried alive; Emperor Caracalla, who was half insane, raped one of them, Claudia Laeta, and had her buried alive for it; Emperor Heliogabalus married and divorced three vestals successively, then remarried the first. On the whole, however, the vestals seem to have led a dignified life and to have been respected.

    8. Ambrose, *Epistola XVIII,* nos. 11-12 (P.L., 16, 975).

    9. Cyprian, *On the Dress of Virgins,* chap. 3 (P.L., 4, 455); see *Fathers of the Church,* XXXVI (New York, 1958), 31-51. Cyprian's treatise is largely dependent on Tertullian.

Id., chap. 5 (457).

bid., chap. 14 (466); chap. 18 (470-471); chap. 19 (471-472).

Ibid., chap. 5 (456).

. *Epistola LXII*, no. 4 (P.L., 4, 380).

4. Ibid., no. 5 (382).

5. *Epistola LX*, no. 2 (P.L., 4, 371).

16. Ibid.

17. Ambrose, *De paradiso*, chap. 10, no. 47 (P.L., 14, 314).

18. Ibid., no. 48 (315).

19. Ambrosiaster, *On the Epistle to the Romans*, 5, 12 (C.S.E.L., vol. 81, part 1 [Vienna, 1966], p. 163). Although the authorship of the commentaries ascribed to "Ambrosiaster" is debated, Ambrosian authorship does not seem to me to be ruled out.

20. *De institutione virginis*, chap. 3, no. 22 (P.L., 16, 325). The *De lapsu virginis consecratae* (P.L., 16, 367-384), formerly ascribed to Ambrose, is now attributed to Nicetas of Remesiana.

21. *De institutione virginis*, chap. 3, no. 24 (325).

22. Ibid., chap. 5, nos. 32-36 (P.L., 16, 327-329).

23. *De viduis*, chap. 8, nos. 49-50 (P.L., 16, 362-363).

24. *De paradiso*, chap. 12, no. 56 (P.L., 14, 320).

25. Ibid.; also chap. 10, no. 47 (314-315).

26. *In Lucam*, II, 28 (S.Chr., 45, p. 83).

27. *De institutione virginis*, chap. 4, no. 25 (P.L., 16, 325-326).

28. Ibid., no. 26 (326).

29. Ibid., no. 27 (326); also *De paradiso*, chap. 14, nos. 71-72 (P.L., 14, 327-328).

30. *De institutione virginis*, chap. 4, no. 29 (P.L., 16, 326).

31. *De paradiso*, chap. 15, no. 73 (P.L., 14, 329).

32. *De Cäin et Abel*, I, chap. 10, no. 47 (P.L., 14, 358).

33. *De institutione virginis*, chap. 17, no. 111 (P.L., 16, 347).

34. *Exhortatio virginitatis*, chap. 9, no. 58 (P.L., 16, 369).

35. Ibid., chap. 10, no. 61 (370).

36. *De virginitate*, chaps. 8-16 (P.L., 16, 291-307).

37. *In hexaëmeron*, VI, chap. 8, no. 45 (P.L., 14, 275).

38. The soul is described in *De virginitate*, chaps. 17-18 (P.L., 16, 307-311); *In hexaëmeron*, VI, chap. 8 (P.L., 14, 274-280).

39. *De institutione virginis*, chap. 3, no. 20 (P.L., 16, 324).

40. *De virginibus libri tres*, bk. II, chap. 4, no. 30 (P.L., 16, 226).

41. *De institutione virginis*, chap. 5, no. 32 (P.L., 16, 327).

42. Ibid., no. 33 (328).

43. *Exhortatio virginitatis*, chap. 4, no. 19 (P.L., 16, 357).

44. *De viduis*, chap. 13, nos. 79-81 (P.L., 16, 272-273); chap. 15, nos. 86-90 (274-276).

45. *Exhortatio virginitatis*, chap. 4, nos. 20-27 (P.L., 16, 357-359).

46. *In hexaëmeron*, VI, chap. 9, nos. 54-74 (P.L., 14, 280-288).

47. Ibid., no. 56 (281).

48. *De Caïn et Abel*, I, chap. 10, no. 46 (P.L., 34, 357-358).
49. *Epistola LXIX*, no. 2 (P.L., 16, 1285-1286).
50. Ibid., no. 4 (1286).
51. Ibid., no. 6 (1286).
52. Ibid., no. 7 (1287).
53. *De virginitate*, chap. 6, no. 34 (P.L., 16, 288).
54. *De viduis*, chap. 4, no. 23 (P.L., 16, 254-255).
55. Ibid., chap. 13, no. 79 (272).
56. *De virginitate*, chap. 6, no. 33 (P.L., 16, 288).
57. *De viduis*, chap. 15, no. 89 (P.L., 16, 276).
58. *Epistola LXIII*, no. 79 (P.L. 16, 1270).
59. *De viduis*, chap. 13, no. 79 (P.L., 16, 272).
60. *De institutione virginis*, chap. 4, no. 30 (P.L., 16, 327).
61. Jerome, *Adversus Helvidium* (P.L., 23, 183-226).
62. P.L., 16, 1169-1171.
63. Ambrose, *Epistola XLII* (P.L., 1172-1177).
64. Jerome, *Adversus Jovinianum* (P.L., 23, 211-338).
65. Ibid., I, no. 3 (224).
66. Ibid., I, no. 5 (228).
67. *Retractationes*, I, chap. 22 (*Oeuvres de saint Augustin*, 12 [Paris, 1950], 488).
68. Jerome, *Contra Vigilantium* (P.L., 23, 339-352).
69. *Epistola XXII*, no. 26 (P.L., 22, 411).
70. Ibid., no. 14 (402-403).
71. Ibid., no. 11 (401).
72. Ibid., no. 18 (405).
73. Ibid., no. 19 (406). See *Adversus Jovinianum*, I, no. 29 (P.L., 23, 262-263), where Jerome admits he does not know God's designs over Paradise. On this question see Michael Müller, *Die Lehre des hl. Augustinus von der Paradiesehe, und ihre Auswirkung in der Sexualethik des 12. und 13. Jahrhunderts bis Thomas von Aquin* (Regensburg, 1954).
74. *Epistola XXII*, no. 19 (P.L., 22, 406).
75. *Adversus Jovinianum*, I, no. 13 (P.L., 23, 243).
76. Ibid., no. 29 (263).
77. Ibid., no. 26 (259).
78. Ibid., nos. 47-49 (288-296).
79. Ibid., no. 49 (293).
80. *Retractationes*, bk. II, chaps. 22-23 (*Oeuvres*, 12, 488-492). See Kari Elisabeth Børresen, *Subordination et Equivalence. Nature et rôle de la femme d'après Augustin et Thomas d'Aquin* (Oslo-Paris, 1968).
81. *De bono viduitatis*, III, chap. 4, no. 6 (*Oeuvres*, 3, 242).
82. *De sancta virginitate*, XVIII (*Oeuvres*, 3, 140).
83. Ibid., XXII (pp. 148-150).
84. Ibid., XXVII, no. 27 (p. 160).
85. *De Genesi ad litteram*, VI, chap. 5 (P.L., 34, 342).
86. *De sermone Domini in monte*, I, chap. 15 (P.L., 34, 1250).

87. *De Genesi ad litteram,* IX, chap. 5 (P.L., 34, 396).

88. *De civitate Dei,* XIV, chaps. 21-24 (*Oeuvres,* 35, 438-545).

89. Ibid., chap. 26 (pp. 458-460).

90. *De Genesi contra Manichaeos,* II, chap. 13, no. 19 (P.L., 34, 206).

91. *De bono conjugali* (*Oeuvres,* 2).

92. *De Genesi ad litteram,* IX, chap. 5 (P.L., 34, 396).

93. *De bono conjugali,* XVI (*Oeuvres,* 2, 65).

94. *De bono viduitatis,* VII (*Oeuvres,* 3, 253).

95. Ibid., XII (p. 265).

96. *De bono conjugali,* XXIV (*Oeuvres,* 2, 93); see *De Genesi ad litteram,* IX, chap. 7, no. 12 (P.L., 34, 397).

97. *De bono conjugali,* XVIII (p. 70).

98. *De civitate Dei,* XIV, chap. 17 (*Oeuvres,* 35, 428).

99. Ibid., chap. 18 (pp. 430-432).

100. Ibid., chap. 16 (pp. 424-426).

101. *De continentia,* chap. 12 (*Oeuvres,* 3, 89-91).

102. Ibid., chap. 9 (pp. 75-77).

103. *De Genesi contra Manichaeos,* I, chap. 19, no. 30 (P.L., 34, 187).

104. *De Genesi ad litteram,* IX, chap. 3 (P.L., 34, 395); *Retractationes,* I, chap. 15, no. 2 (*Oeuvres,* 12, 329).

105. *De opere monachorum,* XXXII (*Oeuvres,* 3, 427).

106. *De Genesi ad litteram,* IX, chap. 37, no. 50 (P.L., 34, 450).

107. *Confessions,* IX, chap. 9, no. 19 (*Oeuvres,* 14, 108).

108. *De bono conjugali,* IX (*Oeuvres,* 2, 65).

109. *De bono viduitatis,* VIII, no. 2 (*Oeuvres,* 3, 254); *De Genesi ad litteram,* IX, chap. 7, no. 12 (P.L., 34, 397).

110. *De Genesi ad litteram,* XI, chap. 35 (p. 449).

111. *De sancta virginitate,* VI (*Oeuvres,* 3, 123).

112. Ibid., V (pp. 117-119).

113. Hefele-Leclercq, vol. I/1, p. 236 (canon 27); pp. 238-239 (canon 33).

114. Ibid., vol. II/1, pp. 71-75.

115. Ibid., p. 77 (canon 2 of the Council of 390); p. 401 (canon 3 of the Council of 401).

116. C.O.D., pp. 166 and 170.

117. C.O.D., p. 371; D.-S., no. 1889. For further illustration of the theme of the last three chapters, see A.-M. de la Bonnardière, *Chrétiennes des premiers siècles* (Paris, 1957); France Quéré-Jaulmes, *La Femme. Les grands textes des Pères de l'Eglise* (Paris, 1968); Georgia Harkness, *Women in Church and Society* (New York, 1972).

NOTES TO CHAPTER 6

1. Kari Elisabeth BØrresen, *Subordination et equivalence. Nature et role de la femme d'après Augustin et Thomas d'Aquin* (Oslo-Paris, 1968).

2. Vincent Yzermans, ed., *American Participation in the Vatican Council* (New York, 1967), p. 202.

3. *Gospel of Thomas,* No. 112 (Robert M. Grant, *The Secret Sayings of Jesus* [New York, 1960], p. 197).

4. Yzermans, pp. 202-203.

5. Karl Rahner and Herbert Vorgrimler, *Theological Dictionary* (New York, 1965), p. 270.

6. *De cultu feminarum,* I, 1.

7. *Summa theologica,* I, q. 92, a. 1, ad 1. See Bǿrresen, op. cit; Josef Fuchs, *Die Sexualethik des hl. Thomas von Aquin* (Cologne, 1949).

8. *Summa theologica,* I, q. 93, a. 6, ad 2.

9. *De generatione animalium,* IV, chap. 3.

10. *Summa theologica,* I, q. 92, a. 1.

11. Ibid., ad 2.

12. Hippocrates (c. 460-c. 377 B.C.), *Oeuvres complètes,* 10 vols. (Paris, 1839-1861); Loeb Classical Library, 3 vols. (London, 1923-1927); Galen (c. 131-201 A.D.), *Opera omnia,* 20 vols. (Leipzig, 1821-1833).

13. *Commentary on the Sentences,* II, D. 20, q. 2. See Thérèse Healy, *Woman according to Saint Bonaventure* (Erie, Pa., 1956).

14. *Commentary on the Sentences,* II, D. 20, q. 6 ad 2.

15. Ibid., q. 6.

16. Ibid., q. 6, ad 1.

17. Ibid., III, D. 12, a. 3, q. 1.

18. Ibid.

19. Simone de Beauvoir, *The Second Sex* (New York, 1953); Gertrude Von Le Fort, *The Eternal Woman* (Milwaukee, 1954). My quotations from Von Le Fort will be borrowed from the French text, *La Femme éternelle* (Paris, 1946).

20. Von Le Fort, p. 30.

21. Ibid., p. 31.

22. Act 3, scene 3. English translation by Wallace Fowlie (*Chicago,* 1960).

23. Act 4, scene 2. Much of Claudel's work deals with the meaning and task of woman; see *Cinq Grandes Odes,* première ode.

24. Von Le Fort, pp. 156-157.

25. F. X. Arnold, *Woman and Man: Their Nature and Mission* (New York, 1963); J. Galot, *L'Eglise et la femme* (Paris, 1965); Willi Moll, *The Christian Image of Woman* (Notre Dame, Indiana, 1967). See also Louis Sahuc, *Homme et femme* (Paris, 1960); Francoise Danniel and B. Olivier, *Woman Is the Glory of Man* (Westminster, Md., 1966); Suzanne Cita-Malard, *Les Femmes dans l'Eglise à la lumière de Vatican II* (Paris, 1968).

26. *Frauenbildung und Frauenberufe* (Munich, 1949).

27. *Osservatore Romano,* December 10, 1965.

28. Ibid.

29. Ibid.

30. *La Documentation Catholique,* 1966, no. 1482, col. 1923.

31. Ibid.

32. Ibid. The doctrine of Pius XII on woman was identical with that of Paul VI, as appears from his two major speeches on the topic, pronounced in

October 1945 and in October 1956. In both cases, the address was delivered chiefly to Italian women, a point which should be held in mind when assessing the limits of their doctrine. In the first case, the pope's concerns were dominated by the problems of the reconstruction of society after the war and the passing of the Fascist era. See *La Documentation Catholique*, **1956**, no. 1238, cols. 1415-1424; see also below, chap. 9, n. 12 and n. 13.

33. *L'Amour et l'occident* (Paris, 1939).

34. This is the ending of *Faust.*

35. Poem "A une Madonne," in *Les Fleurs du Mal.*

36. See above, chap. 5.

37. *Sermon 51 on the Assumption* (P.L., 194, 1863).

38. *L'Eternel Féminin. Etude sur un texte du Père Teilhard de Chardin* (Paris, 1968).

39. Teilhard's text is in *Ecrits du temps de guerre, 1916-1919* (Paris, 1965), pp. 253-262. This quote, p. 255.

40. Ibid., p. 256.

41. Ibid.

42. Ibid., p. 253.

43. Ibid., p. 254.

44. Ibid., p. 255.

45. Ibid., p. 256.

46. Ibid., p. 257.

47. Ibid., p. 258.

48. Ibid.

49. Ibid., p. 259.

50. Ibid., p. 260.

51. Ibid., p. 261.

52. Ibid., p. 262.

53. Ibid.

54. Julian of Norwich, *Revelations of Divine Love,* chap. 57, in Roger Huddleston, ed. (Westminster, Md., 2nd ed., 1952), p. 118.

55. Ibid., chap. 58, p. 119.

56. Ibid., p. 120.

57. Ibid., chap. 59, pp. 122-123.

58. Ibid., chap. 60, p. 124.

59. Ibid., p. 125. On divine motherhood, see Claude Chavasse, *The Bride of Christ* (London, 1940); J. Plumpe, *Mater Ecclesia* (Washington, 1943); Hugo Rahner, *Mater Ecclesia: Lobpreis der Kirche aus dem ersten Jahrtausend christlichen Literature* (Einsiedeln, 1944); Karl Delehaye, *Erneuerung der Seelsorgsformen aus der Sicht der frühen Patristik* (Freiburg, 1958).

60. Victor White, *Soul and Psyche* (London, 1960), chaps. 6-8 and appendix VI.

61. Quoted by Victor White, **ibid.**, p. 124, from *The Adornment of the Spiritual Marriage,* trans. C. A. Wynschenk (London, 1916), p. 177.

62. White, p. 137.

NOTES TO CHAPTER 7

1. *The Creation of Man* (P.G., 44, 181-184), quoted in Vladimir Lossky, *The Mystical Theology of the Eastern Church* (London, 1957), p. 109.

2. G. C. Messerman, *The Acathistos Hymn* (Fribourg, 1958), pp. 30 and 38.

3. Romanos, *Second Hymn on the Nativity* (S.Chr., 110, pp. 93-95).

4. Romanos, *Third Hymn on the Nativity* (S.Chr., 110, p. 125).

5. *First Hymn on the Resurrection* (S.Chr., 128, p. 391).

6. S.Chr., 128, p. 578, n. 3.

7. Ibid., pp. 579-581.

8. Ephrem de Nisibe, *Hymnes sur le Paradis* (S.Chr., 137, *Hymn IX*, pp. 126-127).

9. Ibid., p. 128.

10. Ibid., *Hymn XI*, p. 145.

11. Ibid., p. 151.

12. On the Cappadocian Fathers see Jean Meyendorff, *Le Christ dans la théologie byzantine* (Paris, 1969).

13. See René Roques, *L'Univers dionysien* (Paris, 1954); Introduction to *La Hiérarchie céleste* (S.Chr., 58).

14. Hans Urs Von Balthasar, *Kosmische Liturgie. Das Weltbild Maximus des Bekenners* (Einsiedeln, 1961).

15. Lossky, p. 137.

16. Quoted in Jean Meyendorff, *Introduction à l'étude de Grégoire Palamas* (Paris, 1959), p. 294, n. 62.

17. Ibid., pp. 247-248; italics mine.

18. Sergius Bulgakov, *The Wisdom of God* (New York, 1937), pp. 185-187; Louis Bouyer, *Woman and Man with God* (London, 1960), pp. 46-48.

19. Quoted in *Paracelsus. Selected Writings*, ed. Jolande Jacobi (New York, 1951), p. 87.

20. Ibid., pp. 92, 97-98, 110.

21. Since Auguste Comte (1798-1857) had a dominant influence on Soloviev, we may sum up his ideas on womanhood here. In autobiographical sections of his *Systeme de politique positive*, vols. 1 and 2 (Paris, 1851), Comte stresses the predominant role of three women in his life, his "pious mother," his "holy companion" Clotilde de Vaux, and his illiterate servant. These become symbols of "activity and intelligence freely subordinate to service" (vol. 1, pp. 12-13). In the future, mankind will be ruled by a "double conjunction of the philosophers with the women and the proletarians." Woman represents feeling, love, tradition, permanence, the purpose of life, the ideal of society. "The loving sex . . . is the chief personification of the true Great Being," which is identical with Mankind (vol. 1, p. 21). The masculine type reigns in the area of means and achievements; man, usually unable to perceive the goal, is equipped to reach it. Hence "the sacred formula of the positivists: Love as the principle, Order as the basis, Progress as the goal" (vol. 2, p. 65). Positive philosophy ambitions to guarantee the proper priorities within the polarities

of mankind and to balance the leadership of the male in the area of action and thought, with the prevalence of the female in the area of purpose and love.

22. *Lectures on Godmanhood* (London, 1948), p. 206.

23. Ibid., pp. 173-174.

24. Ibid., p. 206.

25. *La Russie et l'Eglise universelle* (Paris, 1889), p. 256.

26. Ibid., p. 258.

27. Ibid., p. 260.

28. Ibid., pp. 259-260.

29. Ibid., p. 259.

30. Ibid., p. 259.

31. Ibid., p. 260.

32. Ibid., p. 261.

33. I have been able to read this poem only in a German translation, *Drei Begegnungen*, in Wladimir Szylarsky, *Solowjew's Philosophie der All-Einheit* (Kaunas, Lithuania, 1932), pp. 81-87. The German texts for the quotations are the following: "der Gottheit Königspurpur," "heilige Leuchten," "o Blüte Gottes," "ewige Freundin," "Weiblicher Schönheit Urbild." I wish to thank Miss Helen Iswolsky for sending me a copy of the German translation of this poem.

34. Quoted by Peter Zouboff in the introduction to Soloviev, *Lectures on Godmanhood*, p. 12.

35. Serge Boulgakov, *Le Paraclet* (Paris, 1946), p. 343.

36. Ibid., p. 310.

37. Bulgakov, *The Wisdom of God*, pp. 120-121.

38. *Le Paraclet*, p. 314.

39. Ibid., pp. 318-319.

40. Ibid., p. 315.

41. Ibid., p. 350.

42. *The Wisdom of God*, p. 183.

43. *Mystical Theology of the Eastern Church*, p. 62, n. 1.

44. Ibid., p. 112.

45. Ibid., pp. 80-81.

46. Paul Evdokimov, *La Femme et le salut du monde* (Paris, 1958), p. 195.

47. Ibid., p. 229.

48. Ibid., p. 223.

49. Ibid., p. 211.

50. Ibid.

51. Ibid., p. 223.

52. Tatiana Struve, "La vocation de la femme," in Tatiana Struve, Agnès Cunningham, François Florentin-Smyth, *La Femme* (Paris, 1968), p. 14.

53. Ibid.

54. Ibid., pp. 46, 48.

55. Ibid., p. 51.

NOTES TO CHAPTER 8

1. Françoise Florentin-Smyth, "La femme en milieu protestant," in Tatiana Struve, Agnès Cunningham, Françoise Florentin-Smyth, *La Femme* (Paris, 1968), pp. 141, 150. There is an extensive Protestant literature on woman, but most of it is not primarily theological. See Henry Wheeler, *Deaconesses Ancient and Modern* (New York, 1889); Edmund Morgan, *The Puritan Family* (Boston, 1944); Kathleen Bliss, *The Service and Status of Women in the Churches* (London, 1952); Margaret Brackenbury Crook, *Women and Religion* (Boston, 1964); Francine Dumas, *Man and Woman: Similarity and Difference* (Geneva, 1966); Elsie Thomas Culver, *Woman in the World of Religion* (New York, 1967); Margaret Sittler Ermarth, *Adam's Fractured Rib* (Philadelphia, 1970); Georgia Harkness, *Women in Church and Society: A Historical and Theological Inquiry* (Nashville-New York, 1972).

2. *Lectures on Genesis,* in Jaroslav Pelikan, ed., *Luther's Works,* I (St. Louis, 1958), p. 115. *Luther's Lectures on Genesis* were written in 1535-1536.

3. Ibid., p. 116.

4. Ibid., p. 117.

5. Quoted in Roland Bainton, *What Christianity Says about Sex, Love and Marriage* (New York, 1957), p. 76.

6. *Lectures on Genesis (Luther's Works,* I, p. 119).

7. Ibid., pp. 118-119.

8. Olavi Lahteenmaki, *Sexus und Ehe bei Luther* (Turku, Finland, 1955), p. 64.

9. Ibid., pp. 86-92.

10. *De captivitate babylonica (Works of Martin Luther,* II [Philadelphia, 1943], pp. 269-270). See also Lahteenmaki, pp. 73-74.

11. *Lectures on Genesis (Luther's Works,* I, pp. 202-203).

12. Ibid., p. 200.

13. Ibid.

14. Ibid., pp. 202-203.

15. Ibid.

16. *The Bishops' Book, or the Institution of a Christian Man,* 1537 (C. Lloyd, *Formularies of Faith put forth by Authority during the Reign of Henry VIII* [Oxford, 1856], p. 89).

17. *Lectures on Genesis (Luther's Works,* IV [St. Louis, 1964], p. 233). The Latin text seems stronger than the English translation: "Ideoque conjugium propter Christum sanctum et purum, concubitum pudicum et honestum esse necesse est, qui per se est foedissimus" (*Martin Luthers Werke,* 43 [Weimar, 1912], p. 302).

18. André Biéler, *L'Homme et le femme dans la morale calviniste* (Geneva, 1963).

19. *Commentaire sur la Genèse (Commentaires de Jean Calvin sur l'Ancien Testament,* I [Geneva, 1961], p. 83).

20. Ibid., p. 57.

21. Ibid., p. 56.

22. Ibid., p. 58.

23. Ibid., p. 59.

24. Ibid., p. 55.

25. Ibid., p. 60.

26. Ibid., p. 441.

27. Ibid., pp. 61, 462.

28. Ibid., pp. 57, 456.

29. Ibid., p. 456.

30. Ibid., p. 486.

31. Ibid., p. 530.

32. See above, chap. 7, n.20.

33. *Marriage and the Sexes in Both Worlds* (*The Swedenborg Library*, IX [Philadelphia, 1875]).

34. "Wherever I look, it always seems to me that the nature of women is nobler and their life happier, and if ever I toy with an impossible wish, it is to be a woman" (quoted in Karl Barth, *Church Dogmatics*, III/4 [Edinburgh, 1961], p. 155).

35. Odette Grosjean-Darier, in the foreword to the French version of Charlotte von Kirschbaum, *Die wirkliche Frau* (Zurich, 1949): *Découverte de la Femme* (Geneva, 1951).

36. Charlotte von Kirschbaum, Preface to the German edition, *Découverte de la Femme*, p. 8.

37. Ibid., p. 64.

38. Karl Barth, III/4, p. 152. This section of the *Church Dogmatics* has also been printed separately as *Mann und Frau* (Munich, 1964).

39. Ibid., pp. 130-131.

40. Ibid., p. 140.

41. Ibid., p. 150.

42. Ibid., p. 151.

43. Ibid., pp. 151-152.

44. Ibid., p. 154.

45. Ibid., p. 163.

46. Ibid., p. 167.

47. Ibid., p. 169.

48. Ibid., pp. 170-171.

49. Emil Brunner, *The Divine Imperative* (London, 1937), pp. 374-375.

50. Ibid., p. 375.

51. *Man in Revolt* (New York, 1939), p. 347.

52. Ibid., pp. 357-358.

53. *Dogmatics* II (Philadelphia, 1949), p. 63.

54. Ibid.

55. Ibid., pp. 62-63.

56. *Man in Revolt*, pp. 352-353.

57. Ibid., p. 354.

58. Ibid.

59. Ibid., p. 347.
60. Ibid., p. 361.
61. *Dogmatics*, II, p. 65.
62. *Man in Revolt*, pp. 350-351.
63. Ibid., p. 356.
64. Ibid., p. 352.
65. *The Divine Imperative*, p. 379.
66. *Man in Revolt*, pp. 358-359.
67. Ibid.
68. See above, n. 1. This chapter does not include a study of D. S. Bailey's *The Man-Woman Relation in Christian Thought* (London, 1959) or of Helmut Thielicke's *The Ethics of Sex* (New York, 1964), for their topics, although related to mine, are not mine. Likewise, I need not examine at this point the literature dealing with the ordination of women, much of which is more anthropological than theological. To appreciate the nontheological nature of a large part of the discussion about ordination of women, see Elsie Thomas Culver, pp. 325-326.

NOTES TO CHAPTER 9

1. *Summa theologica*, II II, q. 175, a. 2, ad 2.
2. Ibid., I, q. 26, a. 3, ad 1.
3. *Summa contra gentes*, III, chap. 53.
4. *Spiritual Canticle*, 22, 3, in *The Collected Works of St. John of the Cross*, trans. Kieran Kavanaugh and Otilio Rodriguez (New York, 1964), p. 497.
5. *Spiritual Canticle*, 25, 5 (p. 503).
6. *Spiritual Canticle*, 39, 4 (p. 558).
7. *Verbum Dei*, 6 in *Dogmatic Constitution on Divine Revelation*, trans. George H. Tavard (New York, 1966), p. 60.
8. This expression designates the qualities appertaining to the divinity and to the humanity of Jesus as they are predicated of the one Person who is both divine and human.
9. Thomas Aquinas, *Summa theologica*, III, q. 8, a. 5, ad 3.
10. This expression is applied by Gerard Manley Hopkins to the Virgin Mary in his poem "The Virgin Mary Compared to the Air We Breathe."
11. Charles Péguy, *La Tapisserie de sainte Genèvieve et de sainte Jeanne d'Arc*, huitième jour.
12. Pius XII, Address, July 29, 1957 (text in *La Documentation Catholique*, no. 1263, col. 1354).
13. Pius XII, Address, November 26, 1951 (text in *The Pope Speaks* [New York, 1957], p. 45).

NOTES TO CHAPTER 10

1. *Summa theologica*, Supplement, q. 39, a. 1; see *Commentary on the Sentences*, IV, D. 25, q. 2, a. 1, quest. 1. On the general question of the ordination of women, see P. R. Smythe, *The Ordination of Women* (London,

1939); V. Hannon, *The Question of Women and the Priesthood: Can Women Be Admitted to Holy Orders?* (London, 1957); M. Thrall, *The Ordination of Women to the Priesthood: A Study of Biblical Evidence* (London, 1958); J. Laplace, *La Femme et la vie consacrée* (Paris, 1963); James Alberione, *Woman: Her Influence and Zeal as an Aid to the Priesthood* (Boston, 1964); Ilse Bertinetti, *Frauen im Geistlichen Amt* (Berlin, 1965); Sister Vincent Emmanuel, *The Question of Women and the Priesthood* (London, 1969); Haye Van Der Meer, *Priestertum der Frau?* (Freiburg, 1969); Elsie Gibson, *When the Minister Is a Woman* (New York, 1970).

2 *Summa contra gentes*, III, chap. 123.

3. *Commentary on the Sentences*, IV, D. 2, a. 2, q. 1.

4. *In librum IV sententiarum*, D. 25, q. 2, scol. 2 (Wadding, ed., *Opera omnia*, IX, 1639, p. 570).

5. Jean Galot, *L'Eglise et la femme* (Paris, 1965), p. 178.

6. Ibid., p. 181.

7. Thierry Maertens, *La Promotion de la femme dans la Bible* (Tournai, 1967), pp. 216-217.

8. Luc-Henri Gihoul, *Femme, vocation de l'homme. Essai d'une théologie de la féminité* (Brussels, 1965), p. 224.

9. Ibid., pp. 66-67.

10. *Le Monde*, 19-20 September 1965, quoted by H. F. (Henri Fesquet). More recently Yves Congar has supported the ordination of women to the diaconate, in his preface to the French version of Elsie Gibson's book, *Femmes et ministères dans l'Eglise* (Paris, 1971), p. 11.

11. *The Ministry of Women in the Early Church* (London, 1961), p. 31.

12. Gonzague Truc, *Histoire illustrée de la femme*, I (Paris, 1940), p. 165.

13. Address, October 29, 1966, in *La Documentation Catholique*, 1966, no. 1482, col. 1923.

14. "The Non-Encyclical on Birth Control," *National Catholic Reporter*, October 2, 1968.

15. Archbishop Denis Hurley, "A New Moral Principle: When Right and Duty Clash," *The Furrow*, 17 (1966), 619-622; "In Defense of the Principle of Overriding Right," *Theological Studies*, 29 (1968), 301-309.

16. Jean-Louis Leuba, "La dynamique juridique post-conciliaire de l'Eglise catholique romaine," *Verbum Caro*, XXIII, no. 92, pp. 4-42. The *Motu proprio "Ministeria quaedam,"* of August 15, 1972, includes the provision: "In accordance with the venerable tradition of the Church, installation in the ministries of lector and acolyte is reserved to men." This has caused consternation and occasioned protests. However, it should be obvious that the Holy See cannot reasonably alter the traditional discipline as long as a new theological consensus in favor of the ordination of women, and their admission to the ministries of lector and acolyte, has not yet clearly emerged.

NOTES TO CONCLUSION

1. Karl Marx, *Economic and Political Manuscripts, 1844*, in Erich

Fromm, *Marx's Concept of Man* (New York, 1961), p. 126. The great predecessor and adversary of Marx, Pierre-Joseph Proudhon (1809-1865) held a very different view of woman: "half-way between man and monkey" (quoted in Abel Jeannière, *Anthropologie sexuelle* [Paris, 1969], p. 26); "If you wish to marry, remember that the first condition for a man is to dominate his wife and to be the master" (quoted in Yvonne Pellé-Douel, *Etre femme* [Paris, 1967], p. 241, n. 8).

2. The Marxist concept of the family has not in fact followed the insights of the younger Marx. See Friedrich Engels, *Der Ursprung der Familie, des Privateigentums, und des Staates* (1884); August Bebel, *Die Frau und der Sozialismus* (1883). For a full study of the nineteenth-century philosophy on woman, one would have to consider the brief but significant remarks of Hegel, *Die Philosophie des Geistes*, nos. 518-534 (*Hegel's Werke*, VII/2, pp. 393-403); *Grundlinien der Philosophie des Rechtes*, nos. 158-181 (ibid., VIII, pp. 221-246).

3. Yvonne Pellé-Douel, *Etre femme*, with bibliography pp. 261-267.

4. *Collected Works* of C. G. Jung, VII (London, 1953).

5. Edith Stein, *Frauenbildung und Frauenberufe* (Munich, 1956); J. J. Buytendijk, *La Femme* (Paris, 1954); Michael Müller, *Grundlagen der katholischen Sexualethik* (Regensburg, 1968); Elizabeth Gössmann, *Die Frau und ihr Auftrag* (Freiburg, 1961); *Mann und Frau in Familie und Oeffentlichkeit* (Munich, 1964); Michael Schmaus and E. Gössmann, *Die Frau im Aufbruch der Kirche* (Munich, 1964); Françoise Daniel and B. Olivier, *La Gloire de l'homme, c'est la femme* (Paris, 1964); "Conception chrétienne de la femme," *Lumière et Vie*, no. 43, 1959. I have been unable to find P. Idigoras, *La Femme dans l'ordre sacré* (Lima, Peru, 1963).

6. Simone de Beauvoir, *Le Deuxième Sexe*, 2 vols. (Paris, 1949). See also Claude Lévy-Strauss, *Les Structures élémentaires de la parenté* (Paris, 1967); Marcel Mauss, *Sociologie et anthropologie* (Paris, 1950); Abel Jeannière, *Anthropologie sexuelle* (Paris, 1969).

Index

253